FACULTY DIVERSITY

Why do we see so little progress in diversifying faculty at America's colleges, universities, and professional schools? This book explores this important question and provides steps for hastening faculty diversity. Drawing on her extensive consultant practice and expertise as well as research and scholarship from several fields, Dr. Moody provides practical and feasible ways to improve faculty recruitment, retention, and mentorship, especially of under-represented women in science-related fields and non-immigrant minorities in all fields. The second edition of *Faculty Diversity* offers new insights, strategies, and caveats to the current state of faculty diversity.

This revised edition includes:

- New strategies to prevent unintended cognitive bias and errors that damage faculty recruitment and retention
- Expanded discussion on the importance of different cultural contexts, political, and historical experiences inhabited and inherited by non-immigrant faculty and students
- Increased testimonials and on-the-ground reflections from faculty, administrators, and leaders in higher education, with new attention to medical and other professional schools
- Updated Appendix with Discussion Scenarios and Practice Exercises useful to search and evaluation committees, department chairs, deans, faculty senates, and diversity councils
- Expanded chapter on mentoring that dispels myths about informal mentoring and underlines essential components for formal programs.

Moody provides an essential, reliable, and eye-opening guide for colleges, medical, and other professional schools that are frustrated in their efforts to diversify their faculty.

JoAnn Moody PhD, JD, is a national consultant in faculty development and diversity (see www.diversityoncampus.com). She is a former college professor and higher education administrator.

FACULTY DIVERSITY

Removing the Barriers

Second Edition

JoAnn Moody

Routledge
Taylor & Francis Group

NEW YORK AND LONDON

First published 2012
by Routledge
711 Third Avenue, New York, NY 10017

Simultaneously published in the UK
by Routledge
2 Park Square, Milton Park, Abingdon, Oxon OX14 4RN

Routledge is an imprint of the Taylor & Francis Group, an informa business

Library of Congress Cataloging in Publication Data
Moody, JoAnn, 1945–
      Faculty diversity : removing the barriers / by JoAnn Moody.
      p. cm.
      Includes bibliographical references and index.
      1. Faculty integration—United States. 2. Minority college teachers—Selection
      and appointment—United States. I. Title.
      LB2332.6.M66 2012
      378.1'2089—dc23
      2011029455

ISBN: 978-0-415-87845-6 (hbk)
ISBN: 978-0-415-87846-3 (pbk)
ISBN: 978-0-203-80539-8 (ebk)

Typeset in Sabon
by EvS Communication Networx, Inc.

Printed and bound in the United States of America on acid-free paper
by Walsworth Publishing Company, Marceline, MO.

Printed and bound in the United States of America
By Edwards Brothers Malloy on sustainably sourced paper.

TO JOAN, JUSTIN, AND B.B.

CONTENTS

CONTENTS

ACKNOWLEDGMENTS

I wish to express my appreciation to these people who have inspired me and honed my commitment to faculty and student diversity: Naomi André, Neal Armstrong, Pat Aron, Gilda Barabino, Edgar Beckham, Chani Beeman, Suzanne Benally, Harold Bibb, Robert Boice, Ruth Brin, Sheila Browne, Shirley Callado, Susan Carlson, Nancy Carriuolo, Don Cole, Natalie Cooper, Linda DeMeritt, Denice Denton, Estelle Disch, Luis Falcon, Gertrude Fraser, Cynthia Gately, Myra Gordon, Frank Hale, Jr., William Harvey, Jim Henkel, Emorcia Hill, Alice Hogan, Sharon Hogan, David Hollinger, Joe Hopkins, Evelyn Hu-DeHart, Dawn Hunt, J.J. Jackson, Chris Jones, Terry King, Bud Knopf, Lydia Villa-Komaroff, Freeman Hrabowski, Laura Kramer, Judith Langlois, Amanda Lapham, Sarah Willie-LeBreton, Douglas Massey, Christine O'Brien, Bud Peterson, Joan Reede, Kyrsis Rodriguez, Chris Sahley, Ricardo Stanton-Salazar, Elliot Schewel, Rosel Schewel, Elaine Seymour, Peg Boyle Single, Daryl Smith, Mary Deane Sorcinelli, Peter Spear, Jocelyn Sprague, Claude Steele, Susan Stone, Sterling Stratton, Ron Takaki, Richard Tapia, Beverly Tatum, Orlando Taylor, Uri Treisman, Cathy Trower, Caroline Turner, Greg Vincent, Cardinal Warde, Karan Watson, Joe White, Clarence Williams, Chuck Willie, Kelly Wise, and Frank Wu. Also co-founders with me of the Compact for Faculty Diversity: Ansley Abraham and Ken Pepion plus the Compact's allies Frank Abbott and Dewayne Matthews. A few of the above have recently left us; they are sorely missed.

Thanks to Routledge Associate Editor, Heather Jarrow, for her astute help with this book.

Most especially, I express my deepest gratitude to my partner Joan Tonn who has helped immeasurably with this edition and everything else I do.

INTRODUCTION

Organization of *Faculty Diversity: Removing the Barriers*

Second Edition

Since the first edition of this book appeared in 2004, I have been intrigued by the mushrooming of research on cognitive errors and biases that undermine fair evaluations and sound decisions. I have also pondered several in-depth examinations of biases and inequities on campuses, accompanied by the subtle tracing of how these are reproduced. Further adding to my education and to my motivation for writing this second edition are lessons learned from my consulting work extending over yet another decade. Traveling to every region of the country, I have collaborated with faculty, administrators, trustees, student groups, faculty senates, and diversity councils at research and comprehensive universities, community colleges, liberal arts colleges, schools of medicine and law, and government research labs.

Not surprisingly, these interactions have enriched my grasp of the issues and barriers we face in diversifying our faculty. The analyses, caveats, and recommendations I am able to offer the reader in this second edition of *Faculty Diversity* are an interweaving of two strands: recent insights derived from researchers and scholars in several fields braided together with the realities of my on-the-ground professional practice and observation.

In this book, I am determined to enliven the writing and at least occasionally rivet my reader to the page. One way that I will do this is by including more testimonials, reflections, and a few jokes from faculty, administrators, and other leaders. Those appearing from time to time will include billionaire philanthropist Warren Buffet, President Barack Obama, activist and author Frank Shorris, law professor Ian Lopez, poet Maya Angelou, social-cognition expert Susan Fiske, higher education professor Caroline Sotello Viernes Turner, law school dean Frank Wu, history professor Evelyn Hu-DeHart, and others.

In this second edition, I will devote far more attention to cognitive errors and biases found in academe. Unwittingly relied on at times by all of us, these errors propel us to reach flawed and unfair conclusions. Covering a wide range, they include: first impressions, elitism, premature ranking of candidates, psychoanalyzing job candidates and tenure-review candidates, and *pervasive* negative and positive biases based on gender and group membership. When these errors and biases corrupt our evaluations, anyone being evaluated, of course, can be harmed—but in fact some are disproportionately harmed. Those who suffer most from these errors are *women* in predominantly male fields and departments as well as certain *"non-immigrant" groups* who are under-represented in just about all fields (namely, African Americans, Mexican Americans, Puerto Rican Americans, American Indians, and Native Hawaiians).

My thinking has changed since the first edition (2004) where I argued that campuses and professional schools mostly needed to build better departmental and campus practices in order to improve their recruitment and retention of women and non-immigrants. I now realize from my additional years of consulting work that better practices *alone* will *not* prevent us from making flawed decisions. Interventions are needed so that we individuals can refrain from habitually underestimating and penalizing women faculty and job candidates in certain academic fields and especially non-immigrants in *all* fields. Part 2 of this book will give detailed instructions on how to construct a sturdy "stop sign" to more than a dozen cognitive errors and biases manifested in our daily routines.

Two *trouble spots* remain the central focus of both editions of this book. First: the low numbers of women faculty in science, technology, engineering, and mathematics (STEM fields)—especially at the full professor level—despite the steady increase since 1980 of doctorates earned by women in these areas. Second: the downright paucity within faculty ranks and within almost all disciplines of what I term members from "non-immigrant" groups in this country. Members of these groups—named above—steadily earn doctorates, but the rate of increase continues to lag that of women. Current data can be found at the websites and publications of the National Research Council, the Nelson Diversity Surveys, the National Science Foundation, the American Council on Education's Annual Minority Status Reports, and the National Center for Education Statistics. Consider, for a moment, these "local" figures from the 2010 MIT Report: while African Americans, Hispanic Americans, and American Indians account for almost 30 percent of the U.S. population, they made up only 6 percent of MIT faculty in 2009, with that percentage having held flat for decades. But when a closer investigation was done, researchers found a significant complexity in their counting: less than one-half of those in the three groups named above were actually born in this country. Native-born "minorities" accounted for only 2 percent of total MIT faculty.

Professor Donna Nelson in her Diversity Surveys has traced a similar pattern to MIT's in her own study of "under-represented minorities" holding faculty jobs at the "Top 100 Science and Engineering Departments." Despite doctoral degrees slowly but steadily climbing for these three groups, there has *not* been a corresponding upward movement in their faculty numbers at large or small majority campuses. By contrast, women's attainment of graduate degrees continues to rise relatively rapidly, and their percentage of faculty at all four-year institutions is now close to 40 percent. But their attainment to the full-professorship ranks at campuses is still slow, especially in several STEM fields.

The encouraging but at times uneven progress for women faculty has come about for several reasons. Dozens of campuses are currently and diligently working to reduce barriers for STEM women, and some of these are funded for three to five years by a new National Science Foundation program named ADVANCE, whose aim is to advance STEM women faculty. In the late 1990s, Joseph Bordogna, NSF's Deputy Director, took action with his colleagues on the documented need: ADVANCE was the result. From 2001 to 2007, Alice Hogan served as founding program director and guided the new initiative with energy and success, assisted by a coalition of advisors and advocates. While ADVANCE was being launched and strengthened, MIT's parallel pledge to remedy gender inequities on its own campus was also being implemented.

In 1999, MIT's campus president Charles Vest and dean of the science division Robert Birgeneau examined the evidence of inequities regarding lab space, salaries, and leaderships posts which were proffered by the handful of senior women faculty in the sciences (Professor Nancy Hopkins was a key leader). Amazed by what they found, the president and provost quickly mobilized all academic divisions to begin correcting the problems. Regular updates were and still are posted on the campus website so the world can scrutinize the actions being taken. MIT's steadfast progress and sustained attention to these issues since 1999 are remarkable—and most people in higher education agree that it has inspired imitation by other campuses to fix gender inequities in all fields or at least seriously try. It is surely neither coincidental nor random that beginning in the mid-2000s, a number of women took the helm as campus president in institutions across the country, in many cases for the first time in the institution's history. Examples: the universities of Pennsylvania, Iowa, and Virginia; Purdue, Harvard, and Princeton universities; MIT and others.

Today, we see successful innovations within campuses, publishing houses, and federal funding agencies that are resulting in the inclusion of deserving women researchers and professors in important STEM and non-STEM areas: for instance, the winning of Pioneer Awards from the National Institutes of Health; more publications by women in journals because blind peer review is being used (where names and sometimes campus affiliations are removed) and/or because journal reviewers are being coached on how to recognize and rise above unintended gender bias (negative bias) towards women. ADVANCE campuses and others are strategizing about how to ensure that women, especially in STEM fields, get to collaborate more with their male colleagues and are invited into influential professional networks (national and international) that are replete with opportunity-sharing and members' exchanges of favors and mutual aid. At some professional schools and campuses, mid-career women professors (and their department chairs and deans) now receive coaching so that these women move more rapidly and methodically up to the full professor level. Finally, some institutions are finding ways slowly but surely to end their anti-family practices and the expectation that a 24/7 schedule is normal for serious academics.

So what is the bad news? Answer: very little uptick in the hiring and the retaining of members of non-immigrant groups. And I can predict that this regrettable steady-state will hold unless *different steps* are adopted—as opposed to expanding or accelerating the same tired approaches. No comprehensive ADVANCE-like program now exists to enlarge non-immigrant faculty members' numbers and contributions on predominantly majority campuses. There is no national movement, *yet*, that spends energy and intelligence in publicizing, demonstrating, assessing, and teaching others what will work. Yet the need is acute. The Universities of California at San Diego and Los Angeles as well as Stanford and other California schools show little or no overall progress in these areas. Almost annually press releases are issued by places such as Dartmouth, the University of Pennsylvania, Cornell, Tufts, Harvard, and others in which campus leaders lament their frustrating lack of progress in recruiting and retaining "under-represented minorities" or "diversity hires" (their terms).

In the realm of non-immigrant faculty and their recruitment, retention, and advancement, MIT may yet again take the lead. In 2010, that campus forthrightly documented and publicly acknowledged its own internal dysfunctions responsible for the shockingly high attrition rate of its "Black and Hispanic" faculty. (See the MIT 2010 Report of the Initiative for Faculty Race and Diversity at the campus website.) A revolving door seems to be operating at MIT: new "diversity hires" leave fairly quickly and are replaced with brand-new "diversity" recruits. A similar phenomenon has been found on a number of private California campuses participating in an Irvine Foundation program. Even when a campus succeeds in recruiting and hiring non-immigrant faculty, the revolving door prevents the campus from making sustained, measurable progress (Morena, Smith, Clayton-Pedersen, Parker, and Teraguchi, 2006).

Perhaps MIT will *jumpstart* a nation-wide movement focused on retention as well on recruitment of non-immigrant faculty. Perhaps the National Institutes of Health, the National Science Foundation, several foundations, or philanthropists such as Bill Gates, Warren Buffett, or

Oprah Winfrey will financially support some parts of it. Certainly campuses and professional schools must somehow be deliberately motivated to act and then be assisted in adopting good practices.

Unfortunately, there is more bad news: the numbers given for non-immigrant faculty on campuses and at professional schools might be even *more* distressing that most of us realize. For several decades, campuses and government agencies (especially the Equal Employment Opportunity Commission) have lumped together all people in the United States who are non-European in ethnic descent and then characterized this huge aggregation as "Minorities." As a result, campuses that bring on board new scholars and researchers from Argentina, Egypt, Nigeria, China, Japan, Taiwan, Brazil, and Jamaica, for instance, almost always count them as "diversity hires." Such counts are misleading, at best, and lull us into concluding that progress is being made in the hiring of domestic, non-immigrant faculty when, in fact, the opposite is true.

It is crucial for campuses to rethink how their data about faculty hires are collected and interpreted. Such data should be more carefully analyzed and clearly disaggregated so that campuses and schools can know to what extent they are achieving domestic diversity—not just global diversity.

Further, it is crucial for campuses to desist from another data-collecting habit, one that involves false precision and false comparisons. On an annual basis, various sets of so-called peer campuses compare the numbers of their brand-new "diversity hires" with the numbers of those of others in their set. Their comparisons lead to faulty conclusions, such as "oh good, we're four percent ahead of most of our competitors this time around; we're not doing so bad." This comparison exercise is similar to grading student papers on a curve in a class where everyone has performed poorly and has failed to meet standards (see further analysis at Smith, "Orienting the Data," 2009, pp. 244–246).

There is much work to do. And valid statistical methods must be used to track exactly how our recruitment and retention of non-immigrant groups are actually unfolding.

Organization of the Book: Part 1— Barriers to Faculty Diversity

Chapters 1 and 2: Rising Above Cognitive Errors

Chapters 1 and 2 show how cognitive errors and shortcuts form a formidable barrier to the advancement of under-represented women (URW) and also non-immigrant (NI), primarily indigenous groups (that is, American Indians, Mexican Americans, Puerto Rican Americans, Native Hawaiians, and African Americans). The fifteen errors include:

first impressions, elitism, longing to clone, shifting standards and raising the bar, pre-mature ranking, psychoanalyzing job candidates and others, and *above all* negative and positive stereotypes (biases) related to gender and to group membership. In my consulting work, I now use this cognitive-errors approach to help academics develop recognition of typical errors and then rise above them. The first edition of this book had little to say about cognitive errors, but they are a very important focus here.

Of course, the rising above cognitive errors—the self-correction—is *not* easy and takes time and reinforcement. A person's well-worn cognitive habits and shortcuts, to be sure, will resist change. Individuals themselves must muster strong intention and motivation to self-correct. They require coaching and preparation (sometimes called priming) as well as reminders, nudges, and refresher exercises related to memory retrieval and especially to applications to real-life problems. Individual evaluators and committees also can be immensely assisted by the adoption of constructive *organizational* practices such as: no overloading and rushing of committee members; ground rules, coaching, checklists, and check-ins to minimize personal opinions and errors and maximize evidence-based, careful deliberations. More discussion of constructive interventions can be found in my practical, "how-to" Chapters 4–6 as well as in Professor Susan Fiske's 2004 article "Intent and Ordinary Bias" and many of her other publications.

Building new cognitive habits (especially the self-correction of cognitive errors) is demanding but essential. Another new self-correction behavior should be adopted by administrators and faculty: attend to the *different* cultural contexts and *different* political and historical experiences inhabited and inherited by their faculty and students, especially non-immigrant faculty and students.

Chapter 3: Diversifying the Faculty Requires a Focus on Domestic Non-Immigrant Groups

In Chapter 3 I trace the political, economic, and historical patterns responsible for the origins of both *positive group bias* (for immigrants) and *negative group bias* (for non-immigrants). Unfortunately, academic leaders are usually unaware of historical origins of positive and negative bias. If they were, I am confident they would *stop* clumping together all non-European American groups and *stop* characterizing all of them as "minorities." By using the amazingly broad concept of "minorities" and other terms such as "Hispanic" and "people of color," academics mislead themselves and fail to realize and address the issues faced by particular groups. These terms should be replaced with more narrow and historically accurate descriptors, as I show in Chapter 3 with the expert assistance of David Hollinger, Ian Lopez, Frank Wu, Camille Charles, and others.

Also in this chapter, I highlight how the prominent immigrant group—Europeans—was successful at consolidating their political, economic, and educational power in this country while excluding other ethnic groups from full citizenship, political office, high-quality education, and generation of wealth. European Americans over many decades denied other groups the massive and enduring benefits they themselves harvested through "affirmative action programs for whites," such as the Homestead Acts, the New Deal and the Social Security System, and the G.I. Bill for veterans after World War II (*When Affirmative Action Was White*, Katznelson, 2005). Most people in academe express shock when they learn of the preferential bias and exclusion allowed into the implementation of the G.I. Bill. After all, many new campuses across the country were constructed and many others enlarged in order to receive returning war veterans. But in fact, *only* European-American male veterans were received and accommodated in any significant numbers. Academics above all others should know about this decades-long form of "affirmative action for whites" and its consequences within the realm of higher education.

Many decades of predominantly European immigration were followed, of course, by the immigration of non-European groups: Cubans, Asian Indians, Chinese, Japanese, Taiwanese, Central and South Americans, Jamaicans and others from the Caribbean islands, Nigerian and other African immigrants). Their prospects for success in this country depended in significant measure on how European Americans (the dominant immigrant group) regarded and treated them and what economic and political currents they discovered and had to ford. But the secret power that *all* immigrants had and have is this: they chose of *their own volition* to come to this country to start a new life. They came with "extravagant dreams" (Takaki, 1989, pp. 18, 66) and "an abundance of hope" (C. and M. Suarez-Orozco, 2001, p. 122). Despite having to endure varying degrees of hardships, each immigrant group has eventually become a part of the American fabric.

Non-immigrant groups, by contrast, were incorporated into this country by *force* (not choice), as I establish in Chapter 3. The majority group denigrated these non-immigrants and in various ways restricted them to the lowest caste-like levels of society. The omnipresent caste-like status—of African Americans, Mexican Americans, Puerto Rican Americans, American Indians, and Native Hawaiians—has had profoundly debilitating effects on their progress in academe and in American society.

Many power-holders at colleges, universities, and professional schools fail to fully grasp the extra complexities for *non-immigrants*. They tend to lump them together with immigrants and then name the entire assembly "people of color" and "minorities." Thus, instead of diversifying our faculties by successfully recruiting and retaining domestic *non-immigrants*, we all too often make the mistake of merely adding "difference" by hiring international and immigrant scholars and researchers. While global diversity is necessary and beneficial for many campuses, it is not sufficient. More care must be given to adding and retaining domestic non-immigrant faculty. And more skepticism must be given to academics' confusing and daily use of the concept and term "minority." In Chapter 3, with the assistance of several scholars, I offer more narrow and accurate terms that can be adopted.

Organization of the Book: Part 2—Removing the Barriers to Faculty Diversity

Chapters 4–6 make up Part 2 of this book. The blueprints, "nuts-and-bolts" instructions, caveats, checklists, and leadership-development elements laid out in these "action" chapters are derived from my consulting work since 1990 with campuses and professional schools, and since 2004 with a number of ADVANCE grant recipients. In these later chapters, I offer candid insights and strategies that will enable the following individuals and groups to remove barriers:

* search and other evaluation committees;
* senior faculty mentors of early-stage mentees as well as organizers of orientation sessions and mentoring programs for full-time and other faculty;
* provosts, deans, faculty affairs officers, and especially department chairs who are expected to develop talent and ensure retention of early-stage professors.

Chapter 4: Faculty Recruitment

Near the beginning of each action chapter in Part 2, I follow this routine: a list of dysfunctional practices will be followed by functional ones to replace them. For instance, after the "dirty laundry" list of dysfunctions in Faculty Recruitment (Chapter 4), I move to how to coach search committees in several ways about cognitive errors, including the use of the long "Discussion Scenario—Practice Exercise" at the end of the book. Further, I give details about eleven ground rules that should govern faculty search processes including:

* efficient outreach steps to identify URW and NI candidates;
* more effective "diversity hire" language for job ads;

- behavior-based interview questions;
- job-hunting assistance for the candidate's significant other.

These and other ground rules can be adopted or adapted by specific committees. Without such rules, "business as usual" will continue and few if any URW or NIs will be hired.

Chapter 5: Faculty Retention

In Chapter 5 on Faculty Retention, dysfunctional practices are listed and then quickly followed by in-depth details about good ones. These include: how to mount professional-development workshops for all early-stage faculty; and how to ensure that senior colleagues and department chairs attend to the typical stressors faced by early-stage faculty— and especially to the *extra* stressors faced by URW, NIs, and new hires who find themselves in solo situations. I also discuss the *extra steps* that should be taken by chairs and others to diminish these extra stressors.

Chapter 6: Faculty Mentoring

Finally, I provide in Chapter 6 an extensive discussion of mentoring that did not appear in the first edition of *Faculty Diversity*. I have found in my consulting practice that little informal mentoring is actually being done. I also have found that mentors are rarely given any formal preparation for this important responsibility. They deserve better. In their roles as mentors, they can immeasurably advance the job satisfaction, success, and retention of early-stagers, but in particular URWs, NIs, and solos. I begin the chapter with a listing of dysfunctional mentoring practices. But much of this chapter is devoted to helping senior mentors correct dysfunctional practices by becoming more competent and confident in their mentoring roles, especially when assigned to URW, NIs, and solos. I also offer several recommendations for organizing, monitoring, and assessing formal mentoring programs.

At the end of each of my of the chapters in this section, I reserve special attention for provosts, deans, and department chairs. I indicate sometimes novel ways that they, in their roles, can enhance faculty recruitment, retention, and mentorship, most especially of URW, NIs, and solos. They are indispensable to advancing faculty diversity.

In the Conclusion and Next Steps of this second edition, I return to these key leaders and suggest that they deserve regularly scheduled workshops or retreats—where they can renew their commitment to faculty diversity and prepare for the challenges that are sure to follow. In particular, I believe these leaders should become more pro-active in disarming what I present as *twelve* typical lines of resistance and confusion regarding the adding of URW and NI groups to the faculty ranks. To this end, I recommend more practice drills and exercises, more "devil's advocate" debates, and more leadership-development workshops devoted to analysis, problem-solving, and thinking outside their own cognitive boxes.

Appendix

The Appendix to this book includes a few supplements to the conceptual material of the first three chapters, with primary focus on the caste-like experiences of domestic non-immigrants. The Appendix also includes four **"Discussion Scenarios—Practice Exercises for Readers and Groups."** These depict:

- a search committee in an early stage and then a late stage of its deliberations;
- several mentors and mentees as they deal with problems and build their relationships;
- a well-meaning but inept interim chair interacting with a brand-new non-immigrant faculty member.

The Scenarios (and the accompanying discussion questions) are designed as Practice Exercises. They can be used in small or large groups to promote brainstorming, critical thinking, and the application of concepts previously learned. They also give participants the opportunity to design actions that might be taken by a character in the scenario and to role-play particular responses. I have successfully used discussion scenarios such as these in my consulting practice with a variety of groups, including search and evaluation committees; mentors-in-training; deans, chairs, and emerging leaders at retreats; subsets of faculty senates; and entire departments.

* * * * *

Before moving on from this Introduction, I want to climb to the bully pulpit, with an exhortation in hand. *The professoriate should welcome and include far more non-immigrants and under-represented women— and make a place for them where they can add value, through their unique intelligence, enterprise, and creativity. Their contributions are essential for enriching student learning and kindling student ambitions; for framing problems in unconventional ways and generating new knowledge and solutions; and for strengthening American democracy and showing that it works.*
    And now, let us begin.

Part 1

THE BARRIERS TO
FACULTY DIVERSITY

1

COGNITIVE ERRORS THAT CONTAMINATE ACADEMIC EVALUATIONS AND BLOCK FACULTY DIVERSITY

Regarding our job candidates, I just don't think Mercedes would be a good fit. Honestly, I can't see any of us having a beer with her at the corner pub. While it would be terrific to have a teacher and researcher who is Mexican American, we need to find someone who is a better fit.

(An anonymous member of a faculty search committee)

For the first four minutes of Todd's job talk, I noticed that he was shaking in his boots. We certainly don't need a high-maintenance, low-confidence kind of guy around here. No way.

(Another anonymous member of the committee)

The ideal ... of the doctor as a dispassionate and rational actor is misguided. As ... cognitive psychologists have shown, when people are confronted with uncertainty—the situation of every doctor attempting to diagnose a patient—they are susceptible to unconscious emotions and personal biases, and are more likely to make cognitive errors.

(Harvard Medical Professor Jerome Groopman, 2007b, p. 41)

Across the country, I am amazed to find that evaluation committees try very, very hard to <u>read the minds</u> of various candidates they are considering (for instance 'I'm sure she won't accept our job offer because her partner is still in a post-doc in L.A. Have no doubt: she'll turn us down).

(Gilda Barabino, Georgia Tech and Emory University Biomedical Engineering Professor and also Associate Chair for Graduate Studies, conversation with Prof. Barabino, 2011)

Every day at colleges, universities, professional schools, research institutes, and government labs, we find evaluation and decision-making processes underway. Those doing the evaluations will usually be reaching important decisions about students, staff, colleagues and prospective colleagues, and others. Yet we are learning, from the research of cognitive scientists, that many of the selection and evaluation processes we undertake on a daily basis are alarmingly "contaminated," despite our good intentions. The contaminants—generically termed "cognitive shortcuts and errors"—are present as we gather and sort through information, interpret it, and reach decisions about the following: candidates for jobs, tenure/promotion, and contract renewals; applications for grants; nominations for awards and leadership posts; and colleagues' and students' professional and academic performance, mastery of new concepts and skills, publications, exhibits, and other demonstrations of mastery and creativity.

During these cognitive processes, most of us *unwittingly* commit a variety of errors and automatically take shortcuts. A chronic one, regularly showing up in our personal and professional lives, is the confusion between causation and correlation. Who among us is immune from that error? Unfortunately, there are many more confusions and traps. If we are rushed and distracted, then cognitive errors and shortcuts demonstrably multiply. When those involved in evaluation and decision-making are not coached and not given opportunities to be thorough, deliberate, and self-correcting, then dysfunction results and unsound conclusions are reached about colleagues as well as prospective colleagues and potential award recipients.

Cognitive errors, intensified by organizational dysfunctions, can of course bring about the unfair measurement and evaluation of *anyone* included in the selection process. But I will suggest here and in other chapters that these errors have disproportionately damaging effects on under-represented women in predominantly male fields (whom I will abbreviate as URW) as well as especially damaging impacts on members of colonized, non-immigrant groups (NIs). The errors—usually made quickly and automatically—result in the under-valuing and frequent rejection of URW and NIs and therefore inadvertently block campuses' and schools' progress on diversifying their faculty ranks. A very serious roadblock needs to be removed.

Setting the Stage

Before continuing, it's important for the reader to know how I will be using the term non-immigrant (NI). I mean the term, discussed in detail in Chapter 3, to include five groups: African Americans, Mexican Americans, American Indians, Puerto Rican Americans, and Native Hawaiians. These non-immigrant groups were incorporated into this country through force (enslaving, conquering, possessing, dispossessing, denigrating). By contrast, immigrant groups were not subject to such force: they arrived through their own volition.

Who exactly are the fortunate immigrant groups who exercised the choice to settle here, despite encountering hardships and struggles? Immigrant groups include: the dominant European Americans; Asian Americans with their several subgroups, some of whom are now regarded in the United States as "honorary whites"; newcomers from Africa, the Caribbean, the Middle East, Eastern Europe, and so on; and recent and non-so-recent arrivals from South and Central America, some of whom are also regarded as "honorary whites" (Lopez, 2006a; Wu, 2002; and a dozen other scholars). Immigrant groups are motivated by choice and ambition. They are usually accompanied by and aided in establishing their new lives by other newcomers—newcomers who share some of their habits and values because they in fact have also come from the *same* village or area in the old world.

In this first chapter, I will focus on thirteen cognitive errors that show up repeatedly in academe. These have serious consequences for URW and NI groups. In Chapter 2, I will delve deeply into two additional and highly significant errors: negative bias/stereotyping and positive bias/ stereotyping, which also have serious consequences for URW and NI groups. Further, in almost every chapter of this book including this first one, I will outline dysfunctional practices that exacerbate the frequency and severity of the fifteen cognitive errors (such as rushing and overloading evaluation and decision-making committees or failing to adequately prepare, assist, and then monitor those involved in the processes).

Finally, I will suggest ways to end these organizational bad practices as well as to reduce the cognitive errors and shortcuts committed by individuals, in usually innocent and unknowing ways. (For more on this subject see Moody, 2010, *Rising Above Cognitive Errors*.)

An Overview of Cognitive Errors

Consider diagnoses of medical disorders. In examining and interacting with patients and reviewing lab results, practitioners must be able to resist predictable and preventable errors, including first impressions; rushing to judgment; bias based on gender or group membership; and failing to factor in atypical symptoms and instead selectively choosing data that confirm one's original hunches (see Groopman, *How Doctors Think*, 2007; also Dawson and Arkes, 1987; Redelmeier, 2005; Bond, 2004; Croskerry, 2003).

Likewise, behavioral economists and legal and cognitive experts (such as Sunstein, Thaler, Kahneman, Greenwald, Krieger) have identified shortcuts and biases that corrupt "rational" thinking, the estimate of probabilities, and sound decision-making and investing. Who is susceptible to these shortcuts and to what economists Robert Shiller and George Akerlof call "animal spirits" in their book by the same name (2009)? Lawyers, judges, juries, investors (big and small), professional financial managers, Federal Reserve Bank directors, philosophers, campus presidents, and, of course, the general public are susceptible. As one example, how one chooses to frame a problem can easily shut down open-minded exploration and foreclose certain solutions. Anchoring (i.e., fierce adherence to one's first impression) will corrupt deliberations as will a number of other predictable cognitive errors.

Recognizing the prevalence and danger of cognitive errors, several law and medical schools have begun coaching their students and residents to form self-correction habits and to routinely rely on safeguard protocols, reminders, and checklists (Gawande, *The Checklist Manifesto*, 2009). Likewise senior decision-makers at colleges, universities, and professional schools—as well as their gate-keeping bodies such as search committees—are receiving instruction in cognitive errors and in structural ways to minimize the errors and improve peer review. Such instruction of individuals and committees plus larger organizational changes are *long overdue*.

Thirteen Cognitive Errors

I will begin the discussion of cognitive errors by focusing first on *the tendency to rely on first impressions*. I will then examine in turn twelve other errors that evaluation and decision-making committees are capable of recognizing and rising above—when they are appropriately coached, assisted, and monitored.

1. First Impressions

Probably most of us are perennially reminding ourselves to stop judging a book by its cover. Unless we remain on guard, we will unfairly make conclusions about a candidate or applicant or new acquaintance in a matter of seconds, based on whether their dress or cologne or posture or laughter or something else pleases or displeases us. Our own personal values and preferences (and, of course, our learned stereotypes about certain groups, which I will consider in Chapter 2) can inordinately influence us to make fast and unexamined assumptions and even decisions about a person's worth or appeal.

For instance, you might hear a powerful gate-keeper observe: *Well, that ponytail and those blue jeans clinched it for me, as soon as I saw him walk towards us. Clearly, that applicant is disrespecting us and still thinks he's in graduate school.* Responding to the same candidate at the same moment in time, a second person might observe: *I got a kick out of the ponytail and jeans. I bet he'd be a sharp person for our emergency-*

room team. Both of these rapid-fire assumptions could be fuel for sloppy decision-making about the applicant.

2. Elitism

This error involves feeling superior or wanting to feel superior. Elitism (commonly known as snobbery) could take the form of downgrading on the basis of the candidate's undergraduate or doctoral campus, regional accent, dress, jewelry, social class, ethnic background, and so on (Moody, *Rising*, 2010; Padilla and Chavez, 1995). A search committee member might complain: *She's so very Southern—I'm not sure I can stand that syrupy accent. These folks always sound illiterate to me.* Or conversely, giving extra points on the basis of the candidate's alma mater, accent, dress, or other items can be a manifestation of elitism. An evaluation committee member might observe about a candidate: *Isn't it nice to hear his English accent? Always sounds classy. He would be a wonderful choice for our fellowship.*

Other examples of elitism are easy to find: Fearing that a NI colleague from a stigmatized group will somehow lessen the quality and standing of the department, a committee member might say: *Well, shouldn't we always ask if a particular hire like Dewayne is likely to bolster our place in the business school ratings wars? I think that's okay. I mean, Dewayne's scholarship is a bit out of the mainstream and could weaken us.* Another similar example might be: *Are we sure Ricardo will be productive enough to keep up with our publishing standards? I'm not so sure.*

Elitism can, of course, prompt a committee member to feel validated because the candidate will bring some extra snob appeal. *I think Les's doctorate from Princeton is just the kind of boost in prestige that we could use around here. I see no reason why we can't take that degree at face value and forego the so-called 'weighing' of what Les has done at Princeton with what the other candidates have accomplished at their hard-scrabble places. To me, that's an awful waste of our time.*

3. Raising the Bar

This error involves raising requirements for a job or an award *during* the very process of evaluation. The raising is usually felt to be necessary because of the decision-maker's realization that the candidate is a member of a suspect group regarded as inferior (such as URW in science fields and NIs in almost every field). You may hear:

Say, don't we need more writing samples from Latorya? I know we asked for only three law review articles or other compositions from applicants. OK, hers are solid. But I'd feel better, to tell you the truth, if we had a few more in this particular case. I just want to be sure she's <u>really</u> *qualified. I have to admit I'm uneasy for some reason.*

A second instance: Another committee member agrees and says, *Well, I wish Latorya had a doctorate from the Ivy League or maybe Berkeley. Can't we informally decide right now that Latorya and other candidates have to possess those credentials? I think we can.*

My point is that "raising the bar" is unfair and yet unwittingly done in evaluations. Unfortunately, power-holders don't stop to ponder why they may be uncomfortable and why they desire both more evidence and more qualifications for one candidate but not for another. Perhaps group membership is implicated.

4. Premature Ranking/Digging In

All too often, evaluators at every kind of educational institution rush to give numerical preferences to the applicants they are considering. I often wonder if this haste-to-rank brings relief to evaluators and falsely assures them that they have now *escaped* both personal subjectivity and embarrassing vulnerability to cognitive errors. Perhaps they finally feel they have achieved objectivity and fairness. Ranking, after all, gets you "a number" and that guarantees objectivity, doesn't it? Embracing such *false precision* is unfortunately what many of us indulge in.

The superficial rush to rank candidates leads evaluators to prematurely state their position (*he's clearly number one*); close their minds to new evidence; and then defend their stated position to the death. Rather than developing a pool of acceptable and qualified candidates and then comparing, contrasting, and mulling over candidates' different strengths with one's colleagues, some evaluators prefer to simplify their task and go for the simple numbers.

Here is one illustration of premature ranking and digging in: *Well, I don't want to waste time here in summarizing each candidate's strengths and weaknesses, as the dean suggested. That seems to me just a useless writing exercise proposed by our dean, an overzealous former English professor. I've got enough evidence to make up my mind about who should be number one, number two, and number three. I just hope we can hire number one and not be stuck with the others.*

Another illustration: *Let's go through the categories we're using and assign points to each of the serious candidates for this job. I totally trust everyone here so you don't have to give me subtle and complicated reasons for your actions. With this straight-forward, no-nonsense approach, we can quickly add up the points and we've got a decision on our first choice—all in twenty-five minutes or less. I'm a big believer in mathematical, objective approaches to these decisions.*

Rushing to rank is a mistake because it obviates engagement with colleagues in these cognitively beneficial tasks: higher-order thinking, sifting through and interpreting evidence, comparing and contrasting, and "weighing" the importance of different items of evidence on the table.

Rushing to rank easily fades into *rushing to judgment*. Admittedly, this rushing to judgment *could* stand on its own as a cognitive error. But in this publication, I have not treated it this way.

5. The Longing to Clone

The longing to clone (reproduce yourself or your clan as nearly as you can) appears in the search process when committee members undervalue a candidate's educational credentials and career trajectory simply because they are not the same as most of those on the evaluation committee. You might hear a committee member ask: *Hey, have we ever chosen anyone with a doctorate from the University of Southwestern Nevada? We don't know anything about that place. No one here ever went to that school, did they? No way.* Or you might hear during tenure-review deliberations: *I am dubious about this woman's seriousness as a researcher. Her dropping out for several years to raise little kids— this is not a confidence-builder in my book. Alarm bells are going off in my head. None of the rest of us ever had such leaves—it's a dangerous move, no matter what your gender.*

In another instance of cloning, a committee member seeks candidates who resemble a colleague who has retired or died. You might hear: *I can't believe that Tony has been gone for three years now. He was the perfect colleague and tax expert. Isn't it time we found someone just like him?*

While the sentiment about missing Tony's presence is understandable, the danger comes when the committee constructs a very narrow net in order to find a Tony-like replacement and recreate the past. Casting a narrow net can do a disservice to the growth and evolution of the school and will shrink the number of qualified candidates who might be given serious consideration.

6. Good Fit/Bad Fit

Increasingly, gate-keeping individuals and committees ponder and worry whether a job candidate would be a "good fit" or "bad fit" for their department. It is, of course, necessary for a candidate to be able to meet the agreed-on needs of the department, the students, the institution, and perhaps the community. Further, candidates being seriously scrutinized should possess the professional qualifications and competencies listed in the position description. But these elements are usually not what is meant by "fit." Instead "fit" is often stretched to mean: "Will I feel comfortable and culturally at ease with this new hire? Or will I have to spend energy to learn some new ways to relate to this person? Will we have to do a lot of hand-holding with this colleague? Who has the time?"

In other words, the longing to clone and to remain intact as a monoculture within the department may be prompting the complaint that the candidate "just won't fit with us." The same longing to clone can appear in tenure reviews when the candidate is faulted for not being sufficiently collegial. In fact, the American Association of University Professors has begun to warn campuses to resist the slippery use of "collegial" as the reason for denying tenure and/or promotion. The vague term and concept seem to lie in the eyes of the beholder and the power-holder. All of us should be on guard against rampant subjectivity when the question is posed: "Is this a good fit?" The weighing of good fit and bad fit should be done very carefully and with the presence of abundant evidence and details, rather than opinions and personal leanings. I often remark to my consulting clients that I will be pleased if they come to *intensely worry* about how their evaluation committees are handling the good fit/bad fit discussion. Such worry, I hope, will prompt leaders to provide and require more preparation of evaluation committees as well as to issue warnings and reminders about treacherous shortcuts to avoid, such as rushing superficially through the weighing of "fit." Far too often, committees fail to be on guard. Far too often, they use "good fit/bad fit" as what I would call a "trump card" in the evaluation process.

As one illustration, you may hear: *Well, I think Mercedes doesn't deserve tenure. We've lived with her long enough to know that she's really very, very different from the rest of us. Sure, she can do the job and do it rather well. But to be blunt, she's just not the kind of person I like to spend time with, especially socially. She's never going to become a soccer mom in this town, if you know what I mean. We can do better.*

Another example: *Timothy will stick out in our department, as I'm sure everyone here senses. Won't he be hard to relate to? He is so clearly a New York City kind of a person. He's just too different from the rest of us. We've got a bad fit here, I think. On the other hand, Jerry would be great for us. He can hit the ground running and will be able to read our minds—well, at least most of the time. That's the beauty of his coming here. He'll fit right into everything, very fast. He's just like us— that's the long and short of it.*

7. Provincialism

Closely related to cloning, this error means undervaluing something outside your own province, circle, or clan. Several comprehensive studies have shown that evaluation committees often tend to trust only those letters of recommendation or external review that are written by people they personally know (Sagaria, 2002) or who are in certain respected networks. This could be termed an "affiliation bonus" (Wenneras and Wold, 1997).

You might hear a committee member disclose: *Listen, I'm uneasy because I have never met this referee. I have a gut feeling that we shouldn't give his letter much credence. I just have no confidence in what is being said.* In effect, the committee member is announcing: "I trust only those from my own clan or network."

Another example: *Here's a funny, old-fashioned letter. I'm not sure we should really believe all these superlatives. The author writes what could only be termed a 'very peculiar' external review letter. Yes, yes, I know we have debated whether we should give external referees more guidelines. Maybe we should. But anyway, I have the distinct feeling that this particular author wouldn't be able to follow our guidelines. She's clearly living in an earlier century.*

8. Extraneous Myths and Assumptions (Including "Psychoanalyzing" the Candidate)

Personal opinions and misinformation should be suspect during evaluations. So too should second-guessing, mind-reading, or what I prefer to call "psychoanalyzing the candidate." Here are several illustrations of misinformation and of psychoanalysis.

- *Sally is bound to be unhappy with our harsh winters and our family-centered town. I'm certain of that.*
- *Really, there are no qualified women or minorities for us to hire. I wish there were. The pool is bone-dry* (paraphrased from Smith, 1996).
- *No one from Georgia Tech would want to come here. I know some of those folks. I'm positive about that.*
- *Minorities like Tonya will be receiving a dozen early-career awards in the next year or two. After all, we're now in the decade of "Let's celebrate the minority scientist." So I say we by-pass Tonya because she'll be getting plenty of prestigious recognition from other folks.*
- *Zack will find it too rural here. I wish we had cosmopolitan and diverse neighborhoods for him but we don't.*
- *This candidate will turn down our offer in an instant. Our measly salary will insult this finance whiz. Let's not set ourselves up for rejection.*
- *This candidate will not be satisfied with a small medical school like ours, no matter what she said. I can only see her thriving at a huge research university.*
- *Her husband has a great job in New Jersey. So put two and two together. This candidate won't accept an offer from us. We're too far away.*
- *Ricardo is playing us for a fool. What I mean is this: he can't be serious about coming to our campus. He's just adding us to his list of eager suitors. Under-represented minorities like Ricardo get a hundred job offers. We don't have a chance, and we should face up to that painful fact* (paraphrased from Smith, 1996).

11

- *I worry that this campus can't provide Yolanda with a Puerto Rican-American faculty mentor. She deserves a mentor who has the same ethnic background. She needs that kind of person to help her learn the ropes and understand what she's up against here. It would be a disservice to bring her in when we are empty-handed in this area. It just wouldn't be in her best interest.*

9. Wishful Thinking; Rhetoric not Evidence

By wishful thinking, I mean not only holding to a notion in spite of overwhelming evidence to the contrary but also casually allowing this notion to cloud one's cognitive processes. A common form of wishful thinking is this: insisting that America and its colleges, universities, and professional schools operate as a *meritocracy* where whom you know and what status and privileges you start with are immaterial.

An illustration: *There is absolutely no subjectivity or favoritism involved when we seek merit and excellence in candidates. We should be proud that all of our grant winners have cultural anthropology doctorates from Yale and Texas. After all, they're the best and the brightest in my book.*

Another instance of wishful, non-critical thinking occurs when someone insists that they (or the committee) are color-blind and gender-blind and therefore there is no need for them to be more careful than usual in their deliberations. *Listen, I don't really see gender or race in people. Really, I don't. It doesn't matter to me whether a job candidate is black, white, green, polka dot, or purple. Really, it doesn't. I don't see why you're asking me, of all people, to bend over backwards to recruit more and more minority candidates. Give me a break.*

In my other publications, I discuss how the gender-blind and color-blind assertion is almost always a self-serving, disingenuous rhetorical plea by a *majority* person (for non-majorities to make such an assertion would be absurd). With this plea, the majority person seems to be claiming some sort of political innocence and otherworldly infallibility as well as disclaiming any responsibility for past or current discrimination and devaluation of women and minorities. Further, the gender-blind and color-blind assertion deliberately calls into question the wisdom of trying to identify and perhaps hire women and non-immigrants. Faculty search committees should deal with this line of resistance *before* they commence their work. Otherwise, the assertion at certain points can confuse and even unravel the committee's efforts to diversify its departmental faculty.

A number of scholars agree with Penn State Professor Frances Rains that the color-blind assertion attempts to "trivialize the substance and weight of the intertwined histories of Whites and people of color" (1999 p. 93), histories intertwined in the U.S. since the beginning of English settlements in the 17th century (also see Dahl, 2001; Fair, 1997; Guinier

12

and Torres, 2000; Takaki, 1993; Gaertner and Dovidio, 1986; Moody, "Rising," 2010). While *on the surface* the color-blind, gender-blind assertion may sound admirable, it usually plays out as a disingenuous and trivializing stance that, I maintain, can slow down actual diversifying at schools and campuses.

Finally, wishful thinking can also be illustrated when a group of evaluators is satisfied with the mere uttering of one individual's opinions and hunches—and does not insist on evidence and verifiable facts. Perhaps the evaluation committee members don't wish to or feel they can't take the time to do the required digging and hard work that must precede the consideration and weighing of evidence. Accepting opinions and wishful thinking are so much easier.

Ironically, most of the cognitive errors being discussed in this book could be characterized as what happens when time-consuming digging for evidence and then careful sifting through it are in fact *abandoned*. Instead, decision-makers unfortunately allow short-cut stating of opinions, personal likes and dislikes, and standard stereotypes to thrive.

10. Self-Fulfilling Prophecy

Some experts would prefer to call this error "channeling," which has been described as structuring our interaction with someone so that we can receive information congruent with our assumptions or so that we can avoid information incongruent with our assumptions. If you have high expectations for someone, you may unthinkingly set up situations — sometimes called *priming*—so that person is likely to be spotlighted in a positive way and earn extra points. Or conversely, if you have low expectations for someone, you can easily set up situations so that these low expectations will be confirmed (Nahavandi and Malekzadeh, 1999).

An example of self-fulfilling prophecy might unfold in this way. You believe the job candidate coming for an interview tomorrow is head and shoulders above all the other candidates. Consequently, you ask one of your most senior and well-informed colleagues to meet the candidate at the airport. Primed by this colleague, the candidate will be better prepared than other candidates for issues he or she will face in the upcoming interviews and evaluation process.

Yet another illustration of self-fulfilling prophecy might occur in a situation like this: the committee has chosen three candidates to interview. In your judgment as chair of the committee, two candidates look more attractive on paper than the third. Based on your reading of the files, you decide to place personal phone calls to the two you regard as stronger, to answer their questions. But you ask the *department secretary* to call the third one. It shouldn't be surprising if the third candidate doesn't do as well as the others during the visit. Although this slighting of one

13

applicant is probably unintentional, the slighting can activate the self-fulfilling prophecy.

11. Seizing a Pretext

Seizing a pretext is creating a smoke screen to hide one's real concerns or agenda. By seizing on a pretextual reason, a power-holder can come to the decision desired while keeping hidden or obscure the real reason for the decision.

One example involves assigning excessive weight to something trivial, in order to justify quick dismissal of the candidate. Someone might say: *Raquel seemed so nervous during the first five minutes of her job talk. Why keep her in the running for the administrative position? We don't need a timid mouse to work with.* What this evaluator may be really doing is setting up a superficial and false reason for a thumbs-down verdict.

In another example of seizing a pretext, a tenure and promotion committee decides to "selectively exclude favorable [teaching] ratings and focus on the two courses in which a professor had difficulties" and then to use this "contrivance" as a key reason for refusing tenure to the candidate. Such a deliberate and outrageous smoke screen was uncovered by a judge in a case discussed in *Tenure Denied: Cases of Sex Discrimination in Academia* (American Association of University Women, pp. 56–57). Pretextual reasons, when they go unchallenged, ensure contaminated results.

12. Assuming Character over Context

Assuming character over context means that a judge does not consider the particular context and any extenuating circumstances within that context but instead thinks automatically that an individual's personal characteristics explain her or his behavior. (Some social scientists call this an "attribution" error.)

Here is one example of character over context: A committee member might say, *Well, I didn't like the offhanded way that Walter responded to your question about his most recent public health report, at dinner last night. I mean, is he really serious about this job or not?* Here the committee member ignores the social nature of the dinner setting. Perhaps the candidate thought it would be inappropriate to get into a long discussion of his research since that would be the focus of his two-hour presentation the next day.

Another example of character over context: A committee member hastily concludes, *You know, Sheila didn't seem very lively when I saw her after my 4 p.m. seminar. I don't think we want a low-energy person joining our technology-transfer team.* Here the committee person ignores the context that the interview is late in the day after a lengthy series of interviews for the applicant. That context might well have been the explanation for Sheila's behavior.

A third illustration of this particular cognitive error concerns teaching evaluations. Over the years, various personnel and tenure review committees on a campus might have noticed that women and non-immigrant instructors usually earn lower teaching evaluation ratings from students than do male majority instructors who are usually viewed as the "norm." Despite this familiar pattern, few committee members have ever bothered to check external studies to see if group-bias and gender-bias could help explain this pattern (they do). Instead, the committees blithely assume that URW and NIs themselves are totally responsible for their lower ranking and should pay the consequences.

13. Momentum of the Group

If most members of an evaluation committee are favoring one candidate, then it will be more difficult for the remaining members to resist that push towards consensus. The remaining members will have to work harder to get a full hearing for other candidates. Sometimes the struggle doesn't seem to be worth it.

Here is one example: *Okay, this is the last time that I try to call attention to other worthy applicants. Come on, hear me out. Let me go over the strengths and weaknesses, as I see them, of two more promising folks. Hey, listen to me, please.*

The difficulties involved in resisting the group consensus and trying to get the group to extend its deliberations are evident in this example: *Yes, I know we're all exhausted. I know we've spent more time on this stage of the search process that we intended. Nevertheless, I want to make sure we give a full hearing to the only African American in our pool of finalists. Why should he be dismissed quickly when we invested plenty of thought and care in the others? Is he here just for the sake of symbolic value and to reassure our dean that we did indeed try to diversify our faculty? Please, hear me out. Please.*

Another example illustrates the power of the group's considerable momentum: *Stop and think, Patrick. Doesn't it make you wonder why all the rest of us are behind Candidate A and <u>you're</u> the <u>only</u> holdout? Are you sure you're not just trying to make some ideological point or be a royal pain? I'm just kidding, of course.*

Organizational Dysfunctions that Exacerbate Cognitive Errors and Unsound Evaluations

The thirteen errors and shortcuts just named are likely to be made— unwittingly and repeatedly—by *individuals* during evaluation processes.

These contaminants can and often do undermine what should be the evidence-based rigor and equity of evaluation reviews.

But when the larger conditions and practices within a lab, institute, department, division, or larger *organization* are dysfunctional, then the severity of an individual's and a review committee's errors (and the consequences of those errors) is unfortunately magnified. I now want to highlight bad practices frequently manifested at the organizational level that do indeed serve as magnifiers. How to fix these bad practices will receive attention especially in Chapters 4 and 5.

1. Overloading and Rushing the Search Committee

It is common to abruptly "thrust" a search committee or other evaluation entity into its complex task without adequate time to prepare or to execute with care. I have repeatedly heard this complaint from committee members. "No wonder," they tell me, "we can't think straight. No wonder that we keep reproducing ourselves year after year. No wonder that we can't manage to do active searches but just keep on doing wholesale screening out of candidates. We have a mess here."

Unfortunately, it is standard procedure to rush and overwhelm evaluation committees. Cognitive errors and shortcuts will thrive in frenetic situations. "When people are distracted or put under pressure to respond quickly," they become far more vulnerable to cognitive errors and "faulty decision-making," according to Steven Pinker and a number of other cognitive researchers whose work parallels his (Pinker, 2002, p. 205; also Martell, 1991; Croskerry, 2000, 2003; Groopman, 2007a,b).

Rather than committee members being relieved of some of their routine duties, they are usually given their search or other evaluation assignment as an overload to their regular work. Not receiving extra secretarial support or assistance from the dean's office, the members and the chair struggle on their own to plow quickly through applications instead of carefully considering which candidates would bring new skills and strengths to their department or school.

Finally, search and other evaluation committees are sometimes hastily formed. If there is a renewed commitment in the hiring department and school to identify and hire more under-represented women and non-immigrant, domestic minorities, then this renewed commitment should be reflected in those who are chosen to carry out the search (Whetten and Cameron, 2002). To keep the committee alert to opportunities for identifying and hiring more members of under-represented U.S. groups (not international or immigrant) and more women, I recommend that one committee member be designated as the Diversity Advocate. (Stanford Medical School uses the term "Good Practices Monitor" while several ADVANCE-National Science Foundation campuses use the term "Equity Advisor.") After some coaching, this Advocate or Monitor will be able to effectively remind members of the importance of hiring under-represented colleagues and can gently press everyone to do more out-reach to diversify the applicant pool. And, of course, the Advocate can assist the committee chair in helping to keep the evaluation on track and away from cognitive errors and a rush to judgment.

2. No Coaching and No Practice for the Committee

Corporations habitually spend time and money ensuring that the managers who hire new employees are well-trained and practiced in search and interview methods. But professional schools and campuses often neglect this dimension—perhaps assuming that anyone can do a job search, just as anyone can teach. (Not true, of course.)

One single job search often requires enormous "economic, adminis-trative, emotional, and interpersonal resources" from the search mem-bers and the school as a whole. When one accounts for the cost of job advertisements, for the time spent by search members, staff, and deans as they sort and review applications and support materials, for the travel expense of bringing finalists to campus for interview, then the total sum arrived at "is about the same as the first-year salary of that new faculty member (at least in the humanities)" (Dettmar, 2004, p. B8). If the new hire works in a specialty that requires scientific equipment and special resources, then the start-up cost is much, much higher. Thus, it is worth-while to improve search practices in order to increase the likelihood of hiring a sound person who will stay and succeed.

What passes for preparation is woefully inadequate at most places: provosts, deans, human resource directors, or affirmative action offi-cers will distribute to search committees a list of illegal questions to avoid asking job candidates (regarding marital status, age, sexual orien-tation, disability, family, pregnancy, religion) but will do *nothing more* to prepare the committees. With only this cursory list of "don'ts" in hand, the committee members often feel confused and hamstrung. For instance, when they may want to court a candidate by offering to help find employment for his/her significant other, the committee members remain quiet because they believe broaching that topic is illegal. Silence on this topic is a *bad* practice. Numerous studies of new hires, includ-ing Cathy Trower's COACHE program, underscore that assistance with spousal hiring can be a deal-*maker* or a deal-*breaker* during the hiring season (see the Harvard website for details about the Collaborative on Academic Careers in Higher Education).

What the committee desperately needs to know are acceptable and legal ways to discuss this deal-maker or deal-breaker. Some job candi-dates, invariably, will be shy and hesitant about bringing up the dual-hire topic on their own: this is yet another reason for interviewers to take the lead. As one example, Associate Vice Chancellor and physicist Bernice

Durand at the University of Wisconsin-Madison delivers the following deft and perfectly legal statement to every finalist during their campus visit: "If information about dual-career assistance interests you, it's right here in this packet of materials I'm giving you. Please let me know of questions you may have before your campus visit ends, or you can email or phone me after your visit is completed" (conversation with Durand, 2009). Another legal, effective example: "We on the search committee are sending a brochure to *all* candidates being interviewed by us over the phone. This brochure describes how spouses and significant others (of those we hire) will be assisted in identifying and finding jobs in this geographical area. For more info, candidates should contact the person in the provost's office who is named in that brochure."

Failing to coach evaluation committees—and especially committee chairs—is a *dire* mistake. While the provost or the dean may resort to impressive arguments and rhetorical flourishes as they charge the committees to be fair and careful in their deliberations, such an abstract pep-talk does little good, in my experience. Instead of delivering a pep-talk, these power-holders should ensure that evaluation and selection committees engage in thorough preparation as well as in thoughtful review of the cognitive errors and corrupters discussed in this publication. Following this review, committee members should be given *practice sessions* to sharpen their skills and alertness.

Deans and provosts might wish to adapt some new strategies currently being adopted by several medical schools and teaching hospitals. These medical institutions are beginning to coach medical students, residents, and physicians to better understand—and then reduce—their unwitting reliance on cognitive errors and shortcuts. Several approaches have recently been launched, which I will quickly list.

- Simulations with a mannequin can bring to light medical residents' shortcuts and lead them to cultivate *mandatory mindfulness* and resistance to the particular errors each of them tends to repeatedly make. (The use of simulations was borrowed from the aviation industry's training of pilots with computerized flight simulations.)
- Many more active-learning *exercises* are being developed because lectures by experts have proven ineffective. Passive listening does not build skills.
- Clinicians are warned that they must be extra cautious when dealing with a number of predictably complex and ambiguous situations (such as abdominal pain in an elderly patient) that are habitually and quickly mis-diagnosed by novices *and* veterans.
- Medical residents and others are cautioned to seek second opinions and feedback from other experts—so that they can grasp alternative perspectives and treatments and enhance their thinking *out-*

side their own cognitive boxes (Gallagher, 2003; Bond et al., 2006; Croskerry, 2000; Redelmeier, 2005; Pronovost, 2009).

It is also encouraging to see that a subset of medical experts is constructing a new professional society devoted to "Diagnostic Error in Medicine," with its first international conference held in 2008. The quickening attention to cognitive errors is encouraging and overdue. My guess is that some of the self-correction techniques being developed will find their way—and indeed should find their way—into academic evaluations and decision-making.

3. Failure to Consult Relevant Parties

Before the search or evaluation commences, the committee should have time to consult and discuss with the department chair, the dean, the hospital director, the technology-transfer officer (or any other relevant officials) *the various programmatic needs and opportunities* to be considered and decided on before the process goes forward. Because this all-important ground rule is often ignored, committee members in the midst of their work are likely to become flummoxed and even enraged with one another: "Wait a minute! You're dead wrong. That's not the reason we're trying to fill the vacancy. I never heard and certainly never agreed to such nonsense" or "The dean is simply not going to get a patent law expert though he is pushing us relentlessly. He's wasted his time. I refuse to go along with him or with the rest of you. That's my position."

4. No Ground Rules

Other key issues must be clarified before the committee is activated. These clarifications should lead to the construction of ground rules to govern the committee's work. Examples include:

- How will committee members help one another rise above cognitive shortcuts and errors?
- What are the job criteria we agree to use for the selection process? Do we agree that we won't create additional criteria half-way through our process?
- What are the *preferred* versus the *required* credentials, experience, achievements, and/or skills we are seeking? Using the word *preferred* will open the door to "equivalent" expertise—expertise that often goes unrecognized when evaluation groups construct their searches or award selections in the same old way, year after year (Turner, 2002, p. 17)
- How will all committee members (or certain designated ones) undertake pro-active outreach early on in the evaluation process, so that

19

a *broad net is being used*—rather than a cut-and-dried narrow net probably used by previous committees.

A number of other ground rules for evaluation committees will be set forth in nuts-and-bolts specificity in Chapter 4 on Faculty Recruitment. Ground rules usually end up saving time because the evaluation chair can reel in members from wild-goose chases by referring back to what everyone agreed in the beginning. Further, ground rules can put a welcome damper on what one dean vividly labeled the "psycho-dramas" that take place when two evaluators begin to express aggravation and anger towards one another. In this case, the evaluation committee chair will be able to refer back to one or more ground rules that heighten his/her authority and help the committee move ahead.

5. Absence of Reminders and Checklists

Given that cognitive errors and shortcuts are so automatic and deep-seated, there *must* be reminders to committees about the contaminating power of these errors on their evaluation and decision processes. Why not give each evaluation committee member a large index card that lists all the errors, so committee members can handily refresh their memory? Or on the wall of the meeting room, why not hang a banner that lists the errors? Or how about some sort of posted checklist like those often seen in hospitals: *Remember to wash your hands often; confirm the identity of the patient; be sure to operate on the correct leg; check for drug allergies; be sure to carefully monitor this, that, and the other.*

Medical checklists are increasingly regarded as an essential tool for reducing errors, complications, and patient suffering. Drawing on his own work as well as that of other medical experts mentioned directly above, Surgery Professor Atul Gawande (2009) shows that checklists can serve as invaluable precautions against a number of bad practices: the rush to judgment; lazy guessing about the causes of a problem; over-confidence about one's infallible judgment. Moreover, checklists can deflate deference to hierarchy that leads junior associates to stifle their own warnings to senior colleagues about errors and complications they see. (By the way, pilots and co-pilots were infamous for doing this but now use checklists to help diminish the junior's excessive deference to the senior; checklists in use by airlines have influenced the construction of medical checklists.)

At colleges, universities, and professional schools, checklists to prevent errors in peer review and evaluations should be more widely used. As an interesting aside from Gawande, checklists were developed several decades ago by the U.S. Air Force to help pilots fly increasingly complicated airplanes. But my guess is that surely in the past there were a number of experienced craftsmen, alchemists and chemists, farmers, psychologists, teachers, parents, and other experts across the globe who learned—perhaps the hard way—that they needed their own personal checklists to ensure quality control in their work. Checklists, to my mind, are often the sign of a humble but competent practitioner. Discovering more and more about the predictable limitations of the human brain (as well as its astounding capabilities, of course), neuroscientists currently are recommending more checklists, reminders, retrievals, and practice exercises (especially quizzes) to improve cognitive functioning and the daily performances of our trades. In other words, consuming more caffeine isn't enough!

6. Lack of Attention to Internal and External Monitoring/Accountability

In academe, should evaluation committees be better monitored? I would argue *yes*. For instance, an associate dean could check in every two weeks or so with each evaluation committee chair, to see if perennial errors and bad habits are being avoided by the committee. In addition, Equity Advisors (senior faculty leaders who have received special coaching) could provide assistance to search committees when they encounter problems.

The committee chair is seldom expected to update the dean, provost, equity advisors, or diversity council on how the various stages of an ongoing search or evaluation are progressing. Far more disclosure is needed in these processes.

Annual assessments of the job-performance of deans and department chairs rarely consider the results produced by the search and evaluation committees in the units for which these administrators are responsible. Indeed, many institutions do not have any sort of performance reviews of their department chairs or program directors, a puzzling situation that should be corrected.

Committees and schools also should be reminded that the outside world is concerned about critical issues, such as gender imbalance. The media and legislative groups may begin to scrutinize their behavior. For example, in 2004, after media criticism of gender imbalance, Canadian universities heard the wake-up call: they nominated and chose a much higher number of women to be Canada Research Chairs (see "Women Make Gains," 2004). Likewise, several California state legislators a few years ago called on the University of California System to disclose the representation of women in all faculty ranks. Not surprisingly, gender imbalance was evident in the numbers, and pro-active steps were launched to resolve that imbalance.

Recently, a number of campuses and professional schools have started collecting data regarding hiring results by gender and ethnicity, and are making the information readily available to those involved in hiring, to the campus community, to state legislators and auditors, and to regional

21

and national accrediting associations. The provost and others should also periodically review data regarding start-up packages offered and accepted by new hires in all fields. Regular reviews such as these will usually lead to the detection of patterns that need explanation or correction.

7. Lack of Debriefing and Systematic Improvement

Year in and year out, most searches and evaluations go forward without considering the past experiences and hard-earned wisdom of those who have gone before.

At the present time, only a few schools tap into the wisdom of former search and tenure review chairs and invite these leaders to meet with new search and tenure chairs. Why not make these leaders' caveats and recommendations available in a comprehensive evaluation primer? Within the demystifying primer could be other important items: case studies of actual successful and unsuccessful searches, practice exercises, and a summary of model ground rules that other schools and departments have used to govern evaluations and decision-making.

There could be debriefing of every evaluation committee in order to add its own "lessons learned" to the primer. Because so little institutional history and wisdom are being recorded at the present time, each committee packs up and sets out on its own—with the likelihood that it will make some predictably amateurish mistakes. Job candidates themselves have insights to share. An associate dean (or perhaps several Equity Advisors) could make it a habit to interview from time to time a number of candidates who turned down the campus's job offers as well as candidates who were not offered jobs.

* * * * *

The *organizational* bad practices just sketched (overloading; no preparation as well as no practice, ground rules, checklists, reminders, monitoring, or debriefing) will boost the spread of the contaminating thirteen cognitive errors. These bad practices will also appreciably intensify the reliance on positive and negative biases by *individuals* in during evaluation and decision-making processes. The biases are rampant in academe; they are routinely applied to gender and to group membership. In Chapter 2, I will delve into negative bias/stereotype (Cognitive Error #14) and positive bias/stereotype (Error #15). In that next chapter, I will trace how these biases both subtly and frontally manifest themselves and then suggest how organizational reforms could reduce their power. In Chapters 4–6, I devote a great deal of attention to how academics and committees—step by step—can prevent or shrink these two biases as well as the other thirteen cognitive errors.

2

NEGATIVE BIAS AND POSITIVE BIAS

Two Powerful Cognitive Errors that Impede
the Advancement of Some Faculty and
Speed the Advancement of Others

Intellectually, any woman and any black person must [constantly] prove that she or he is not dumb ... it is tiresome in the extreme ... and even attending social gatherings—where one is always on show, always standing for The Negro—saps one's energy.

(Princeton History Professor Nell Painter, who has African-American ancestry; quoted in Reiss, 1997, pp. 6–7)

We European-American males have the experience of "having our voices heard, of not having to explain or defend our legitimate citizenship or identity, of seeing our images projected in a positive light, of remaining insulated from other people's realities, of being represented in positions of power, and of being able to tell our own stories.

(Western Washington State University Adjunct Professor of Social Justice and Education Gary Howard, 1999, p. 62)

I was born white, male, and in America. I won the lottery.

(Billionaire investor and philanthropist Warren Buffet, quoted in Miles, 2004, p. 89)

As these observations make clear, some individuals in this country (such as Painter) are assigned a negative bias which means that their worthiness, intelligence, and leadership potential will be questioned and often undervalued. I find it helpful to refer to these unfortunate experiences as "penalties." By contrast, those sufficiently lucky to be assigned a positive bias, such as Howard and Buffett, will usually reap the opposite. Penn State University Professor Frances Rains has called these fortunate experiences "hidden profits" (1999).

Individuals encountering negative bias about their capabilities will usually number only a few among faculty members; boards of trustees of campuses and professional schools; legislators in Congress and in the states; investment teams at Goldman Sachs and other Wall Street and financial corporations; CEOs, members of boards of directors, and entrepreneurs of large and medium-sized businesses, and on and on.

By contrast, those with a positive bias will probably be over-represented in these spheres—or, if you prefer, they will exhibit far-above-average representation. (U.S. President Barack Obama is an "interesting case," I readily admit. In Chapter 3, I will explain why I believe the president as well as Colin Powell, the former head of the Joint Chief of Staffs, mostly escaped the negative bias and stigma that would have curtailed some of their ambition and success.)

Negative bias and positive bias are two enormously important cognitive traps that all of us wander into unknowingly and frequently. *Negative bias* will be classified as Cognitive Error #14. *Positive bias* will be Error #15. I would venture a guess that these two errors actually outweigh—in frequency and importance—any of the other errors discussed and illustrated in the previous chapter. My goal in this chapter will be to briefly review some of what scholars and researchers have learned about negative and positive biases and how they are manifested.

At times, my discussion will fold in findings from neuroscientists (some are named in Chapter 1) who are probing ways to reduce the power and effects of cognitive errors. In general, researchers conclude that our brains (especially the amygdala and its allies) prefer to stick with familiar and quick-to-access categories. To form new categories and cognitive habits, we must muster considerable concentration and engage in retrieval, reminders, priming and practicing, testing, and above all constant *self-correction*. It's not easy. (Consult especially the prolific work of social-cognition expert Susan Fiske described at the Princeton website.) Later in this chapter, I want to concretely illustrate how negative and positive biases are experienced on a daily basis by faculty members and how the biases produce predictable disadvantages for members of some groups and predictable advantages for members of others. In this last section, I hope that faculty members' personal testimonies and disclosures about the two biases as well as broader ethnographic evidence will move our understanding from the conceptual realm to the "on-the-ground" realm. This seems important.

SECTION A

Negative Bias (Cognitive Error #14) and Positive Bias (Cognitive Error #15)—and their Application to Gender and to Group Membership

What exactly is a bias or a stereotype? (I will use these two words interchangeably.) Most of us are probably familiar with the notion of a stereotype—that's been a part of our vocabulary and thinking for decades. All of us have probably heard some of the following generalizations:

Tall men make better leaders. Asians and Asian Americans are innately better at math and engineering than any other ethnic group. White men can't jump. Women are emotional. Men are rational. People in wheelchairs are usually mentally handicapped, too. Those who can, do; those who can't, teach.

In that short list, notice that we heard negative stereotypes (also called negative biases) about some groups but also positive stereotypes (positive biases) about others. This illustrates an important fact to remember: stereotypes can be positive as well as negative. A stereotype can be defined as a broad generalization about a particular group and the assumption that a member of the group embodies the generalized traits of that group. Just how pervasively these generalizations enter into and contaminate our cognitive processes of evaluating, judging, and deciding is the concern of dozens of experts—brain specialists, social scientists, cultural anthropologists, lawyers and law professors, courtroom judges, medical diagnosticians, and management experts. I recommend the findings of experts listed in the Bibliography, such as: Biernat; Blair and Banaji; Delgado; Fiske; Foschi; Fried; Greenwald; Groopman; Hollinger; Kahneman; Kanter; Kobrynowicz and Biernat; Kunda, Sinclair, and Griffin; Martell, Lane, and Emrich; Martell; Massey; McIntosh; Mervis; Moskowitz, Gollwitzer, and Wasel; Nahavandi and Malekzadeh; Nosek; Pinker; Rosser; Sagaria; Sanchirico; Steele and Aronson; Sturm and Guinier; Trix and Psenka; Valian; Wenneras and Wold; C. Williams; C.L. Williams; Wilson and Brekke.

Negative Bias: Regarding Gender

Believing women are innately less competent than men is a pernicious assumption found in many countries and cultures. U.S. society, for instance, is still male-dominated, male-identified, male-centered, and systematically devalues women especially in traditionally male fields. "Most organizations have been created by and for men and are based on male experiences" (Meyerson and Fletcher, 2000, p. 132). Quickly review in your mind who in this country holds almost all the powerful political, economic, legal, religious, intellectual, and military positions (Lopez, 2006, p. B7). It is deemed extraordinary when a woman achieves such a position. Men rule, most especially European-American males. Further, conventional male values—strength, decisiveness, aggression, thick skin, self-sufficiency, control over emotions, forceful leadership—are frequently accepted as the norm in this society. For women, the conventions are almost the exact opposite, and women's care-giving propensity is expected and in fact vigorously reinforced by the larger society. Further, women's inferiority to men is broadcast and accepted in countless ways.

Remember former Harvard President Larry Summer's *faux pas* a few years ago? At a national conference, he mused that women are perhaps innately inferior to men in science areas and therefore they would not rise to top posts. Many faculty on his campus immediately and vociferously protested; the presidents of several major universities published a letter of reprimand. After reflection, Summers retracted his claim and observed: "I think it was, in retrospect, an act of spectacular imprudence." He says that he deeply regrets if girls and women have been discouraged by his off-the-cuff remark (quoted in Leonhardt, 2007, p. 25). Like Summers, many of us aren't fully cognizant of our gender biases (though fortunately there are ways that we can learn to recognize, self-correct, and rise above them).

Negative bias against women is ubiquitous, as numerous studies have documented. An ambitious enterprise to detect this and other patterns of biases (and recommend how to overcome them) has been launched by three major researchers and their labs at the universities of Washington and Virginia and at Harvard. These three researchers have created a website for self-administered Implicit Association. More than five million visitors in various countries have taken the on-line tests since 1998 (see http://www.projectimplicit.net/generalinfo). The website contains articles (written by members of the U.S. labs and also by scholars throughout the world) about how to recognize and correct for these automatic biases.

How does gender bias manifest itself in academic life? Admittedly in the 21st century, it would be rare for us to hear virulent anti-woman rhetoric in academe and observe pernicious behavior toward women. But nevertheless, subtle undermining and shortchanging will occur. For instance, disparagement of women applicants for medical school posts was spotlighted in a comprehensive study of more than 300 letters of recommendation used in hiring and promotion processes at a large medical school. The study found that competent women faculty were underestimated and stereotypically described as "caring," "refreshing," and "diligent." By contrast, competent male faculty were praised in specific ways for their research brilliance and for their concrete career achievements (Trix and Psenka, 2003). A recent study by Rice University researchers finds the same situation in their analysis of 624 letters of recommendation submitted for applicants seeking junior faculty positions at a research university (Madera, Hebl, and Martin, 2009).

The two anthropologists who conducted the medical school study went on to issue these four warnings to academics involved in the gate-keeping processes of screening, hiring, making awards, and reviewing candidates for tenure and promotion: (1) double-check and eradicate from your own verbal and written evaluations superficial assumptions related to gender schema; (2) be on guard against omitting essential topics (such as concrete career achievements) that are related to gender schema; (3) make sure that colleagues understand how the evaluations of applicants may be typically positively biased towards males and negatively prejudiced towards females; (4) coach female colleagues on how they can ensure that department chairs evaluate their individual promise and professional accomplishments rather than fall back on belittling gender stereotypes (Trix and Psenka, 2003).

Job evaluations can in fact be riddled with subjectivity and involve shifting standards. The result is that "only super-duper women rise to the top," according to a female vice provost for faculty affairs, "because the mediocre ones are beaten out by the mediocre men. They [the women] have to prove themselves, to have published 26 articles, look the part, be assertive, tough-minded." A female presidential candidate, the vice provost adds, would be assumed by college trustees to possess far less business sense than a male candidate, though their backgrounds were almost identical (quoted in Glazer-Raymo, 1999, p. 161).

A similar point is made by Joan Steitz, Professor of Molecular Biophysics and Biochemistry at Yale University. Women "superstars" in predominantly male departments, she observes, seem to have an easier time in advancing their careers than do "sort of average" women who are bunched in the middle with "most of their male colleagues." Steitz believes that women, unlike men, seem to have a difficult time in the middle being accepted as equal colleagues. Their evaluations do not result in their being granted fair and full recognition for their accomplishments (2001, quoted in "Tomorrow's Professor" Listserve operated by Professor Richard Reis and headquartered at Stanford University). To adapt a quip attributed to former Congresswoman Bella Abzug, "Our struggle today is not to have a female Einstein get fairly evaluated and promoted in academe. It is for a woman *schlemiel* to get as quickly promoted as a male *schlemiel*."

The shabby treatment of female tenured science faculty at MIT reveals "the lens of prejudice and discrimination" unwittingly used by male colleagues. The MIT senior women in the science division numbered just over a dozen among almost 200 male faculty. The women's investigation in the late 1990s demonstrated that they had been "marginalized, excluded from full participation in the academic process, and undervalued" at their home institution even though they had been inducted into the National Academies and recognized as international experts. The MIT President and the Dean of Science both expressed shock when they found these gross inequities: the women faculty members' lab areas, bridge funding from the Institute, and actual salaries were much smaller than their male colleagues; and no woman had ever chaired a science department. Clearly, these women were being constricted by gender bias and a glass ceiling not affecting their male co-workers (see MIT Newletter website for details about how the inequities are being resolved).

Inequities mount up and have a cumulative effect. This fact has been proven by computer modeling, when only a tiny 1 percent discounting is shown to result in women's slower advancement in the professions (Martell, 1991). Certainly the MIT women were being discounted at a *much higher* percentage rate. The National Academy of Sciences, citing dozens of studies about gender bias, concludes that the *accumulation* of biased discounting has a substantial effect on the careers of women in science and engineering fields (see the Academy's *Beyond Bias and Barriers: Fulfilling the Potential of Women in Academic Science and Engineering* (2006). Two quotations from the report (p. 114) are especially telling:

> *Through a scientific or engineering career, advancement depends on judgments of one's performance by more senior scientists and engineers. A substantial body of research shows these judgments contain arbitrary and subjective components that disadvantage women. The criteria underlying the judgments developed over many decades when women scientists and engineers were a tiny and often marginal presence and men were considered the norm.*

> *Incidents of bias against individuals not in the majority group tend to have accumulated effects. Small preferences for the majority group can accumulate and create large differences in prestige, power, and position. In academic science and engineering, the advantages have accrued to white men and have translated into larger salaries, faster promotions, and more publications and honors relative to women.*

In short, the repeated discounting of women's accomplishments and innate abilities produces a cumulative effect. The cumulative effect even of small slights and shortchanging will mount up ("molehills create mountains," to use a helpful metaphor from Hunter College Distinguished Professor Virginia Valian). The result can demoralize women and derail their careers and their contributions to science, medicine, law, arts and humanities, business, government, and other domains (Glazer-Raymo, 1999; Valian, 2000a,b).

How do women business leaders fare in their various workplaces? Details abound in *Our Separate Ways: Black and White Women and the Struggle for Professional Identity* by Ella Bell, Visiting Professor of

Business at Dartmouth College and Stella Nkomo, Professor of Business at the University of South Africa. In their study comprising 120 black and white women in business careers, the authors found that women in business continue, as a matter of course, to have their authority and judgment questioned and their ideas undervalued. Undermining of their expertise is especially true for African and African-American women (Bell and Nkomo, 2001).

A comprehensive study of 3,200 engineers in 24 U.S. corporations demonstrates how negative bias prominently threads through job evaluations of women workers (DiTomaso, Farris, and Cordero, 1993). The study demonstrated that not only access to constructive work experiences but also positive evaluation of job performance were secured most often by majority U.S.-born males. They were followed, in invariable order, by: European-born majority males; then U.S.-born majority women; then East Asian men; Hispanic men; African-American men. At the bottom were *African-American* and other non-immigrant *women* who were the most disadvantaged in their access to constructive work experiences and positive evaluation of job performance. In short, the thinking processes of corporate power-holders (usually majority males) together with conventions and customs in the workplace clearly influence who gets ahead in the corporation and who does not.

Organizational behavior Professors Afsaneh Nahavandi (Arizona State University-West) and Ali Malekzadeh (St. Cloud State University) reenforce this point in their textbook (1999). One extremely common manifestation of negative bias occurs through a psychological process called "channeling"—this is "the process of limiting our interaction with another so that we avoid receiving information that contradicts our judgment." In other words, we set up a situation to gather the data needed to confirm our notion about the other person.

Professors Malekzadeh and Nahavandi continue: "Women are generally perceived by both male and female managers to be less competent, less capable of leading, and more likely to quit because of family pressures." The negative perception quickly leads to action that confirms these perceptions: managers "provide women with fewer training opportunities, limited exposure to diverse experiences, and more routine, less challenging assignments. In many professions, women are bypassed for key promotions because the position requires that they supervise men." Can it be surprising, the authors ask, that many women leave less challenging jobs or feel stymied by underemployment? The clear caveat is this: "Organizations that channel women's behavior because of gender stereotypes assure that the stereotypes become reality" (1999, p. 167). This process could be called self-fulfilling prophecy, as I discussed in Chapter 1.

29

Another shortchanging of women appeared in an audit at the Swedish Research Council. Peer reviewers, it was discovered, usually assumed that women applicants for post-doctoral grants possessed less scientific competence than men applicants with the *same* credentials and qualifications. To be competitive, the women had to be extraordinary. They had to have "published three extra papers" in high-impact journals like *Nature* and *Science* or "20 extra papers" in excellent but less prestigious journals. In short, a female applicant "had to be 2.5 times more productive than the average male applicant to receive the same competence score as he" (Wenneras and Wold, "Nepotism and Sexism," 1997, p. 342; also see Rosser, 2004). The ratio of 2.5 to 1 is astounding.

What is one remedy for such inequity? Removing names from the applicant proposals (called a "blind review") quickly resulted in women receiving close to one-half of the Swedish grants. A parallel remedy has been implemented in another venue: symphony orchestras. During musical auditions for orchestra employment, a new procedure has resulted in far more women being hired: the procedure requires applicants to play *behind a curtain*. The structural change (the curtain) guarantees anonymity and defeats the evaluators' unexamined tendency to devalue women's performances and promise. Several academic journals have switched to blind review (no names appear on the articles submitted for review and publication). The result has been a significant increase in published papers by women scholars (Budden et al., 2008).

Blind review is also recommended by Zurich researcher Lutz Bornmann who has extensively studied the biases within peer review in science. Peer review is widely regarded as the best way to be sure of "good science" and be sure taxpayers' money is wisely spent on grants. But in fact, as Bornmann points out, "there are robust gender differences in grant peer-review procedures" that result in women receiving far fewer grants (2007, p. 566). Blind review is one remedy for the gender inequity. Another remedy is to widen the rules for submitting nominations for awards (the U.S. National Institutes of Health's Pioneer Awards Program now accepts only self-nominations rather than institutional submissions because women were very rarely nominated). Third, some funding and award agencies are spending more time in training peer reviewers. These simple steps have already resulted in greater equity (Bornmann, 2007).

Negative Bias: Regarding Group Membership

Before turning from gender bias to group bias, I think it wise to interject a brief discussion about semantics. In this book, readers will probably notice that I deliberately avoid several popular terms (like "the white race" and "the black race") and choose instead other ways to identify certain ethnic groups. There are certain terms I myself try to avoid: *minority, under-represented minority, people of color, Hispanic, Latino/a, Black, White.* And wherever possible, I avoid using the word "race" because it is, as most of us agree by now, not a real biological category. But, of course, it remains a very powerful social construction. One has only to look at the U.S. Census's use of the word to see how pervasive it is. (As one expert has mused, if we agree that "race" was socially and politically constructed, then why can't we undo that construction, piece by piece? This is beyond my power but not beyond my wishing.)

In this book, I will eschew "race" and instead employ the following words and hyphenated descriptors: *non-immigrants* (NI); *majority group* which signifies the *European-American group; under-represented women* (URW); *colonized groups* which to me means the same as non-immigrant groups; hyphenated ethnicities such as *European-American, Mexican-American, Chinese-American, Cuban-American individuals and groups,* and so on; and finally *communities of descent,* which will mean ethnic lineage traced to specific places such as India, Korea, China, Haiti, Ireland, and so on (this is historian David Hollinger's term, 2005, 2011).

As a further clarification, when I use the interchangeable terms *non-immigrant groups* or *colonized groups* in this country, I am intending to include only these five: **African Americans, Mexican Americans, American Indians and Alaskan Natives, Native Hawaiians, and Puerto Rican Americans.** Chapter 3, I trust, will make very clear why only these five should be described as non-immigrant, colonized groups and why and how these groups came to be associated with a negative bias regarding their intellectual capabilities and promise. In fact, these groups were forcibly and unfairly assigned an extraordinary negative bias called a "stigma." This is the term used by sociologist Erving Goffman (1963) to denote the assignment of a spoiled identity that disqualifies members of a particular group from full societal acceptance and respect. Obviously dealing with and pushing back on a negative bias—let alone a more intense stigma—turns into an unenviable and "tiresome" task, as Professor Nell Painter has phrased it (Reiss, 1997). Earlier in this chapter, I described how under-represented women in predominantly male settings and departments have to spend extra time and energy in order to push back and cope with their under-valuation and short-changing. And I listed some strategies (such as blind peer review and heightened self-correction by evaluators) that are bringing about greater equity and recognition for women.

In this next section, I will do the same as I spotlight the colonized, NI groups listed above. Let us begin. One stunning example of negative group bias has been sketched out by MIT Emeritus Management Professor Thomas Allen, himself European American. As both a faculty member and administrator, he observed that "racism is so ingrained in this society that people don't see it in themselves." Repeatedly he saw the following scenario play out: "Without even thinking, two people will walk in—one's white, one's black—and they [his colleagues] assume the black isn't capable. Yet they don't know a thing about either one of them, nothing." As a dean, he was repeatedly frustrated and angered by his majority-group colleagues. When he would bring in an African-American job candidate, Allen's colleagues in subtle but unmistakable ways "would discount that person right away." They would assume that this candidate was "not as capable" as the majority candidate.

While Allen didn't see this behavior in everyone, he saw it "in so many people who you wouldn't expect it from, people who espouse liberal values." He strenuously and wittily underscores: "These aren't rednecks I'm talking about." Rather, these are educated colleagues who "make wonderful talk" about equal opportunity and democratic values but unconsciously make "simplistic and damaging assumptions" about who can be competent and who cannot (quoted in C. Williams, 2001, pp. 314–19).

As several cognitive scientists have pointed out, for those surrounded by a negative stereotype "far more evidence is required for a judge to be certain that an individual possesses an *unexpected* attribute." The unexpected attribute is *competence* while the expected attribute is *incompetence*, according to University of Kansas Psychology Professor Monica Biernat (2003, p. 1020) whose lab does meticulous tracking of shifting standards. (See also Sagaria, 2002, on filters applied differently to different groups of job candidates.) If a member of a search committee assumes a job applicant from an under-represented group is possibly substandard, then that committee member will predictably raise the bar and insist on far more evidence than required before he/she can accept the applicant as worthy of consideration. It is a common practice for faculty search committees to seek from under-represented candidates (but not others) extra assurances that they are qualified, such as additional writing samples, letters of recommendation, and so on (Reyes and Halcon, 1991). This sort of raising the bar is one of the cognitive errors discussed in Chapter 1.

Negative group bias regarding competency can also lead search committees to insist that non-immigrant, under-represented candidates must have earned doctorates and must have performed their residencies or post-doc training at the most prestigious places—a requirement that is not usually essential for other applicants. Majority candidates will probably enjoy the assumption of being competent and well-qualified and will have *extra points added* to their evaluations, albeit unwittingly. On the other hand, those with negative bias will have *points subtracted* by evaluators, albeit unwittingly.

University of Pittsburgh Emeritus Law Professor Richard Delgado has observed similar standard-shifting in law schools' academic searches and decision-making. He points out that when the archetypal academic search committee is seeking a new colleague and after several months of work has not located the "superhuman, mythic figure who is Black or Hispanic," then the committee turns to a non-mythic, *average* candidate who is almost always "white, male, and straight." The committee has confidence that the choice they are reaching is a sound one: this is because the lower standard of evidence—applied to a positively stereotyped person—is being unwittingly used (Delgado, "Storytelling," 1998, p. 265).

Another manifestation of negative bias was uncovered by Robert Haro, an educational researcher in the Southwest. He interviewed "Latino/a leaders in higher education" as well as a number of European-American trustees and members of hiring committees at twenty-five colleges and universities. (I will use the word "Latino/a" here because Professor Haro does so.) On the basis of 120 personal interviews, Haro found that Latinos/as are often stereotypically and negatively treated: their academic credentials and experience are viewed as suspect and their styles of personal interaction discounted as inappropriate. For instance, European-American job candidates for a college presidency were not required to have had previous experience as an academic dean or provost but Latino/a candidates were. European-American candidates might squeeze by with a doctorate from less than a top research university but *not* a Latino/a. Latina candidates were sometimes pronounced to be inappropriately dressed and wearing "cheap and distracting" jewelry, in the words of a trustee and a member of a search committee (Haro, 2001, p. 32).

What is the negative stereotype being spotlighted in these studies and anecdotes? *It is, of course, the presumption of inferiority and incompetence*—and this presumption about URW and non-immigrant groups NIs endures and endures even in the face of abundant evidence of their accomplishments and leadership. Internal surveys of University of Michigan faculty repeatedly reveal that professors in these categories at the Big Ten University frequently feel they are discriminated against, scrutinized far more than majority male professors, and undervalued as intellectuals. A number of European-American male faculty members at Michigan agree that they too had seen such undervaluing and intense scrutiny of their colleagues. Other campuses' annual and biennial climate surveys reveal very similar patterns.

Can it be any wonder that colonized, non-immigrant groups in the faculty ranks often lament that they are never given the benefit of the doubt, that they are always "on stage," and that they feel they are always being sternly judged? Sociologist Lois Benjamin found that almost all of the one hundred of African-American professionals she interviewed for her book *The Black Elite* felt they were indeed on "perennial probation" and had to prove themselves twice as accomplished as majority colleagues in academe, law, and medicine (Benjamin, 1998, p. 28; see also Cooper and Stevens, 2002; Hollinger, 2011).

In his decades of faculty-development work on campuses throughout the country, Robert Boice has found that under-represented faculty from colonized groups have to deal constantly with insinuations that they are unworthy. They must brace themselves for almost daily snubs and putdowns, both large and small. Boice's finding is compellingly reenforced by two nationally distributed films that feature more than twenty minority professors in various academic disciplines: *Through My Lens* (produced and distributed by the University of Michigan) and *Shattering the Silences* (produced by the Public Broadcasting Company and now distributed by several outlets). These two eye-opening films make painfully clear the costs exacted from under-represented male and female faculty as they undertake their daily struggles for professional recognition and dignity and for fair evaluations of their teaching and scholarship.

Both male and female members of colonized, non-immigrant groups in this country often have to deal with "stereotype fatigue." In a study of African-American physicians and professors in academic medicine, the professionals could not recall a single positive "race-related experience" within any of the medical institutions where they had worked, but they easily recalled an abundance of negative ones.

Apparently, medical workplaces and their administrators diligently ignore the negative stereotype (the proverbial elephant in the room). Every under-represented doctor in the above study reported that the relevance of race is *never* acknowledged and that no informal or formal discussions are ever held about the elephant and how to shrink its size or even remove it from the room. A family medicine physician observed: "We have, as a society, figured out ways to systematically deny that racism exists. And so have the medical institutions that train us. There is no way to have a discussion about it because it has been decided that it doesn't exist." Stereotype fatigue results from having to accept this heavy silence and avoidance while simultaneously having to "deal with the pressure of whatever stereotypes people may have about race ... and it is a daily stress at work. It's exhausting for me" (both quotes included in Nunez-Smith et al., 2007, p. 49). This is surely a classic crazy-making situation: silence on the one hand and omnipresent stereotyping on the other.

Well-known cognitive scientist Steven Pinker will be given the last word about negative stereotyping. He warns: "If subjective decisions about people, such as [college] admissions, hiring, credit, and salaries, are based in part on group-wide averages, they will conspire to make the rich richer and the poor poorer" (2002, p. 206).

Positive Stereotype/Bias: Regarding
Gender and Group Membership

Now let's turn to positive stereotypes and to the experiences of those who enjoy such a positive assumption by others about their capabilities. As you would guess, those with what might called a "positive halo" are *presumed to be competent and bona fide*. They will not bump up against implicit quotas limiting their representation to no more than three or so, in a department or on a campus. They will collect more positive points for their achievements, relative to those coping with a negative stereotype. Their extra points will mount up and result in cumulative advantages and advancement, relative to those viewed negatively.

Those with the positive bias are anointed, in a way, with the presumption of competence and deserved authority. The phrase "well-qualified white man" is simply *not* in the lexicon (conversation with Professor Nell Painter, 2005). Due to this presumption of worthiness, it can be easy for those with the positive bias to slip into a state of feeling entitled to success and deference. This entitlement can be understandably viewed as arrogance by those lacking the positive halo (Thompson and Louque, 2005; Boice, "Lessons," 1992; D. Smith, 1996, 2000, 2009). By contrast, those with a negative bias are often doubted by others and sometimes by themselves ("maybe I'm an imposter?"). While in graduate school, James Bonilla felt he did not belong; in fact, he felt at times like he was play-acting. He repeatedly mulled over: "What is a working-class, New York Puerto Rican trying to do entering the ivory tower?" Only with the bolstering and encouragement of the other two members of his writing support group was he able to overcome his "internalized fear and racial vulnerability" (Bonilla, quoted in Moody, 1996, p. 8). Bonilla now works as an associate professor at Hamline University.

A European-American professor, Frederick Frank, discloses that "while I worked like a Trojan to earn my way in this life, I nevertheless assert that a good measure of my success" results from societal perception. This professor is surrounded by the favorable stereotype of being competent. In such an advantageous position, he is sure he has gotten "breaks" and at times received "more positive evaluations" of his job performance, more positive "than I expected or deserved." He concludes: "I try to be grateful" (Frank, 1999, p. 148).

Expressing similar gratitude, Management Professor Peter Couch admits that his being a white male has brought him "extra" points and extra opportunities at every stage of his academic career. "I have always found myself in a world of opportunities—opportunities that I [naively] thought were available to anyone energetic and capable" (Couch, quoted in Gallos and Ramsey, 1997, p. 21).

The fundamental privilege of being in the European-American majority group, according to Wellesley College researcher Peggy McIntosh, is that you "take for granted" the legitimacy and power that such social status automatically bestows on you. In fact, those with such status are taught to be *oblivious* to their social privilege and unearned advantages (1989, p. 3). "To be white in America is not to have to think about it" (quoted in Doane, 1999, p. 75). Being oblivious means you believe you are the norm. You don't think of yourself as having race, privilege, and perhaps even ethnicity—you're an American.

Numerous reports have shown that there are glass borders, glass ceilings, "Keep Out" signs, and jealously guarded stations of inside information at every turn, for women seeking to enter male occupations and for under-represented groups seeking high-paying and prestigious occupations and professions (Massey, 2011). In seeking desirable jobs, majority males will be aided by the phenomenon that *like people hire like people*. Employers tend to hire those who look, think, and speak like themselves, unless they become conscious of this evaluative bias and concentrate to overcome it. Without a doubt, majority employers faced with equally qualified applicants "prefer white to black or Latino job applicants three to one" (Fischer et al., 1996, p. 182). A wry story captures the *reproduction* principle of hiring: An elderly, European-American manager is preparing to meet job candidates. Leaning into the intercom on his desk, he instructs his secretary to "Send in someone who reminds me of myself as a young buck." In other words, this employer is putting up a "Welcome" sign for those who are clones of himself.

In his national research studies, Sociology Professor Ronald Breiger at the University of Arizona has found that professional, managerial, and even technical workers are almost three times as likely to have secured their jobs through personal contacts as through direct application or responding to newspaper advertisements. The jobs with "the highest pay and prestige and affording the greatest satisfaction to their incumbents, were most likely" to be filled through personal contacts (Breiger, 1988, p. 78). Because URW and NI faculty usually are outsiders with fewer personal contacts, they have to work extremely hard to secure academic posts and promotions. In recognition of this, I make it a point in my consulting to help them build very wide professional networks to compensate for being outside the usual circles of academic tradition and influence.

Many European Americans realize on a "gut" level that they are indeed fortunate to belong to the majority group imprinted with the positive bias.

I grew up in an affluent Connecticut suburb in the 1960s. Secure behind old stone walls and trimmed hedges, safeguarded by burglar alarms, this was a world far removed from any dis-

cussion of race. It was a world of good schools, safe streets and perfect teeth…. In this world, people of color were the ones who came to your house to work, and they worked hard … [but] the better jobs went to the plumbers, the electricians, the painters: people from the ethnic white working class of the town, most of them Italian…. There were also a few Black kids at the school, but almost no one knew them…. Everyone liked them, wondered how they did it, but most thanked God every day that they had been born white. (Correspondents of the *New York Times*, 2001, pp. 335–36)

These illustrations point out the clear and daily benefits of belonging to a group viewed as competent and sound. Members of such a positively regarded group, according to a number of experts, are likely to:

- receive the benefit of the doubt if there is ambiguous evidence about how well they performed or behaved;
- receive more "points" for their achievements;
- find that their "points" accumulate faster and produce a sturdy base of successes;
- are assured that their successes are unlikely to be questioned or suspected;
- find they do not face a quota system that restricts them to only token representation (meaning one of a few) and restricts them to marginal power in an organization;
- find they do not have to worry about their race and in fact can be oblivious to it; and
- finally, enjoy greater deference inside and outside their traditional venues, whether that is the college classroom, the laboratory, the boardroom, the courtroom, the operating room, or the legislature.

Reflecting on this state of affairs, a European-American professor confesses that "for all of us white guys who are honest enough to admit it, we know in our heart that we have been blessed by birth to have had options not available to those who are not white and not male" (Frank, 1999, p. 75). In a similar vein, President John F. Kennedy once archly observed that majorities who touted the astounding progress being made by non-majorities in this society, nevertheless, would not for a moment consider exchanging places with them. Being a majority insider has its incontestable privileges and hidden profits.

But what about a male with a positive bias who chooses to work in a female-dominated profession such as nursing, social work, or librarianship? Certainly he would be a "token" (meaning he is the only one or one of a few "others" who are different from the rest). A solo or one of

37

a few, according to organizational experts, usually occupies a stressful and awkward position because those in the majority give skewed attention to the solo and often misinterpret his/her real motives and performance. Yet this man, albeit unusual in nursing or library work, nevertheless brings his higher status and positive stereotype of competence with him. Instead of being devalued and hitting a glass ceiling (as a woman, for instance, in science and engineering would almost certainly experience), the male solo will typically find himself on a *"glass escalator"* that somehow brings quick recognition, promotion, and a corner office as a dean or director (C. L. Williams, 1992; Yoder, 1994; Kanter, 1977, 1997).

In short, those assigned a positive stereotype will receive substantial hidden profits that advance them on a cumulative basis in both traditional and *non-traditional* settings. Those assigned a negative stereotype will be dealt extra penalties, taxes, and glass ceilings that will hamper their advancement on a cumulative basis (see C. L. Williams, 1992; C. Williams, 2001; Steele and Aronson, 1995; McIntosh,1998 and 1999; Valian, 2000a,b; Rosser, 2004).

European-American males' privileges and positive-bias "halo" are givens. Yet increasingly, *certain* Asian-American and Central and South American subgroups have privileges and positive bias that they too can take for granted. These groups, beneficiaries of exceptional conditions, have recently sought and been granted the high status of "honorary whites" meaning honorary European Americans (Lopez, "Colorblind," 2006, p. B8). In Chapter 3, I will return to this development.

How do negative and positive stereotypes about groups arise and then endure? The stereotypes are the outcomes of political power exercised at various times by the dominant European-American group in this country. In Chapter 3, I will make this clear through synthesizing the work of dozens of anthropologists, political scientists, economists, historians, novelists, and sociologists. These experts have found that those American citizens whose ancestors started out in this country as the conquered, dispossessed, and enslaved (that is, incorporated by *force, not choice)* are usually branded with a long-lasting negative stereotype. This stereotype continues, generation after generation. The groups treated with overwhelming force by the dominant majority group include: American Indians, African Americans, Puerto Rican Americans, Mexican Americans, and Native Hawaiians.

By contrast, voluntary immigrants who exercised choice in settling here usually enjoy a positive stereotype, much higher status than colonized and conquered groups, and societal expectations that they are likely to succeed in attaining the American dream. Immigrants benefit because they and their ancestors exercised varying degrees of choice as they entered the country. These groups include members of the very powerful and dominant European-American group as well as some Asian-American groups and many recent immigrants from Central and South American who have come to be regarded as "honorary whites" in this country (see Takaki, Lopez, Wu, Hollinger, Tapia, Waters; citations in Bibliography; also see Chapter 3 of this book).

What about European-American women's status and treatment? These will vary, largely depending on whether the women are trying to enter and succeed in fields and in institutions traditionally closed to them. Some of the situations in which negative bias and glass ceilings severely restrict majority women were discussed earlier in this chapter.

SECTION B

How Negative Bias and Positive Bias Affect Faculty Members' Professional Lives on a Daily Basis

This section moves from the *concept* of bias/stereotype to the *effects* of bias. I provide here personal observations and disclosures from faculty who enjoy a positive bias but also from those who chafe under a negative one. Let us start with a stunning observation from a professor of surgery at an academic institution. Asked how he is viewed by others at work, he explains: "I think race permeates every aspect of my job; so ... when I walk onto a ward or on the floor, I'm a black guy before I'm the doctor. I'm still a black guy before I'm the guy in charge, before I'm the attending of record, so that permeates everything" (quoted in Nunez-Smith et al., 2006, pp. 46–47). Pushing through that dynamic on a daily basis requires enormous energy and patience. This is a hidden penalty. Those with a positive group bias find themselves enjoying a hidden profit when they escape that dynamic.

Another substantial and predictable penalty is meted out at professional schools, colleges, universities, government labs and institutes: URW and members of NI groups are asked and expected to symbolically serve as "the diversity member" on numerous tasks forces and committees. This overload can weaken a professor's career, whether she/he is a brand-new hire or a mid-career, seasoned veteran. Another physician/faculty member vividly recounts how the requests play out: "At work ... whenever they want to diversify something, they call me. When they don't need that, when they would need someone purely for individual intellectual capacity, I am not the first person they think about." This committee overload is a widespread burden for URW and NIs, as countless studies have demonstrated. Yet again, a severe penalty is being meted out. In Chapter 5, I advise department chairs and other leaders why and how they must deactivate this penalty and service overload.

In the remainder of this chapter, I will touch on other penalties (for those with a negative bias) and on other profits (for those with a positive one). Contrasting one disadvantage/penalty with a *corresponding* advantage/profit is the way I will organize this section.

1. Disadvantage: Professors dealing with negative bias will frequently experience <u>unfair evaluations</u> of their work and have to deal with the suspicion from some colleagues and students that they are perhaps innately incompetent.

Advantage: Professors dealing with positive bias will usually be granted unfair, overly <u>generous evaluations</u> and will enjoy others' presumption that they are perhaps innately competent or superior.

Early on, University of Massachusetts-Amherst Professor Sonia Nieto recognized the stereotypical reactions that she knew she would have to overcome on a regular basis. While she proudly speaks Spanish and proudly claims her Puerto Rican heritage, she nonetheless has "strived to make it very clear that I was intelligent" *in spite of* these cultural markers that distinguish her from mainstream scholars (2000, p. xxiv). As one African American on a majority campus puts it, "Man, from the day we're hired until the day we're retired, we are on probation!" (quoted in Moore and Wagstaff, 1974, p. 9). Hampton University sociologist Lois Benjamin likewise found that almost all of the one hundred African-American professionals she interviewed for her book *The Black Elite* felt they were on "perennial probation" and had to prove themselves *twice* as accomplished as majority colleagues in academe, law, and medicine (Benjamin, 1999, p. 28; also see Cooper and Stevens, 2002; Hollinger, 2011). My conversations with a score of non-immigrant faculty reenforce this sense of being kept on never-ending probation.

Unfair evaluations deeply concern Cornell University Environmental Studies/Biology Professor Eloy Rodriguez (the first U.S.-born Mexican American to hold an endowed science chair). He warns that women and minorities still face formidable obstacles to succeeding at majority campuses. Throughout his academic career, based first on the West Coast and now on the East Coast, Rodriguez has seen "sexism" and "racism" operating in a host of recruitment committees and tenure and promotion committees at various campuses. To level the playing field, he urges departments and campuses to reduce the *enormous subjectivity* that academic decision-makers can indulge in as they make personnel decisions: "The measurements being used for the tenure decision must be clearly set forth, and campuses and departments must be mindful and vigilant against exclusionary patterns in their evaluations and their granting of tenure" (personal conversation, 2008).

Because positive-biased colleagues do not suffer from these formidable obstacles in their reviews by power-holders, they can be more relaxed and at times "fade into the woodwork" without anyone noticing. They can be irritable or aggressive at times without worrying that such atypical behavior will be used against them in future evaluations. They can win professional society or book awards and not have to endure whispers behind their back that their work is actually over-rated. As one majority professor anonymously disclosed to me, "Even getting a Pulitzer Prize would not count as much for a recipient of color as for a white male. I'm certain of that." In other words, that negative presumption subtracts points from the achievements and recognition of under-represented minorities and women.

Job evaluations have been the object of study by several medical experts and national task forces. "Medical school faculty of African descent have lower job satisfaction and are promoted less frequently than their nonminority counterparts who have similar productivity and similar academic accomplishments" (Nunez-Smith et al., 2007, p. 45). This conclusion—and recommendations for remedying the situation— appear *regularly* in editorials in medical journals. It is typical for under-represented physicians and professors to underscore how much energy and intellect they must expend as they push back on the stereotype that follows them from the classroom, to grand rounds, to the surgical area, and on and on. "It's exhausting." Their majority colleagues almost always have no clue and no interest in the extra expenditures required of them.

In fact, medical and academic institutions concentrate on ignoring and denying that negative and positive stereotypes may be operative in their workplaces. After reviewing a score of studies, medical professors Joseph Betancourt and Andrea Reid call on institutions to hold "open and honest dialogue" and to "openly acknowledge that race matters as much in the health care workplace as it does in society." They continue: "All health care professionals should be taught about the impact of stereotyping and prejudice as part of their employee orientation and ongoing in-service training (for example, in grand rounds)." And finally, organizations should make sure that senior colleagues and chair are developing, mentoring, and monitoring the progress of negatively stereotyped professionals (Betancounrt and Reid, 2007, p. 69). In other words, the elephant in the room should be attended to.

Evaluation of Job Performance in the Classroom

Students are very likely to hold and act out stereotypical views about who is the norm and who is intellectually worthy—and who is *not*. Professor Painter observes that in academia "students of all races and genders seem extremely judgmental toward non-white, non-male faculty ... Time and time again I've seen white women and people of color harassed,

41

questioned, and rebuked by students who accept just about any behavior from white male faculty" (quoted in Reiss, 1997; the same point is discussed in Harlow, 2003 and Moody, *Demystifying,* 2010). Even *established, tenured* professors from disfavored groups also have to deal with this continuous jousting and testing by students and at times receive lower-than-deserved ratings (source: my conversations with dozens of such faculty, during my consulting work). In fact, some non-majority students may participate in this testing and jousting because they, too, have internalized the norm that *only* majority males (and no one else) are automatically entitled to legitimacy and authority. Because of the internalization of the norm, some students in their written evaluations of courses taught by under-represented faculty may be disproportionately harsh. Several provosts have shown me just how outrageously cruel some students' additional comments can be. Not surprisingly, course instructors with a negative bias may have to devote extra energy and concentration to psychologically managing classroom dynamics—dynamics that are more complex that those faced by other instructors (Harlow, 2003; Stanley, 2006; also my own conversations with non-majority instructors, both adjunct and tenure-track).

Those with a positive bias usually avoid these taxes. "Professors of the dominant group are assured of addressing (in classroom lectures or other settings) individuals and groups of their own racial and ethnic composition." They do not have to expend extra energy and are likely to receive deference and the benefit of the doubt when they stumble (Turner, 2001, p. 122). They are the norm, after all. They are allowed to be average. By contrast, to beat back a negative presumption calls for exceptional endurance. New Mexico State University Professor Herman Garcia has joked that progress will be reached when Mexican-American and other under-represented groups throughout academia can save energy and feel as relaxed "about being mediocre" as many majorities now seem to feel (quoted in Padilla, 1995, p. 156).

Evaluation of One's Research and Scholarship

National studies have underscored the shortchanging that URW and NIs often receive in their evaluations, as I mentioned earlier in this chapter. As one remedy for gender inequities, blind peer review is being tried (blind review means no names or affiliations appear on articles to be reviewed for publication or on grant proposals being considered for funding). In addition, there is increasing vigilance by reviewers to recognize and rise above their own negative and positive biases and slow down their deliberations so they can reach more evidence-based results. Some federal funding agencies now circulate reminders and give training sessions for their peer reviewers. All of these, as I observed earlier, are hopeful signs.

But other stumbling blocks remain. One is the difficulty of being invited into national and international networks of researchers where one's work can be discussed, critiqued, promoted, and published. These networks are also essential if one, in order to earn the rank of full professor, must build up an international reputation in a field. Further, career-advancement interactions constantly take place within these webs: "science like other institutions depends on the exchange of personal favors" (Stephen Cole, *Making Science*, 1992, p. 81) and on being embedded in opportunity-rich "network ties" (p. 176).

More steps must be taken to ensure that URW and NIs are able to join internationally and nationally powerful networks. (Various ADVANCE campus recipients are beginning to take exactly these steps; see the ADVANCE-National Science Foundation website.)

One clear pattern of academic advantage/disadvantage is observed again and again. The *super-star* academic role is almost totally reserved for majority men who possess a positive-bias halo. The department chair or others seem to pamper and groom this person to become the golden boy. "He is not a minority or a woman, and that person is regarded as the great star of the future, and he is given just a little bit more or even a lot more. He is the head of the parade." Such a star gets extra institutional funding and support; finds that promotion comes quickly; and enjoys a high salary. What is at work here? "Sometimes those 'golden boys,' in my mind, are not necessarily better than anyone else, but it becomes a self-fulfilling prophecy" (quoted in Maher and Tetreault, 2007, pp. 100–1). Self-fulfilling prophecy is, of course, another cognitive error, as I discussed in Chapter 1.

Not every European-American man is, of course, being groomed to become an academic super-star. Nevertheless, it is clear that average men still enjoy privileges related to how they are evaluated in the workplace: they "are more likely to be given early opportunities to show what they can do at work ... to be mentored, to be given a second chance when they fail, and to be allowed to treat failure as a learning experience" (Johnson, 1997, p. 31). They enjoy more breathing room and latitude.

2. Disadvantage: Faculty with a negative bias are often viewed and treated as "outsiders" and, because of this, they have to endure extra psychological stresses and the general feeling of not belonging. This uneasy psychological context can undermine their confidence and success.

Advantage: Faculty with a positive bias are often viewed as "insiders" who belong and thus feel comfortable and accepted. This psychological context can boost their confidence and success.

Constant reminders that certain people do not belong in academe are highlighted in national studies and turn up in my consulting visits to various campuses. A NI senior male faculty member at a Midwest university tells this story: "People ask me '*Why do I speak English so well?* ... They've already superimposed on me that I don't belong here.... I used to think it was a harmless little question but now I feel that the message that I've received is that I don't belong. I don't look like I belong" (quoted in Turner and Myers, 2000, p. 120). An African-American scientist reflects on his stressful experience in a majority setting: "Regarding racial prejudice in science, you should know that although people I work with are pretty open-minded and we have a lot in common (family, professional interests, politics, kids, etc.) ... as a black person you are never over the hump." Feeling that he must always be on guard, he tries to head off tensions and to stay on common ground with his colleagues—because "a split can always develop" (quoted in D. Smith, 1996, p. 103).

Assistant Professor of Education Ana Martinez-Alemán has written: "To be a professor is to be an anglo; to be a Latina is not to be an anglo. So how can I be both a Latina and a professor? To be a Latina professor, I conclude, means to be unlike and like me. *Que locura!* What madness!" (1995, p. 75). Dr. Martinez-Alemán, formerly at Grinnell College, is now at Boston College.

Law professor Patricia Williams expands on this point. "Those who privilege themselves as Un-raced—usually but not always those who are white—are always anxiously maintaining that it doesn't matter." Nevertheless, they feel pity towards those who are raced because they view race as a "social infirmity" (1997, p. 8) or "some sort of genetic leprosy or a biological train wreck" (p. 9). With such an attitude, those in the majority often feel a vast distance between "us" (other majorities like themselves) and "them" (non-majorities). Professor Williams, as an African American, sees no choice but to deal incessantly with that divide: "[I] have little room but to negotiate most of my daily lived encounters as one of 'them.' How alien this sounds. This split without, this split within" (p. 13).

For many years, Ethnic Studies Professor and Department Chair Evelyn Hu-DeHart was one of only three tenured non-majority women (a "solo" clearly) at the University of Colorado where there are more than one thousand faculty. (She is now at Brown University as Professor of History and Director of the Center for the Study of Race and Ethnicity.) At Boulder, Hu-DeHart had ample chances to observe that new faculty hires who are European-American males usually begin their careers as *insiders* and are the most easily accepted by departments already dominated by European-American males. This is because "a common language and other shared codes of communication already exist between them ... the risks of miscommunication, mistrust and missteps are minimal on both sides of this evolving relationship" (Hu-DeHart, 2000, p. 29). In other words, the insider is likely to save energy and time and enjoy a sense of belonging in the enterprise.

But for outsiders such as under-represented faculty, a much longer and more daunting cultural distance must be bridged, with great potential for mishaps, slights, and misunderstandings. To put it starkly, these faculty are frequently treated as "aliens" who do not belong in academe. This disheartening finding—from a survey of more than three thousand African-American faculty and administrators on majority campuses—still in my experience holds unfortunate validity (Moore and Wagstaff, 1974; Vargas, 2002).

3. Disadvantage: Those with a negative bias often have to spend precious time and energy deciphering the complex psychological dynamics and possible micro-aggressions unfolding between them and some of their majority students, colleagues, and administrators.

Advantage: Those with a positive bias tend to save time and energy by not being overly concerned about these dynamics.

Psychologists who have studied disfavored populations find that many suffer incessant "micro-aggressions" and put-downs by some members (but not all, of course) of the majority clan. These micro-aggressions function to reassert the supremacy of the dominant group over subordinate ones. Managing these slights plus sorting through and weighing what they might mean consume precious psychic energy. "In addition to maintaining an internal balance, the [slighted] individual must continue to maintain a social facade and some kind of adaptation to the offending stimuli so that he can preserve some social effectiveness," according to New York University Law Professor Peggy Davis who has African-American ancestry. "All of this requires a constant preoccupation" (2000, p. 145).

In addition, many URW and NIs find another management task to master: they must perform almost constant "smile work." That is, they must spend extra energy in being congenial and easy-going so that their majority colleagues do not view them as aggressive, threatening, or overly sensitive about the particular group membership allotted to them (Tierney and Bensimon, 1996, p. 83). Smile work is still part of the unspoken job description for URW and NI groups. I have no doubt of that.

Yet more energy must be expended as one ponders and tries to determine whether the perceived micro-aggression was in fact deliberate or accidental. Sorting through the dynamics and interchanges takes thought and care. Questions like the following race through one's head:

Did the dean just insult me or was that merely a canned joke she trots out for every new assistant professor?

How in the world could the computer for my office not be up and running when I arrive the week before I start teaching?

Is this just a typical technical snafu, or is this a sign that they don't really want me here?

Why was I not consulted before that report was sent off— doesn't my opinion count around here?

Faculty from non-immigrant groups must activate their emotional radar in order to think through, on a daily and at times an hourly basis: "Is this (event, person, demand, slight, racist remark, incident of exclusion, lack of professional opportunity, etc.) important enough to give it my energy?" (Turner, "Defining," 2001, p. 122; also see P. Williams, 1991). Following this mulling-over and sorting-through process, faculty members have to decide what they should do: perhaps confront the person who has harmed them; perhaps express their hurt or rage; perhaps assume the role of "cultural worker" and try to process the incident with the majority person (Martinez-Alemán, 1995, p. 70; the term "cultural worker" was coined, I believe, by Giroux, 1992). Of course, *any one* of these responses has the potential to boomerang and bring on even more stress. Yet another option is to swallow the pain and internalize the perceived slight. It is no wonder that "stereotype fatigue" is a major concern for under-represented faculty, as I have amply learned from my consulting practice.

4. Disadvantage: A quota system will often block the faculty hiring of those with a negative bias. Some departments, already having one member from a disfavored group, are likely to subscribe to the "one is sufficient" policy.

Advantage: Majority job candidates do not face such a quota barrier and thus enjoy improved chances of being hired.

Most of us probably would guess that a quota means more than one. But real life shows that a quota can be indeed "only one." Law Professor Derrick Bell has repeatedly called attention to an unspoken and rigid quota in academia: only one or only a very small handful of faculty from NI groups will be tolerated at mainstream law schools. This can be referred to as a tolerance for only *token* diversity, I suppose. An organizational psychologist would probably theorize that power-holders in the law schools (such the Harvard Law dean, in Bell's case) dread the power shift that might occur if the number of colonized, non-immigrant group members in their midst continues to climb.

When Bell persisted in bringing extraordinarily qualified job candidates in this category to the dean's attention, *the administrator complained and told Bell that Harvard Law School was not now and would not become a Woolworth's lunch counter in the South, destined to become integrated by non-majority activists.* Possessing such an attitude, the dean could not see and genuinely appreciate the strengths of any new job candidates who possess non-majority status. Bell understandably maintains: once a token or very low number of such faculty is hired, a "real ceiling" is reached that prevents the hiring of any more "regardless of their qualifications" (Bell, 1992, p. 141) and thus blocks fair access and fair evaluation. A positively biased group such as European Americans would not be subject to such a ceiling that metaphorically permits only crawl space.

Other analysts have also focused on this unusual *quota* system. "Many colleges and universities operate under an unwritten quota system that manifests itself as reluctance to hire more than one minority faculty member per department." This "one-minority-per-pot" syndrome is best illustrated by the refrain heard from numerous department chairs across the country that "we hired a minority last year" and thus diversity has been satisfied (Reyes and Halcon, 1991, p. 75).

Being the lonely "quota" person in a majority department can understandably bring psychological disquiet. Tenured Professor Caroline Turner muses: "I have been at the University for thirteen years; in that period, I remain the only faculty member of color in my department. I listen to the assurances [that the department is open to hiring more minority candidates]. I look at the statistics." Yet the numbers, sadly, do *not* change (Turner, 2001, p. 133). How can a professor in such a situation not come to suspect departmental colleagues of paying merely lip service to equity? How can a professor not suspect from time to time that he/she is indeed being *used* as the symbolic token?

Notice this sad pattern: extra steps will probably have been taken to include non-immigrant job applicants in a hiring committee's candidate *pool*. But these special candidates have been placed there for show and will be restricted to serving as metaphorical *bridesmaids rather than brides*: "apparently, an applicant pool that includes minorities is considered by White faculty as evidence of a 'good faith effort' in hiring and integrating minorities—even if minorities are not ultimately hired." In fact, it is predictable that these "show" applicants will *not* be hired. The one-minority-only rule restricts the "career goals and aspirations of Hispanics and other minority faculty" and is partly to blame for the lack of diversity on America's campuses (Reyes and Halcon, 1991, p. 75). This is a reasonable assertion.

A quota system—that restricts certain groups to miniscule representation and marginal power in the organization—actually serves to privilege majority members and reserving for them far more latitude (no ceiling to hit, in other words). Competition for faculty posts is artificially manipulated in this way so that majority candidates are more likely to be *hired* and then, once hired, more likely to professionally thrive as a result of their majority status and positive bias.

5. Disadvantage: Because those with negative bias are typically under-rated and treated as outsiders, they often need *visible and formal affirmative action programs* in order to have the chance to prove themselves. But a backlash is often involved.

Advantage: Those with a positive bias are often overrated, treated as insiders, and given privileged access to set-aside benefits. Thus, they enjoy de facto and *invisible affirmative action* on a continuous basis. There seems to be no backlash.

When under-represented women and non-immigrants are hired as faculty on predominantly majority campuses and professional schools, many of them, from time to time, will be characterized as political hires or affirmative action hires. Either characterization can be translated in this way: they are actually under-qualified for their posts. This dynamic plays out because of the confused and superficial debate about how faculty diversity will/may weaken intellectual excellence and the academic meritocracy. Being the subject of such a hurtful characterization causes considerable hurt, whether expressed openly by students or colleagues in a hallway, whispered loudly at cocktail parties, or assumed automatically by senior power-holders in closed-door deliberations. In Chapters 5 and 6, I outline how department chairs and assigned senior mentors must take pro-active steps to unravel this characterization and ensure that URM and NIs (at all levels) feel welcomed and valued.

Ironically, those who have benefitted enormously from *invisible* affirmative action programs—the European-American group (especially men)—rarely if ever are subject to teasing, assumptions, or judgments that they are in fact under-qualified for their positions. In Chapter 3, I will discuss the many ways that invisible affirmative action has boosted the advancement of this dominant immigrant group, including: the Homestead Acts, the G.I. Bill, the easy access to institutions denied for centuries to NIs and women (such as Harvard, the University of Virginia, and so on), and the fraternity-like exclusive networks where personal favors are exchanged that advance careers.

Currently, we are beginning to see the public questioning of one hitherto invisible affirmative action practice: preference in college admissions being granted to student applicants who are "legacy admits" (so-called because one of their parents previously graduated from that college or university). Legacy applicants, on average, have *seven* times the odds of being accepted than do non-legacy applicants (Lewin, 2011). The legacy practice, of course, gives even greater advantage to those already advantaged. Furthermore, these students—almost always of European descent—readily escape being discounted and stigmatized, simply because they blend into their larger majority group. In a real way, legacy students are being guaranteed "invisible" affirmative action.

Berkeley Professor Takaki insists in his publications that "throughout American history, there had always been affirmative action for white men." For centuries, European-American men in educational, political, and employment realms did not have to compete with women or colonized groups. "Many of them are the beneficiaries of their history of exclusion based on race and gender, and pass their economic and social advantages on to white men in the next generation" (Takaki, 1987, p. 231). Academe is becoming more aware of this reproduction within its structures.

6. Disadvantage: A negatively stereotyped faculty member often has to deal with an uninviting territory in academe where there is little or no mentoring, inside information, or introductions to valuable connections and networks. Such deprivation is likely to hamper professional growth and satisfaction.

Advantage: A positively stereotyped faculty member in an accepting academic climate will receive numerous benefits that speed along professional achievement and satisfaction.

Because I have already touched on several disadvantages that impede non-immigrant, disfavored groups, I will be brief in this section. "Uninviting territory" does indeed await many as they enter and pursue their academic careers in majority settings. This is the conclusion of Harvard education professor Richard Chait and Harvard educational researcher Cathy Trower. Their comprehensive studies confirm what many others have found: social isolation, a dearth of mentors, and even explicit discrimination are common experiences for non-majority faculty in academe (Trower and Chait, 2002, p. 35; Gregory, 1995; Moore and Wagstaff, 1974; Turner and Myers, 2000; also the current COACHE findings at the COACHE website).

When senior leaders do reach out (an uncommon practice), they sometimes make superficial assumptions. One analyst found that prospective allies on medical school faculties, for example, "made assumptions about the [NI] physicians' career goals on the basis of race ... presuming they would want to work directly in underserved communities of color rather than pursue academic careers of administrative and leadership positions" (Nunez-Smith et al, 2007, p. 48). Yet I want to point to heartening instances where under-represented faculty members are being magnificently mentored by European-American male and female faculty in the senior ranks. Go to University of Colorado-Denver Professor Brenda Allen's second edition of *Difference Matters: Communicating Social Identity* (2011) and her article "Learning the Ropes" (2000) as well as Texas A&M University Professor Christine Stanley's article "Cross-Race Faculty Mentoring" (2005). In my consulting, I make it a point to ask URW and NIs about the mentoring they have cultivated and are receiving. Some are being well served by their departments and colleagues. Many are not.

Usually as a *rule* rather than as an exception, *majority insiders* anointed with a positive bias find that their backpack is filled with mentors and allies, roadmaps, a compass, emergency numbers to call, and other valuable contents—rather than a backpack containing extra taxes and penalties. Insiders can feel they already belong to a high-status club. A majority person can spend most of his/her time with majority people and not have to allocate extra energy to learning the language and customs of non-majorities. Being a member of the majority club also brings instant acceptance and validation, according to McIntosh and other analysts.

Networks for Insiders and Exclusion for Outsiders

Professional networks are a key to one's success. I have already cited several studies that show exclusion to be a serious deprivation. An African-American medical professor is well aware of this when he observes: "We don't get invited to the picnic or to the dinner parties ... and that is where those [leadership] jobs come up. We've not in the corridors of power ...We are not in those pipelines, and it has nothing to do with intellectual capacity or ambition" (quoted in Nunez-Smith et al., 2007, p. 48). Again, dozens of researchers have validated this observation.

The clannishness detrimental to URW faculty is captured in a no-nonsense manner by this Stanford female professor:

> *There are some groups of men ... tied by personal friendship and professional collaboration, with no women in their networks, who scratch each other's backs and put each other up for things and it works. They understand each other, they share interests, and they bond. They don't even notice how highly gendered this is.* (quoted in Maher and Tetreault, 2007, p. 62)

Nor do these and like-situated male professors realize how ethnically exclusive their clans are. They claim repeatedly that individual merit and entrepreneurial behavior explain why they advance quite methodically. "Basic to this style is a profound public silence around the idea that White males belong to, or benefit from, any kind of group membership or that standards of accomplishment as articulated by that group may be culturally based and biased" (Maher and Tetreault, 2007, p. 62).

7. Disadvantage: A faculty member assigned a negative bias is often thought to represent his/her whole group and, as such, has to worry that

his/her behavior or performance can open or close doors of opportunity for an entire generation.

Advantage: A faculty member possessing a positive bias has far more latitude and tends to worry only about him/herself.

So many times, undergraduate and graduate students from disfavored groups are embarrassed when their majority professors naively call on them to provide the "Black viewpoint" or the "Puerto Rican" or "Latino/a" or "American Indian" perspective on an issue or a class assignment. The professors mistakenly assume that all members of a group think and behave similarly—but they, of course, do *not* assume the same about members of the European-American majority group. As one New England doctoral scholar complained to me, "I feel like I'm being asked to stand for my *entire* tribe. Is this goofy or what?" He explained that when this happens, he feels trapped in a no-win situation: if he scoffs at the professor's question, he can trigger hostility from some his classmates and the instructor. If he responds as complexly as he can to the question, he wonders if "his people" will be honored or dishonored by his answer.

More than four dozen faculty (whom I have recently interviewed) report that they, too, have been asked to speak for their "entire tribe." Moreover, women and members of under-represented groups often feel that any performance problems they might have as individuals will have important negative consequences for all members of their group or for *all* women. As one person anonymously observed to me: "If a minority person does something magnificent, then it's an exceptional event. But if a minority person does something awful, then it's a typical event for 'those people.'" In other words, it is much easier to accrue lasting impressions of inferiority or incompetence for people in marginalized groups.

A majority person, in short, has far more latitude in this situation as well: "I can do well in a challenging situation without being called a credit to my race. I am never asked to speak for all the people of my racial group. My culture gives me little fear about ignoring the perspectives and powers of people of other races" (quote from McIntosh who has European-American ancestry, 1989, pp. 65–67).

8. Disadvantage: Faculty with an assigned negative bias are often unfairly constrained in their choice of scholarly pursuits and in fact face a "brown-on-brown" taboo.

Advantage: Faculty enjoying a positive bias can set themselves up as scholars of almost anything and expect fair evaluation of their scholarship.

Emeritus Professor of Political Science Willard Johnson recalls his lifelong struggle with his own department to "appreciate the quality and relevance and significance of black scholarship. It is just an overwhelming problem." Why the "blinders" on many majority colleagues in those departments? Johnson believes it's because only scholarship on *their* majority group seems worthwhile to them (oral history interview, C. Williams, 2001, p. 191).

A Native American tenured professor, at a large four-year southwestern university, reports a continuous battle with most of his departmental colleagues over his research projects. They devalue his work for two reasons: because it is on American Indian topics and because he himself is American Indian—so in their minds he could not possibly perform "objective scientific research on his own people." Editors of mainstream journals also resist publication of his work because they believe that scholarship on Indian issues should be done by "objective non-Indian" academics. Needless to say, most editors of such journals are European American (see Shin, 1996).

The irony here, of course, is that majority academics can study and publish to their heart's content on issues related to majorities. Why is their objectivity not suspect? (Peterson-Hickey and Stein, 1998). Hisauro Garza, formerly a professor of Chicano and Latin American Studies at California State University-Fresno and now President of Sierra Research and Technical Services in California, analyzed the responses of 238 college faculty throughout the United States who were included in the National Latino Faculty Survey. Almost one half of these faculty felt that any kind of social science or humanities scholarship, if undertaken by Mexican Americans and Puerto Ricans, is viewed as intellectually *inferior* by most members of their departments. If the scholarship focuses on minority issues, then the value of that research shrinks *even more*. But then a incredible shift of valuation happens: if European-Americans undertake research on minority issues, the value of that investigation *rises* dramatically (Garza, 1993, pp. 37–38).

Several analysts have graphically named this phenomenon the taboo against "brown-on-brown" scholarship, a taboo not affecting majority intellectuals who are granted great latitude to study *anything* of interest to them. For example, majority scholars are presumed to be objective and competent when they scrutinize majority group members' criminal activity and Ponzi schemes, mortgage-derivatives funds, musical and cultural contributions, political maneuvers, philanthropic causes, and so on. No one would say they are "too close" or "too similar" to their subjects.

9. **Disadvantage: Because faculty with an assigned negative bias are likely to be treated as both super-visible and invisible, depending on the circumstances, they will have to cope with psychological dissonance. When deemed super-visible, they will be overloaded with student**

advising and academic committee work. When deemed invisible, their opinions will be ignored.

Advantage: Majority faculty escape this psychological dissonance, the work overload from service and student advising, and the demoralization associated with being voiceless.

Being treated as "both super-visible and invisible," according to Simmons College Professor Sarah Nieves-Squires, is a jarring experience. "On the one hand," Nieves-Squires discloses, "a Hispanic's comments in classrooms or at staff and faculty meetings may be ignored; on the other, she or he constantly may be called upon to present the 'minority view' or the 'Hispanic woman's view' rather than her own views" (1991, p. 12). Such a crazy-making situation is also routinely experienced by several minority professors interviewed by Pennsylvania State University Professor Frances Rains and reported in her article, "Dancing on the Sharp Edge of the Sword: Women Faculty of Color in White Academe" (1999). Being ignored and being regarded as inconsequential can be characterized as "imposed" invisibility, according to Rains. One of her interviewees explains that "I am on several committees—and I can go to a meeting and if they're talking about anything other than minority issues, I'm invisible *even when I'm verbal.*"

But dissonance can be just around the corner. If the conversation in the same committee meeting "turns to minority issues, then the talking stops, and the eyes drift to wherever I am, and I am supposed to expound on 'what it is to be a minority' or 'what Hispanics think'" (quoted in Rains, 1999, p. 160). The shift has clearly been made at this point so that the under-represented colleague is now assigned, according to Rains, "designated" visibility (p. 161).

Business expert Rosabeth Kanter, in her superb book *Men and Women of the Corporation*, elaborates on several aspects of this heightened visibility that tokens—the numerically rare— have to cope with in "skewed" organizations where they compose 15 percent or less of the total population. Kanter explains that tokens suffer from high *visibility* because they are a very few "Os" greatly outnumbered by "Xs"; from artificial *contrast* because the dominant group members tend to exaggerate, in their minds and their perceptions, the differences between themselves and the tokens; and from rampant *stereotyping* because the dominant group tends to deny the token any individuality and uniqueness and instead fits the token to the group stereotype (Kanter, 1997, pp. 206–42). I discuss the Solo Phenomenon at length in Chapter 6, where I argue that senior faculty mentors must understand and then take steps to reduce the extra stressors that solo mentees (one of a numerically few) often confront in majority settings.

Majorities in the corporation or academic department should be thankful they do not have to struggle with high visibility, artificial contrast, or stereotyping—all of which their non-majority token peers are likely to face. These vulnerable colleagues, moreover, are very likely to be regarded by high-ranking administrators on a majority campus as embodiments of "diversity"—another form of designated super-visibility. Carrying such symbolic weight, they are asked or appointed to serve on an excessive number of departmental and campus committees so that each committee will have at least one "diverse" member in its composition. National studies have documented how frequently under-represented professors are *overloaded* with service and committee requirements which impede their scholarship, publishing, and assuming of leadership roles.

This is a most significant cultural tax that majority faculty escape, along with the excessive advising of students that usually falls again to non-majority faculty. In fact, department chairs often direct all under-represented students to the very few or the one token faculty in the department. Preventing both these overloads is the responsibility of the department chair, mentors, and administrators of mentoring programs. Another strategy (rarely followed, unfortunately) is to give solo faculty, when they come up for tenure-and-promotion review, considerable credit for the exceptional advising load they may have carried and the exceptional service contributions they may have made to various committees and the campus overall.

* * * * *

To recap, this second section of the chapter has isolated and examined nine important ways in which majority faculty members (with a positive bias surrounding them) are usually privileged and favored at majority colleges and universities—at the same time that faculty from certain other groups (with a negative bias around them) are usually disadvantaged and disfavored.

What must be seen *as a whole* is the elaborate and interlocked *system* of disadvantages/advantages that favor some and disfavor others. Institutional discrimination, as we have seen, "involves patterns of resource allocation, selection, advancement, and expectations" that perpetuate higher status and likely success for the favored group but just the opposite for all others (White and Cones, 1999, p. 81).

Conclusion and a Segue

The two enormously significant cognitive errors—positive bias and negative bias—deserve much more attention in academe, together with the thirteen other errors outlined in Chapter 1. All of us should spend more time and brain power in resisting these errors and in reducing their power through our own *self-correction.*

But self-correction is not enough. I suggest that we need to dig deeper, to understand the origins of negative and positive biases. How did they take shape in this country? How and why were some people anointed with the positive bias and others branded with the negative bias? The answers are historical and political. The next chapter will provide detailed answers, derived from the findings of distinguished scholars in a variety of disciplines.

The next chapter will underscore that academics, at all times, must remain mindful of the enormous differences between, on the one hand, *European Americans and other immigrant groups* who chose to settle in this country and, on the other hand, *non-immigrant, colonized groups* who had no choice but were instead forced into subordinate roles in this country. If campuses wish to hire voluntary immigrants and international scholars as faculty, this is perfectly acceptable. But counting them as "diversity hires" is not. In Chapter 3, I will maintain that only members of five colonized, non-immigrant domestic groups should be regarded in this manner: **African Americans, Puerto Rican Americans, American Indians, Mexican Americans,** and **Native Hawaiians.**

Academics must become thoroughly grounded in the differences between voluntary, immigrant groups and involuntary, non-immigrant groups *before* they develop strategies for remedying the paucity of "diverse" faculty at their colleges, universities, research institutes and labs, and professional schools. Faculty Diversity Action Plans currently in place at many institutions are unsound primarily because their well-intentioned authors and implementers are "unclear on the concept." That is, on a daily basis they confuse immigrant groups with non-immigrant groups.

Gaining clarity on the concept should not be the exclusive domain of a few dozen highly regarded researchers, authors, and analysts. Instead, all of us in academe should gain more clarity—this is the aim of Chapter 3. Only then are we ready to move on to consider what I refer to as my nuts-and-bolts, "how-to" chapters on faculty diversity. Chapters 4–6 will address these questions: What are the barriers to the recruitment of members from colonized, non-immigrant groups? What are the perennial barriers to retaining and mentoring them? How can careful and pro-active strategies enable academic leaders to push aside these particular barriers to recruitment, retention, and mentorship? What caveats and precautions (arising from my own consulting practice) should be shared with prime movers throughout the country who are intent on diversifying their faculty ranks?

3

DISADVANTAGES FOR NON-IMMIGRANT GROUPS BUT ADVANTAGES FOR IMMIGRANT AND "HONORARY WHITE" GROUPS

Asian Americans are for the most part voluntary immigrants ... most of us had the luck to enter the country during an economic boom period [following the Immigration Act of 1965]. *Many Asian Americans are well-educated, have resources, or both. We have not been held in bondage* [in the U.S.] ... *Asian Americans also may benefit just by not being black. The decreasing significance of race for some Asian American ethic groups does not mechanically correspond to the decreasing relevance of race for African Americans. It may be that the ability of Asian Americans to pass into whiteness depends on their ability to distance themselves from blackness and from the caste-like status of African Americans ... Richard Pryor, one of the most successful African American comedians, joked that the first word an Asian immigrant learned was the n-word.*

(Frank Wu, 2002, pp. 66–67; in 2010 Wu became dean of Hastings Law School, part of the University of California System; formerly he was law school dean at Wayne State University)

Immigrant black students are 'hugely over-represented' at selective colleges and universities. Twenty-five percent of the total black student sample were immigrant or children of immigrants [primarily from Jamaica, Haiti, Ghana, and Kenya] *but only five percent of the total U.S. Black population are immigrants. Of Latino students enrolled at these selective campuses, fifty percent are immigrant.*

(Camille Charles et al., *Chronicle*, 2009, p. A32; Charles is a sociology professor at the University of Pennsylvania)

I think [President] *Obama has an edge that many of us don't have. He has not inherited the slave experience* [he grew up in Hawaii, with a brief period in Indonesia; he is the child of highly educated parents—a European-American mother and an African father from Kenya]. *Those of us whose ancestors were part of the whole slave institution, we have built a resilience. But we also carry baggage. It's as if he* [President

Obama] *didn't get the memo: that I am inferior, as some people portray African Americans.*

> (Sylvia Rousseau, Principal of Santa Monica High School,
> quoted in Remnick, 2009, p. 22; I provide more
> information about President Obama later in this chapter)

In the U.S., honorary-white status seems increasingly to exist for certain people and groups. The quintessential example is certain Asian-Americans, particularly East Asians...the model-minority myth and professional success have combined to free some Asian-Americans... at least as measured by professional integration, residential patterns, and intermarriage rates.... Latinos in the U.S. have long been on the cusp between white and nonwhite. It seems likely that an increasing number of Latinos—those who have fair features, material wealth, and high social status, aided also by Anglo surnames—will both claim and be accorded a position in U.S. society as fully white.

> (Ian Lopez, 2006, p. B8; Lopez is a law professor
> at the University of California-Berkeley)

Because boundaries [in the U.S.] *are loosening for some nonwhite groups* [primarily Asian and Latino/a], *this could lead to the erroneous conclusion that race is declining in significance for all groups or that relations are improving at the same pace for all racial ethnic minorities...we must recognize that race and the color line have difference consequences for different minority groups.*

> (University of California-Irvine Sociology Professors
> Jennifer Lee and Frank Bean, 2007, p. 580)

Not all ethnic groups, as the quotations above clearly underscore, possess the same standing and same regard from the dominant European-American group in power. Immigrants and immigrant groups who, of their own volition, choose to settle in this country automatically enjoy much higher status in the eyes of the majority group. By contrast, a caste-like, rigid, low status is assigned to *internal* groups who were incorporated by the dominant group through the use of "force, not choice" (to use political scientist Jennifer Hochschild's memorable phrase, 1995, p. 82).

This chapter will discuss *how* and *why* members of internal *colonized* groups (that is, those forcibly incorporated into the United States through enslaving, conquering, decimating, dispossessing, or possessing) often face greater disadvantages inside and outside academia. These colonized, non-immigrant groups (NI) are: African-American, American Indian, Puerto Rican-American, Mexican-American, and Native Hawaiian. Shortly, I will provide details on why these NI groups are best described as colonized groups and why other groups are more favorably viewed as immigrants and as honorary whites (that is, honorary European Americans). But first, some semantics should be addressed.

SECTION A

Avoid Certain Misleading Terms: People of Color; Minority; Hispanic; Latino/a; Diversity or Multi-Cultural Faculty Hires

Concurring with two dozen scholars and practitioners, I maintain that it is critically important for administrators and faculty—at professional schools, colleges, and universities—to attend to the *different cultural contexts and political histories* inhabited and inherited by their students, faculty, and staff. The first step in attending to these various contexts and histories is this: eschew convoluted and inaccurate terms superficially used in academe on a daily basis.

"*People of color*" and "*people of non-white races*" and "*minorities*" are three examples which obscure cultural and historical differences of a number of ethnic groups. These three terms are overly broad, overly inclusive, and indeed homogenizing in their effects: they imply that all non-European Americans (so-called people of color) have had to struggle against the oppression of the majority group and possess the same or similar subordinate status in relation to that dominant group. This is just not true. Groups assembled under the "minority" term have widely divergent political and economic experiences and histories with the dominant European Americans, depending on when, how, and why these new groups arrived and how they were received and viewed (Massey, 2011; Lee and Bean, 2007; Hollinger, 2005, 2006, 2011; Skrentny, 1996; H. Graham, 2002; Wu, 2002; Takaki, 1989, 1993).

By the way, most of us in academe currently accept that "race" is not actually a biological fact or category—but indeed a very powerful social and political construction that affects our personal and professional lives on a daily basis. (I am trying to wean myself from using the word "race" or related racial words like "black," "white," "red," and "yellow.")

For another alternative, we can follow the lead of social psychologist Claude Steele who sometimes uses the term "non-immigrants" when talking about certain ethnic groups in this country (2000). Non-immigrants refer to those specific colonized groups who had *no choice* but were incorporated by force. This term, I believe, is very helpful because it may remind the listener of *force not choice*. As the result of being colonized and conquered, several "non-immigrant" groups in this country continue to deal with devaluation and with demoralizing conditions that have resulted from their ancestors being conquered and thereby stigmatized.

In light of such a painful history, it is clearly insulting to characterize the United States as a wonderful and exceptional "land of immigrants," as a number of politicians invariably do when on the stump. To leave out non-immigrants who labored in so many ways to build this country is a serious mistake. As Steele reminds us: "Blacks and Native Americans have always been here" (1992, p. 121). It is in fact immigrants (myself included) who are the newcomers. So, too, we should remember that Mexicans in the Southwest preceded all European Americans. This ethnic group saw their national boundary in the 1860s forcibly moved much further south, with the resultant loss of one-half of the Mexican homeland to the land-hungry and often slave-holding European-American settlers moving westward. A clever and poignant way to describe what happened to Mexicans in the Southwest comes from a Mexican-American professor from Arizona: "Well, my people were here the whole time in the Southwest. That's for sure. But the line was moved on us!"

Moreover, the terms "*Hispanic*" and "*Latino/a*" should be avoided because their scope is gargantuan and their meaning too entangled and dense to parse. The two terms indiscriminately melt down numerous groups' cultural differences, national origins, and social statuses (H. Graham, 2002, p. 181). For instance, a scholar from Argentina should be described as immigrant or international—not incorrectly as a minority or Hispanic or Spanish-speaking. Possessing immigrant or international standing, such a person typically will enjoy higher status in this country and in academe. By contrast, a Mexican American with a complex historical and political experience with this country is a member of a *domestic, colonized* group or, put differently, a member of a *non-immigrant* group.

Social historian David Hollinger underscores this fact: "So great is the variety of experience among Hispanics that the Census bureau would do well to think carefully about the basis for continuing to treat Hispanics as a single category at all." The Census, he continues, should drop this quasi-racial category and count instead those inhabitants who identify with their "*descent communities*" (Hollinger, 2006) in Mexico, Cuba, Puerto Rico, the Dominican Republic, Haiti, so on. This is after all the specific way that people with these descent lineages describe *themselves*. In addition, instead of counting Asians as one huge, monolithic group, the Census might count people who trace their descent specifically to China, Japan, Korea, Vietnam, India, Iran, the Philippines, Pakistan, Turkey, and so on. And the Census bureau, maintains Hollinger, should also distinguish among these three groups: domestic African Americans, Caribbean blacks, and immigrant blacks from various countries in Africa and elsewhere (2002, p. 25). The first group (domestic African Americans) is a U.S. colonized group and the other two are immigrant groups.

To Hollinger's and others' credit, the 2010 U.S. Census reflected a few of these constructive changes. But one change in the Census is truly non-sensical and muddled: in Question Five of the 2010 Census, both "race" and "origin" are mentioned but not defined (such hopelessly bureau-cratic ambiguity reminds me of the slippery language used by the U.S. Internal Revenue Service in its dreaded tax return forms).

Question Five in the 2010 Census is aimed at "Hispanic, Latino, or Spanish origin" people who are at least offered more finely detailed choices about origin, such as "Puerto Rican, Cuban, Argentinean, Dominican, Salvadoran, Spaniard," and so on. Question Six, on the other hand, does not mention origin in any way but instead is aimed at people who have one of the following so-called four "races": "White; Black, African American, or Negro; American Indian or Alaska Native; and Asian." Asians are indeed given choices by the 2010 Census about their descent community, but Question Six characterizes these choices as not about origin but about "race" and then gives examples of "races" such as "Asian Indian, Chinese, Native Hawaiian, Hmong, Thai, Paki-stani" and so on. *Four times* in Question Six, the word "race" is used but never once is "origin" mentioned. Very odd indeed. Very confusing. But at least Asians are given ways to distinguish their cultural origins. Question Six does not, however, allow any distinction among immigrant Africans (coming from Africa or some part of the African diaspora), Jamaican Blacks, and domestic African Americans, as Hollinger had recommended and I applaud.

Be Careful with the Term "Diversity Hires"

Thus far, I have recommended the use of these terms: *descent communi-ties, non-immigrant groups, immigrant groups, U.S. colonized groups* as well as hyphenated terms referring to specific ancestries/origins, such as *Chinese-American, European-American, and Puerto Rican-American* groups. Superficially assuming that all or most groups are alike—and that they face similar challenges and opportunities as they interact with majority European-American institutions and power-holders—is a big mistake. For that reason, I advise against using these overly broad and misleading terms: *Hispanic, Latino/a, minority, people of color, Whites and Blacks.*

Likewise, I suggest it is a mistake to lump together all groups that descend from somewhere *other* than Europe—and then characterize all of these *non*-European American groups as the pool from which so-called *"diversity hires"* can be drawn during faculty search processes.

Unfortunately, such superficial and confused counting of faculty hires happens at most campuses (Yoshinaga-Idtano, 2006, pp. 348–49).

The data about new faculty colleagues must be disaggregated so that campuses and schools understand the descent communities of those they are hiring or considering to hire. If they do not, then the hiring authorities are very likely to feel more comfortable with and to make quick offers to immigrants and international scholars (who usually enjoy a positive bias about their intellectual abilities). Then the shocking discovery and disappointing pattern will come into view: over the past few years, the campuses and schools have inadvertently hired none or only a very few members of domestic, colonized groups. In short, disaggregating data about the descent communities of new faculty hires must be done in order to protect against the shortchanging of domestic, colonized groups. In the next section, I will discuss at length what I and others mean by "colonized, domestic" groups

SECTION B

Distinctions Among Groups from Europe, Asia, India, Central and South America, the Middle East, the Caribbean, and so on

Differences Between Colonized Groups and Immigrant Groups

Why are some groups and clans more likely to be accepted and respected by the dominant, European-American group at our colleges and universities? Why do other groups often encounter higher obstacles and a chilly climate within academic departments? Why do teachers and professors often believe that students from certain groups possess good prospects for future success while students from other groups have unpromising prospects?

To begin grappling with these large questions, I will continue to draw a distinction between *immigrant/voluntary* groups and *colonized/involuntary* groups. I rely on a number of thinkers, but especially on Robert Blauner, who, in the early 1970s, wrote a stunning analysis entitled "Colonized and Immigrant Minorities." For the insights below, I also thank: Alvarez; Berreman; Brown; Bruner; Carter and Segura; Charles; Cruz; Cummins; DeVos; Fischer et al.; Franklin; Gibson; H. Graham; Grosfoguel; G. Loury; Hochschild; Hollinger; Jacobson; C. Lee; Y. Lee; Lee and Bean; O. Martinez; Massey; Matute-Bianchi; Montero-Sieburth; Nieto; Ogbu; Oquendo; Powell; G. Rodriguez; R. Rodriguez; Shorris; Shibutani and Kwan; Stanton-Salazar; Steele; M. and C. Suarez-Orozco; Takaki; Vélez-Ibáñez; Waters; C. Williams;

61

Wu; and Yetman (complete citations are in the bibliography). A host of novelists, scholars, and journalists continue to remind us that the immigrant model for this country is shortsighted and obscures the stigmatized status of several minority groups. Nevertheless the model continues to be invoked—especially by U.S. politicians who claim "we are all immigrants" and all enjoy the fruits of American democracy and the possibility of realizing the American dream. This is not true: it is empty political rhetoric. Within our boundaries are internal, colonized groups who find their life chances and opportunities to advance very sparse. "The colonized became ethnic minorities *en bloc*, collectively, through conquest, slavery, annexation, or a racial labor policy." Their cultural practices and ways of life are to varying degrees decimated, exploited, degraded, and controlled, generation after generation (Blauner, 1972, p. 151). They are not immigrants.

Immigrants have *chosen* to relocate to the United States—or any other society—because they desire a better future: more money and property; more opportunities for themselves and their children; higher social standing; safety and relief from political war, starvation, or religious persecution. Immigrants usually do not come alone but rather with relatives or neighbors from their Old World villages and counties. They are usually ambitious and believe they will be making a fresh start. They typically possess an "abundance of hope" (C. and M. Suarez-Orozco, 2001, p. 122) and "extravagant dreams" (Takaki, 1989, pp. 18, 66)— despite encountering usually daunting, exhausting, and unexpected challenges.

The first immigrant group to settle in the Eastern region of this country was of English heritage. In short order, the English as well as German, Irish, and Scottish settlers came to predominate, with their Christian and Jewish cultural and religious allegiances. Other voluntary groups in this country trace their descent from Spain and other European countries, China, India, Japan, Korea, Africa, Central and South America, the Middle East, and the Caribbean, namely Jamaica, Trinidad, Haiti, and the Dominican Republic (Takaki, 1989, 1993; Hollinger, 2005, 2011; Waters, 1990, 1999, 2000).

European-Descent Immigrants Become the Dominant Group and Consolidate their Economic and Political Power

The first European immigrants, of course, found the New World already populated with aborigines (I will refer to these natives as American Indians). But the American Indians were forcibly pushed aside. The Europeans overwhelmed them with their germs (smallpox, measles, chicken pox, and so on), sophisticated weapons, belief in the rightfulness of European "white supremacy," and legal and political guile. American

Indians' lives, territories, and cultures were forever changed and nearly decimated—a few scholars have referred to their removal as the "American Holocaust" and as the largest genocide in the history of the world (Stannard, 1993).

Many European Americans, both common folk and power-holding leaders, rejoiced in this removal of Indians under the banner of Manifest Destiny and empire-building. Several U.S. presidents in fact took part in the removal and decimation. In the late 1800s Teddy Roosevelt, like many of his Harvard professors and peers, celebrated the extermination of American Indians as a sign of European-American superiority and reason. Inspired by this original and comprehensive victory over the aborigines, Roosevelt longed for the imperial conquering of other native peoples in other lands (James Bradley, *The Imperial Cruise*, 2009).

In short, American Indians were the first—but by no means the last—colonized group in this country. By "colonized" I mean physically conquered, culturally weakened, and even pushed at times to the point of extinction by the dominant group. American Indians were certainly incorporated into this society *by force and certainly not by choice.* Indian leader Carlos Montezuma in the late 1800s, sadly reviewing his peoples' suffering and demoralization, came to this conclusion: "Indians would be much better off, if they could be put on boats and then allowed to reenter the country as immigrants, with the same treatment and entitlements as new arrivals from abroad" (quoted in Maddox, 2005, p. 75). Needless to say, American Indians are still marginalized and many have been forced to live on reservations on the edge of the mainstream society. They often encounter very high barriers to economic and political autonomy and struggle to this day with demoralization.

The first European Americans settling on the Eastern seaboard quickly created another colonized group: Africans who were kidnapped from their homeland and forced as slaves to work in European Americans' businesses, homes, farms, and especially plantations. Regarded as subhuman and incapable of reason, slaves were treated as *property*, pure and simple, and their forced labor was used to build both the Northern and Southern economies for more than three centuries!

European Americans—in their legal system and courts, businesses, labor unions, and religious institutions—constantly reinforced the exploitation of African Americans and forbade their education and advancement. By doing so, they could constantly elevate their own privilege and increase their hidden and not so hidden profits and advantages. Their assets came to be viewed as European "Whiteness" and concomitant superiority. This sense of superiority and entitlement was created through the denigration, undervaluation, shortchanging, and dispossession of colonized groups who were treated as grossly inferior and deserving of harsh treatment.

As UCLA professor Cheryl Harris analyzed so astutely in her law review article "Whiteness as Property" (1993), whiteness in this country brought political privileges, relatively high social status, and personal identity—as well as the right to exclude those deemed as non-white people from some or all of these privileges and rights. Harris found that the concept of whiteness, early in our country's history, came to mean *white supremacy* and that the courts and legislatures took deliberate steps to protect this supremacy and ensure that it passed on to subsequent generations.

In addition, large property owners manipulated working-class European Americans, because they feared them as potential disruptors of the rigid class/caste system in place. In a maliciously savvy manner, affluent Virginia slave-holders and others methodically endowed working-class European Americans with "whiteness" and spotlighted their new status through preferential practices (e.g., a non-white could not give testimony against a white in a court of law; small plots of land at affordable prices were available when poor European-Americans completed their indentured work service).

Those of privilege and high-economic status took these steps in order to transform the working class into steadfast allies and to activate them as militant enemies of Indians and African slaves who might overthrow the system at any time. Because these power-holders had no professional troops to defend the status quo, they had to carefully build local militia made up of locals newly accepted into the *white-supremacy clan.* This manipulation worked seamlessly (Taylor, 2001, pp. xiii–xiv). It still does: working-class European Americans take deliberate steps to protect their white supremacy and pass it to their offspring. "They define themselves in opposition to African Americans and measure their status in terms of the distance between themselves and black schools, neighborhoods, and people" (Massey, 2011; see also Massey and Denton, *American Apartheid*, 1993).

Just as methodically, the exclusion and disadvantaging of those deemed as non-whites is carefully preserved by those in power, and this regrettable legacy is passed on to future generations (Harris, 1998). Agreeing that white supremacy allows "the spoils of discrimination" to be inherited, University of California-San Diego Professor George Lipsitz concludes that European Americans "are encouraged to invest in whiteness, to remain true to an identity that provides them with resources, power, and opportunity." Whiteness, while not a biological or anthropological fact, is indeed a most powerful "social fact" and social identity (1998, p. vii). Races are social constructions and indeed very powerful.

Over many generations, those with a European-American identity have benefited from governmental legislation and policies—federal, state, and local—that have blocked African Americans and other disfavored groups from acquiring wealth. By contrast, the very same legislation and policies have granted unearned advantages to *majority* male members of the society. This is why numerous scholars maintain that there has *always* been Affirmative Action for European-American men. For instance, American Indians and Mexican Americans were officially forced from their lands, to make way for European-American farmers and ranchers; government policies and courts paved the way for that comprehensive dispossession.

African Americans, once freed from slavery, did *not* receive the promised forty acres and a mule for farming, which some political theorists believe would have been the genuine start of an American democracy. Ruthless discrimination—both in economic and social spheres—continued with Jim Crow laws against colonized groups. And, of course, these unfortunate groups were blocked from participating in the huge land-giveaways (of formerly Indian land) in the Midwest and West, under the homesteading acts. Because only European Americans were allowed to lay claim to new ranches and farms, they were granted a head-start on accumulation of land wealth that continues to accrue to this day (Ignatiev, 1995; Roediger, 1999; Woodward, 1966; Oliver and Shapiro, 1995).

In modern times, the Servicemen's Readjustment Act of 1944—more widely known as the G.I. Bill—together with the Federal Housing Administration (FHA) prevented colonized groups from seizing any ways to quickly advance. After World War II, European-American male veterans exclusively enjoyed the splendid educational, housing, and financial benefits of the G.I. Bill (Katznelson, 2006, *When Affirmative Action Was White*) because of the local ways in which the benefits were distributed. By means of low-cost mortgages, European-American veterans who settled in "white suburbia" have been particularly fortunate (whites-only suburbia was deliberately constructed by the FHA and the Veterans Administration). Quite modest homes, especially suburban tract homes that were bought in the 1940s and 1950s, have appreciated beyond their owners' wildest dreams. Shapiro and Oliver in their book *Black Wealth/White Wealth* calculate that "between 1987 and 2011 the baby boom generation stands to inherit approximately $7 trillion." Much of this wealth has accrued to them through appreciation of their elderly parents' residences (1995, p. 181).

But the elderly parents of African Americans, Mexican Americans, and other stigmatized groups were blocked, sometimes subtly and more often blatantly, from acquiring houses in suburbia where housing appreciation was and probably still is the greatest. (The places where many stigmatized and poor groups were and are concentrated—apartments, low-income homes segregated from European-American settlements, Indian reservations, barrios, slums, or migrant worker camps—realize no such build-up of equity.) In dollars alone, Oliver and Shapiro maintain that discriminatory practices in the residential housing industry "are costing the *current* generation of African Americans about $82 billion" (1995, pp. 9, 151). Two other scholars—Kenneth Jackson in *Crabgrass Frontier* (1985) and Bruce Haynes in *Red Lines, Black Spaces* (2001)—make similar points.

How mostly mercantile-skilled immigrant Jews moved from the margins and were accepted into the U.S. mainstream is discussed by Katznelson (2005), by Yuri Slezkine in *The Jewish Century* (2004), and by David Hollinger in his article "Rich, Powerful, and Smart: Jewish Overrepresentation Should Be Explained Rather than Mystified or Avoided" appearing in the *Jewish Quarterly Review*, 2004. I agree with Hollinger, who maintains in many of his publications, that the *over-representation* of some groups (such as Jews and certain Asian-American groups) in higher education, the professions, and science is a valuable phenomenon for cultural study, as valuable as the study of *under-representation* of other groups. Rather than superficially grasping genetics as an explanation, it is wise to ferret out informal affirmative-action practices such as the G.I. Bill which are often pervasively implicated in both the "over" and the "under" situations.

Another kind of affirmative action for European Americans is at work when selective colleges and universities show favoritism in admission acceptances to children of alumni, as I mentioned in the previous chapter. A number of law reviews have recently focused on how legacy admissions can and should be challenged. Richard Kahlenberg in *Affirmative Action for the Rich: Legacy Preferences in College Admissions* (2010) delineates how the legacy practice rewards those who already have advantages and thus reproduces a kind of aristocracy. (For other ways that the ruling class reproduces itself, see the discussion of the S.A.T. and other high-stakes tests in Sacks (2007); E. Garcia (1991); and the website of the National Center for Fair and Open Testing.)

European-American Labor Unions and Their Creation of Wealth or Poverty

European Americans have also benefited over several generations—and still do—if they belong to labor unions. The unions usually bring them some financial protection and the means to steadily build up wealth. For example, "what especially boosted the Irish as a class was their opportunity to participate in the higher-waged skilled and unionized trades" (Takaki, 1993, p. 163). But these organizations, designed to protect powerless workers, were very *exclusive* in their policies. In the early twentieth century, written clauses in the by-laws, for example, of the Brotherhood of Locomotive Firemen, Brotherhood of Railway

Carmen, and the Clerks, Mates and Pilots Union permitted only white male members. The bigotry in unions, made illegal by the 1960s anti-discrimination laws, continued as unwritten policy and remained just as effective: "By 1970, Blacks in construction unions made up only 1.7 percent of ironworkers, 0.4 percent of elevator construction workers, and 0.2 percent of plumbers." Even today, labor unions in this country remain close to 90 percent European-American in their membership (White and Cones, 1999, p. 42; also see Thurow, 1969).

As European immigrants struggled to create unions in order to protect and advance their interests, they deliberately excluded all others, including women. For example, in 1870 in New Orleans, there were 3,460 African Americans listed in the city directory as carpenters, cigar makers, painters, clerks, shoemakers, coopers, tailors, bakers, blacksmiths, and foundry hands. Yet by 1904 the number was below 346, although the African-American population of the city had increased by more than 50 percent. The new construction unions ensured that the jobs within their jurisdiction became "white men's work"—whereas prior to the Civil War, there had been a "concentration of black workers, both slave and free, in the building trades" (Hill, 1989, p. 214).

This conversion to "white men's work" occurred in many cities along the Eastern seaboard and throughout the Southern states. In New York City between 1890 and 1910, African-American workers were steadily forced out of employment as longshoremen, caterers, tailors, brickmakers, wagon drivers, stable hands, house painters, and hotel and restaurant waiters. Organized labor unions and corporate managers and owners—working together as partners—relegated African Americans to a severely exploited class of workers and blocked them from entering all-white skilled occupations. The government did little or nothing to stop this exploitation. Economist Herbert Hill believes that the chronic poverty and social disorganization found in African-American ghettos over generations has been caused and perpetuated, in large measure, by corporate leaders and by European immigrants and their labor union policies that locked African Americans into the lowest caste position (Hill, 1989).

The same pattern—creating a permanent underclass of Mexican-American laborers—occurred in the Southwest. European-American migrants to California and other parts of the Southwest soon learned that by playing up their "whiteness," they could receive the best paying and more permanent jobs while Mexicans would receive the worst paying and most erratic (Takaki, 1993). Some economists quaintly call this a "dual-wage system." In domestic servant jobs, African-American women were also pushed out. While in New York City in 1830, they held most cooking and cleaning jobs in affluent households, by 1850 Irish immigrant women did. In San Francisco, Irish men organized anti-Chinese activities and shouted that the Chinese threatened the employment of Irish women: "Chinese Must Go! Our Women are degraded by coolie labor" (Takaki, *A Different Mirror*, 1993, p. 154).

Several leaders, including Frederick Douglass as early as 1853 and W.E.B. Du Bois in the early twentieth century, repeatedly complained about this displacement of African-American workers by German, Irish, Jewish, and other immigrants. Douglass noted that "every hour sees the black man elbowed out of employment by some newly arrived immigrant, whose hunger and whose color are thought to give him a better title to place, and so we believe it will continue until the last prop is leveled beneath us" (quoted in Hill, 1989, p. 216). In fact, "it is not just that various white immigrant groups' economic successes came at the expense of nonwhites, but they owe their now stabilized and broadly recognized whiteness *itself* in part to these nonwhite groups" (Jacobson, 1998, p. 9).

The book *How the Irish Became White* (1995) by Noel Ignatiev (Professor of Liberal Arts at the Massachusetts College of Art) details how the Irish Catholic—brutally treated in Ireland as a caste-like and oppressed people by the dominant English—*re-enacted* oppression once they arrived in America. Quickly the Irish immigrants realized the pernicious wisdom of *their* adopting anti-black sentiments. While at first they themselves (despite often very pink complexions) were denigrated by the majority group here as a "black" race which was intellectually and morally inferior, the Irish struggled against this stigma and climbed the implicit "chain of being." Through persistence, violence, political organizing, and other means, immigrant workers like the Irish Catholic pushed to take over the better jobs, achieve some political power, and reap higher wages. "The greater rate of exploitation of the black worker, locked into an all-black labor classification, subsidized the higher wages of whites, a process repeated in many industries and codified into collective bargaining agreements" (Hill, 1989, p. 233).

European immigrants like the Irish gained preferential treatment because their unions routinely refused to consider Mexican Americans, African Americans, Native Americans, and Puerto Ricans for membership or to refer them for employment. By guaranteeing these preferential advantages along with higher wages, the unions enabled many European immigrants to escape crushing poverty and consolidate their power and position. This economic pattern of dominance remains: European-American males still make up the vast majority of tenured full professors and top administrators; senior managers of Fortune 500 and 1000 companies; school superintendents; elected and appointed political leaders; Wall Street investors and managers; Hollywood and Broadway directors, producers, and investors; and on and on (Massey, 2011; Waldinger, 2011). The dual labor system—that structurally enhances wealth-production for the favored group and undermines such production for the disfavored groups—explains why wealth as well as poverty can be predictably inherited by succeeding generations.

Advantages Enjoyed by All or Most Immigrants
(whether from Europe, Asia, India, or Elsewhere)

Immigrants can be aptly described as "migration machines" (Foner, 2001, p. 5) because they usually relocate in the presence of and with the support of others from their home village or county. It is a common mistake to visualize a single, desperate sojourner inching her/his way to the promised land. Once the first immigrant group is settled, these members create "receiving networks" so they can reach back to encourage and welcome a stream of new arrivals from the homeland. Newcomers are comprehensively sponsored—this is, they are assisted in finding jobs, temporary housing, and all-important social, communal support. Basically, the very first immigrants form a "beachhead" that eases the way for more arrivals (Model, 2008, p. 61). Then the tightly knit fabric of immigrants' networks acts to quickly channel newcomers into employment positions and residential settlements (Waldinger, 2011). In a way, these close-knit networks contain benefits and profits that somewhat parallel the "knapsack" of unearned privileges, passports, checks, and hidden profits carried by European Americans, especially males (as discussed by McIntosh, 1989).

Despite the cultural shock and the demands of starting a new life in a strange new world, immigrants usually are sustained by several practices. They usually settle where they have allies, friends from the homeland, financial support, and familiar community-shared habits of daily living. Second, most newcomers can hold on to a Return Exit as an option—that is, they can continue to identify with their homeland and believe that they have the flexibility and option to return, if the new land does not work out (as many Italian newcomers and others did, according to University of Notre Dame Professor Walter Nugent, 1992). Because immigrants are not fully invested in the new home (at least in the beginning), they can "brush off barriers as temporary problems," according to Hunter College immigration expert Nancy Foner, and muster amazing persistence and resilience in the face of roadblocks (2001, p. 183).

Because immigrants are new, they do not have bruises and historical wounds (metaphorically speaking) accumulated by grappling with the majority group in the new land. In a way, immigrants are blank tablets because they lack a history and political relationship with the new world and its European-American dominant group. They believe they will achieve a better life than they experienced in the old world.

Moreover, immigrants have an immediate way to elevate their status and prospects for success. They can disassociate themselves from those colonized groups which they readily perceive have been conquered and now remain stuck at the bottom of America's caste-like system: namely, American Indians (in the beginning of the European settlement), then African Americans, Mexican Americans, Puerto Rican Americans, and Native Hawaiians (Wu, 2002; Takaki, 1987, 1989, 1993; Hollinger, 2011; Massey, 2011).

Disassociation and denigration of those at the bottom—this is the exact strategy that the Irish in the 1800s used as they made America their home. In fact, "it is not just that various white immigrant groups' economic successes came at the expense of nonwhites, but they owe their now stabilized and broadly recognized whiteness *itself* in part to these nonwhite groups" (Jacobson, 1998, p. 9). This dynamic was discussed earlier. A similar pattern of elevation—through a colonized group's denigration—can be detected with the arrival of immigrants hailing not from Europe but from *other areas* of the world. Several examples follow.

West Indians from the Caribbean (Category: Immigrants)

Immigrants from the Caribbean, for instance, typically disassociate from low-caste African Americans. Thus, stigma for the non-immigrant, domestic group gets reinforced because many West Indians persistently insist that they are culturally *different from and superior* to African Americans though there may be some visual resemblance (Model, 2008). West Indians, in a way, position themselves as a "model minority" (Waters, 1999, p. 342). In fact, some second- and third-generation youth with West Indian ancestry cleverly choose a protective strategy: they cultivate and maintain a West Indian (British-related) accent because it announces that they are not African Americans. Their exotic accent can "open doors" to housing and employment—doors that remain shut to non-immigrant African Americans from the same neighborhoods (Waters, p. 332).

U.S. employers often say they feel more comfortable and less guilty when they hire and interact with West Indians. Why? Majority-group employers can look at a West Indian face "without seeing the sorry history of American race relations mirrored back" (Waters, p. 172). Preferring to avoid a sense of guilt and discomfort, some employers shy away from hiring and interacting with home-grown U.S. minorities (Skrentny, 2002; also Dovidio and his studies of stand-offish, "aversive" behavior, listed at the Yale University website). These employers prefer to interact with West Indian immigrants—and they often reap a bonus: from time to time they can tap into the West Indians' strong immigrant networks when they need to quickly find new immigrant employees on a part-time or full-time basis (Waters, p. 332).

Immigrants clearly enjoy privileges. For instance, in his autobiography, Colin Powell (U.S. Secretary of State in President George W. Bush's administration and Head of the Joint Chief of Staffs in President George H. W. Bush's administration) captures vividly the psychological advantage and cultural context he reaps as an immigrant. Powell's parents voluntarily moved here from Jamaica. Although born in New York City, Powell as well as his parents and extended family continue to regard themselves as immigrants who take great pride in having roots in the homeland of Jamaica. He explains:

> My Black ancestors may have been dragged to Jamaica in chains, but they were not dragged to the United States. Mom and Pop chose to emigrate to this country for the same reason that Italians, Irish, and Hungarians did, to seek better lives for themselves and their children. That is a far different emotional and psychological beginning than that of American Blacks, whose ancestors were brought here in chains. (1995, p. 23)

Reinforcing Powell's observation, cross-cultural studies have definitely shown that it is far more psychologically draining for groups to live in the same country where the dominant clan has invaded, subordinated, decimated, or colonized their ancestors and where they themselves continue to have painful interactions with their former colonizers or enslavers.

It is predictable that many U.S. leaders would feel *very comfortable* with Powell who insists that he is still an immigrant. European Americans expect Powell and other Caribbeans to be "better blacks." In addition, many whites find common ground with West Indians' immigrant experiences and, relatedly, their deep faith in the American Dream (Waters, p. 190). But note: West Indians living in England do *not* reap these immigrant benefits. Living in the country that colonized them, they are the "most stigmatized group in Britain" (Model, 2008, p. 66; see also Grosfoguel, 2003; Foner, 2001).

The 2000 U.S. Census underscores that the number of recent immigrants from the Caribbean and Africa has become substantial: foreign-born blacks now number 2.8 million whereas in 1980 they numbered 816,000. What is even more noteworthy is that the newest immigrants from Africa "are the best-educated immigrant group in America," with most possessing advanced degrees (Robinson, 2010, pp. 8–9). Predictably, an accumulation of advantages will be reaped by these well-situated newcomers and their offspring. And predictably, many of them on America's campuses—whether faculty or students—will probably wish to segregate themselves through aversive behavior and clearly distinguish themselves from members of U.S. low-status colonized groups (see publications by Richard Tapia, Lani Guinier and Susan Strum, Camille Charles, Douglas Massey, and Henry Louis Gates, Jr.; citations in bibliography).

U.S. President Barack Obama

Is the president a member of a colonized group? No. Like Colin Powell, he was born in the United States but has collected immigrant dividends. His childhood was spent in multicultural Hawaii and for a short time in Indonesia. His highly educated and worldly mother was European American (raised in Kansas, Washington State, and then Hawaii). His highly educated father was from Ghana and is the subject of the son's best-seller *Dreams of My Father: A Story of Race and Inheritance* (1995). With such a background, the president has several obvious advantages over native African Americans whose ancestry includes slavery, Jim Crow humiliating segregation, discrimination, and micro-aggressions of many kinds.

Janny Scott's impressive biography *A Singular Woman: The Untold Story of Barack Obama's Mother* (2008) documents the personal and family life of Stanley Ann Dunham as well as the anthropological and community-organizing work that engaged Obama's mother for decades in Indonesia. Duke University Press in 2009 published her University of Hawaii doctoral dissertation *Surviving Against the Odds: Village Industry in Indonesia*. Working as a professional for the Ford Foundation and other agencies in that part of the world, Dunham painstakingly created micro-credit practices to advance the work and wages of poor women. Several major anthropologists and economic developers have characterized her efforts as stunningly successful.

In raising her son, Dunham emphasized above all the values of empathy and a rigorous education. She expressed love as well as particularly high expectations for his adult success: perhaps he would become the *president of the United States*. When young Barack lived for a time with his Midwest grandparents, he received the same messages. His grandmother, during her career, climbed to a high position in a local bank.

In short, President Obama was provided numerous assets and lessons, as a child of highly educated parents whose ancestry was immigrant African as well as domestic European American. Because President Obama is not a member of a colonized group in this country, he lacks the wounds, scars, and legacies from that experience. Nevertheless, U.S. Congressman and paramount Civil Rights Movement leader John Lewis (who does indeed have many scars) is proud because Obama has chosen to "digest the spirit and the language of the movement" (quoted in Remnick, 2009, p. 22).

Cuban Americans (Category: Immigrants) and Puerto Rican Americans (Category: Colonized)

Cubans fleeing Fidel Castro's Communist revolution of 1959 voluntarily settled in several countries. Those coming to the United States were delighted to find an extraordinary welcome, probably more positive and preferential than that received by any other immigrant group. Because of the Cold War and the U.S. government's fierce competition with the U.S.S.R., federal officials took unusual steps to ensure that the highly educated Cubans fleeing Fidel Castro's Communist regime would succeed impressively here. The Cubans received amazing subsidies (such as generous European-like welfare payments, special Small Business Administration loans, and special housing) that were *never* extended to Puerto Ricans, African Americans, and others. The U.S. government deemed it vital for Cubans to acquire substantial social capital and social mobility so that their success could be quickly broadcast to the world, to point up the difference between the U.S. and its Communist, Cold War enemy (Grosfoguel and Georas, 2000).

On the other hand, Puerto Rican Americans were not met with this Welcome Wagon of remarkable subsidies. In his book, *Latinos, A Biography of the People*, Earl Shorris explains: "Puerto Rico has been a colony for almost five hundred years ... in no remembered, recorded time did the people of Puerto Rico control their destiny; they have always belonged to someone, been a possession" (1992, p. 144).

Following the U.S. invasion of the island in 1898, Spain transferred its colonial dominion over the area to the victor. Becoming a possession-by-force of the United States did not, of course, allow Puerto Ricans to escape "the monolith of their history" and "the prison of colonialism." Their travel back and forth between the Island and the mainland, while voluntary, can not be characterized as immigration. They "remain colonized" as second-class citizens (Shorris, p. 144). Like other oppressed groups named above, they were engulfed by the dominant group: Puerto Ricans "became an underclass, systematically perceived and treated as a conquered people" in the U.S. (Oquendo, 1995, p. 70).

In short, the power-holders in this country granted the immigrant Cuban Americans much higher political and economic status than the non-immigrant Puerto Rican Americans. Today, Puerto Rico is a U.S. territory. Some Puerto Ricans feel they are treated as an inferior colony incapable of governing itself (as a separate country) or of becoming a true state of the U.S. Those Puerto Rican Americans living in New York City and other parts of this country fare no better: they occupy a kind of "internal colony" status and comprise, in fact, a conquered underclass (Grosfoguel and Georas, 2000). Their situation and their status are much lower than that of *immigrant* minorities hailing from other parts of the Caribbean, such as Jamaica, Haiti, and the Dominican Republic.

Mexican Americans (Category: Colonized)

In 1830 the Mexican government outlawed slavery and prohibited further American immigration into the Mexican region that is now Texas. Americans were outraged, and thousands continued to push into Texas—ironically—as settlers who were in fact *illegal aliens*. These new settlers rose up against Mexican rule in 1836 and, although initially defeated, were eventually victorious. Texas was annexed by the United States in 1845. The Mexican-American War (1846–1848) transformed the Mexican inhabitants of the northern half of Mexico (now California, Texas, Nevada, Utah, Arizona, New Mexico and portions of Wyoming, Colorado, Kansas, and Oklahoma) from independent ranch-owners and workers into a "conquered and "colonized" group within U.S. territory (Martinez, 2001, p. 5; see also Alvarez, 1973).

Following the war, the Treaty of Guadalupe Hidalgo slyly required the original Mexican owners to defend their land ownership in land courts run by their enemies. According to lawyer and University of Arizona Professor Vine Deloria, Jr., "The Court of Private Claims, established in 1891, by a variety of legal technicalities dispossessed almost all the landowning Mexicans and eliminated the common lands of villages that had been their heritage for centuries" (1987, p. 95). Mexicans lost one half of their homeland. Systematically and ruthlessly, corrupt European-American lawyers and judges used devious means to deprive the natives of their farms and ranches in the Southwest.

Usually in one generation, Mexicans were diminished from large and small landowners to "seasonal serfs" and "the mongrel race" who labored on the farms and ranches of the conqueror (Deloria, 1987, p. 95; also G. Rodriguez, 2007). In effect, the original settlers became "foreigners in their own land," a theme of dispossession that remains strong today in Mexican-American writings, according to John Chavez in *The Lost Land, the Chicano Image of the Southwest* (1984, p. 43).

To countenance such dispossession, leaders such as Texan Sam Houston embraced the doctrine of Manifest Destiny and argued that Mexicans, like Indians, were patently inferior and thus European Americans were justified in pushing them off their land in the same methodical and ruthless way they had done the Indians. To cut back Mexican Americans' political rights, legislators of the majority group hastily passed racial-restriction citizenship laws that reserved U.S. citizenship to whites or those who could pass for white. "Ironically, the political privileges [and citizenship] that the Spanish and Mexican governments had previously given people in the Southwest were abolished by the U.S. racial laws. The Mexican *mestizos* and Indians entered a new racial caste-like order," asserts University of Texas-Austin Anthropology Professor Martha Menchaca (1998, p. 392).

Up to the present day, many Mexican Americans living in the Southwest and especially Mexicans crossing back and forth across the U.S.-Mexico border have been reduced to a low level of worker: *disposable* and cheap migrant labor that is first pulled and then pushed according to the needs of the dominant European-American ranchers, farmers, miners, industrialists, and homeowners seeking regular maintenance of their homes and lawns. In summary, Mexican Americans occupy a low caste-like position wherein they have suffered "economic exploitation, occupational segmentation, social segregation, miseducation, political and legal mistreatment, and cultural and linguistic erasure" (Vélez-Ibáñez, 1996, pp. 86–87; also Alvarez, 1973; G. Rodriguez, 2007). In other words, they remain a colonized group and have been assigned an unenviable low place in the caste-like system.

American Indians (Category: Colonized)

European Americans' germs, violence, and land lust, as already mentioned, had a devastating impact on Native Americans. Before Columbus, the population of natives was estimated at 18 million. But by 1630, that number had declined 95 percent. Having no immunity to common European diseases, natives succumbed to smallpox, chicken pox, measles, influenza, pneumonia, scarlet fever, yellow fever, and typhus (Berger, 1991, p. 28). Those who survived this onslaught of germs were subject to extermination through "ethnic cleansing." For instance, the Massachusetts Puritans in 1637 began paying a bounty to those who brought in scalps of Pequot Indians. Many other towns and counties throughout the country followed suit over the next 250 years.

Pushing Indians from their tribal lands became government policy. In 1830, President Andrew Jackson spearheaded the removal of the so-called civilized tribes: Cherokee, Choctaw, Creek, Chicasaw, and Seminole. Trails of tears and massive deaths replayed dozens of times as European Americans drove the natives into oblivion (French, 2003, p. 11). As New York Governor Horatio Seymour crowed,

> *Today we are dividing the lands of the native Indians into states, counties, and townships. We are driving off from their property the game upon which they live, by railroads. We tell them plainly, they must give up their homes and property, and live upon corners of their own territories, because they are in the way of our civilization.* (quoted in Takaki, 1993, p. 205)

The history of California, where I live now, is polluted with ethnic cleansing. In 1848 California Indians numbered 100,000. The discovery of gold in 1848 proved disastrous. By the end of 1849, thousands of gold-seekers had flocked into the state, and many were ruthless in their treatment of Indians. Ten years after the gold rush, natives in the state had dwindled to 35,000. Ethnic cleansing indeed became the *official* policy of the state legislature and the new governor. The first California Governor Peter Burnett observed "that the war of extermination between the two races will continue to be waged until the Indian race becomes extinct, must be expected.... The inevitable destiny of the [White] race is beyond the power and wisdom of man to avert" (Bradley, 2009, p. 87).

Millions of dollars was paid by California and other legislatures to local militia within their states to keep the peace—that is, to kill Indians of any age wherever they were found. In addition, counties and townships throughout the country continued to pay a reward for anyone who brought in Indian scalps. Those Indians still standing and surviving were put on reservations, as non-citizens who were bound to wherever European-Americans directed them to live.

For those Indian children who strayed very far, California passed a law holding that they could be arrested and then placed in the custody of European Americans for employment and training. The custody was very long term: it lasted until Indian men reached 40 years of age and Indian women 35 years. The predictable consequence of the law was the stealing of Indian children and then their sale to the highest bidder (Stannard, *American Holocaust*, 1993; see also Berger, 1991; Blackmon, 2008).

Native Hawaiians (Category: Colonized)

Germs, violence, land lust, and the ideology of white superiority also transformed the Hawaiian Islands. The first European-American James Cook (English, Christian) "discovered" the Islands in 1778. Captain Cook and his crew found a handsome and very healthy people, whose life expectancies were greater than their European contemporaries. But tuberculosis, venereal disease, smallpox, typhoid fever, measles, and other European diseases immediately began decimating the Native Hawaiians. Seven years after Cook and his men had left, a French ship reached Hawaii. The ship surgeon gave stunning details (about tumors, swellings, ulcers, blindness, rickets) that underscored the wide-spread suffering from European diseases. Not long after, New England whalers, merchants, and then missionaries arrived. One missionary wrote that the Hawaiians were "exceedingly ignorant; stupid to all that was lovely, grand and awful in the work of God; low, naked, filthy, vile and sensual; covered with every abomination, stained with blood and black with crime" (quoted in Bradley, p. 149).

The University of Hawaii's Social Science Institute estimates that the population in Captain Cook's time was more than a million. Tragically, the first missionary census of 1832 found only 130,000 native survivors and noted that annual deaths were at least double the number of births and that the mortality rate of young children was severe. Coming from a country driven by Manifest Destiny, the American missionaries viewed the sickly decline of the Hawaiians in the same way they viewed the demise of American Indians: it must be God's will (Bradley, 2009, p. 150).

Two of the earliest New England missionaries, Amos Cooke and Samuel Castle, found ways to deprive the Hawaiian natives of their rich land. Within 20 years, they had amassed vast holdings and become one of the world's largest sugar producers through the importation of contract laborers from China and Japan. In the previous century they would have undoubtedly brought in African and African-American slaves.

European-American wealth on the islands translated into political power. Believing that only they ("Aryans" of course) could reasonably rule, the newcomers took steps to overthrow the Hawaiian monarchy, backed up by U.S. Marines then aboard the ship the USS Boston anchored in Honolulu harbor. A short time later, on January 17, 1893, Sanford Dole (a son of European-American missionaries) became the Governor of Hawaii. A month after that, "his" brand-new government together with the U.S. Senate approved the Annexation Treaty. And finally in 1898, at the urging of Assistant Secretary of the Navy Theodore Roosevelt and others, the Annexation and colonization of Hawaii were made official and binding.

There were a few criticisms of this overthrow, from author Samuel Clemens and several U.S. senators. For instance, one legislator called for a repeal of the treaty, to no avail:

> There is a native population in the islands of about 40,000. They are not illiterate; they are not ignorant. A very large majority can read and write both languages, English and Hawaiian, and they take a very lively and intelligent interest in the affairs of their own country.... Any treaty which had been made without consulting [native Hawaiians] should be withdrawn and ought never to have been sanctioned. (quoted in Bradley, 2009, p. 162)

African Americans (Category: Colonized)

Early in his relationship with President Abraham Lincoln, the African-American leader Frederick Douglass complained in one of his publications that Lincoln held obvious "contempt for negroes" based on his own "pride of race and blood." Douglas attempted to educate the President about the huge differences between enslaved, colonized people and immigrant, non-colonized people.

> *The president ought to know that negro hatred and prejudice of color are neither original nor invincible vices, but merely the offshoots of that root of all crimes and evils—slavery. If the colored people instead of having been stolen and forcibly brought to the United States had come as free immigrants, like the German and the Irish, never thought of as suitable objects of property, they never would have become the objects of aversion and bitter persecution.* (quoted in Goodwin, 2005, p. 470)

African Americans are the only colonized group that has been constitutionally enslaved (though the holocaust-like reduction in the numbers of American Indians is no less horrible). African Americans are the only group that has had to face miscegenation laws and the pernicious "one-drop rule" that enforced the "color line" and the sharp division between "black and white." This one-drop rule, originating with Southern slave-holders, provided that a person was actually 100 percent African no matter how small and remote their blood connection to an African. This rule served to enlarge European-Americans' property—that is, the increase of human slaves—even when the biological fathers were frequently European-American slave owners themselves who had raped their women slaves.

While this one-drop, outrageously constructed color-line rule should have become null and void at the end of the Civil War, in fact the rule still lives on in a perverse way. Despite their emancipation, African-Americans have not been able to easily intermarry with European Americans and other groups. Their out-marry rate has always been very low and still remains that way: 6 percent in 1990 and 10 percent in 2000. By contrast, from the very beginning of the immigration waves in the late 1960s, Asians and Latinos found it easy to out-marry, especially with European Americans, and their rate now approaches almost 50 percent. Such intermarriage of course tends to increase the number of people who come to be regarded as mixed ethnics and "honorary whites." But such intermarriage also holds very steady and separate the number of African Americans occupying the lowest slot in a caste-like system. Intermarriage rates are a breath-taking manifestation of who is socially accepted and who is not (Hollinger, 2011; Massey, 2011).

African Americans were also the group most targeted and demoralized by Jim Crow segregation practices, housing restrictions, and inferior schools (all of these serve to reinforce the sharpness of the color line). Further, this is the only group to have endured *enforced* illiteracy—meaning that it was illegal for centuries to teach members of the African-American colonized group how to read and write. (On the other hand, we should not forget the barbaric forced-literacy boarding schools for American Indians in the U.S. and Canada. Recently Canada's Truth and Reconciliation Commission as well as Anglican/Episcopalian churches in Canada have apologized for cruelties perpetrated in the schools whose doctrine was "to kill the Indian in the child.")

African Americans have suffered the most severe and long-lasting stigma: the stigma produced by their treatment as *property* from the very beginning of the European-American settlements in this country. This stigma and legacy linger on, generation after generation, as hundreds of scholars have shown. In fact, right after being "liberated" by the Civil War, many African Americans were forced into another version of slavery. Instead of receiving reparations to underwrite a new start and a new life (such as the promised 40 acres and a mule), emancipated African-American men were terrorized by quickly constructed *vagrancy laws*. For non-existent or petty crimes, newly freed men were jailed and then bound over to Southern cotton farmers, Western ranchers, coal mining companies, and others who paid a small fee to turn them into *forced and enslaved labor* (see the Pulitzer-Prize winning book *Slavery By Another Name: The Re-Enslavement of Black Americans from the Civil War to World War II* by Douglas Blackmon, 2008). Clearly, such re-enslavement over *more than half a century* would reinforce abject poverty and prevent economic advancement of any kind. To a lesser extent, Mexican Americans and American Indians (especially in California and the Southwest) also were vulnerable to these vagrancy laws as well as Jim Crow segregation practices.

With all these unjust offenses and barriers, African Americans still profited very little from what should have been a turning point: the heartening passage of the Civil Rights Act of 1964 that was created for their benefit. This landmark Act was, of course, made possible by the remarkable Civil Rights protest movement, with photos broadcast around the world of police and their dogs attacking and of water hoses blasting young and old African Americans and other protesters in the movement.

Implementation of the Civil Rights Act, by the newly created Equal Employment Opportunity Commission, unfortunately took an unexpected and sardonic turn—far from what Congress and other sponsors intended. The EEOC's affirmative action programs—related to schooling, vocational training, and business formation—did not provide restorative justice and reparation to African Americans, the intended beneficiaries. What happened? A massive wave of immigrants

The mid-1960s Collision of _Domestic_ Affirmative Action and _Global_ Immigration

Those sponsoring the Immigration and Nationality Act of 1965 (the Hart-Celler Act), especially U.S. Sen. Ted Kennedy, argued that this Act was the symbolically right thing to do. All over the world, people would applaud America and its democratic and humane values in contrast to its Cold War enemy, the U.S.S.R., and its communistic and inhumane values. In addition, Kennedy and others maintained that the flow of new immigrants who chose to enter under this new Act would be very small; they would be required to possess and bring with them highly skilled, marketable expertise; and their numbers would not disrupt any existing demographic patterns in the country.

This was not the case. "We get a sense of the magnitude of this new migration since 1965 if we contemplate the fact that the number of non-black, non-European immigrants [from Asian and Latin America] arriving between 1970 and 2000 roughly equals the number of African Americans already residing in the U.S. in 1980, about 26 million." Because of the U.S. practice of giving preference to immediate family members, these original immigrants were quickly able to bring in more newcomers as part of a "chain migration" (H. Graham, 2002, p. 98).

The sponsors of the hard-won Civil Rights Act did not have a clue that the new and huge wave of immigrants—80 percent of them—would benefit the most from the Civil Rights Act. As affirmative action programs were implemented in accordance with the Civil Rights Act—to increase educational attainment, economic development, and formation and expansion of small businesses—a clear pattern took shape: the new immigrants "pushed out the natives" (Maher and Tetreault, 2007, p. 17). Sophisticated and educated immigrants reaped most of the benefits of these specially created initiatives (H. Graham, _Collision Course: The Strange Convergence of Affirmative Action and Immigration Policy in America_, 2002, p. 5).

How did this surprising development happen? Two reasons seem to make the most sense. First, the federal agencies in the mid-1960s building the new affirmative action programs took a _shortcut_: they decided to use eligibility language developed in 1956 by President Dwight Eisenhower's Committee on Government Contracts. In an attempt to make sure employers granted federal-government contracts were diversifying their workforces, the Eisenhower Committee had asked that employers report the background of their workers. The choices were these: "White; Negro; or Other Minority." The "other minority" was specified as "Spanish-Americans, Orientals, Indians, Jews, Puerto Ricans, etc." Certainly, Orientals (Asians) at this point in time would have been a tiny part of the U.S. population.

A short time later, Eisenhower's Committee removed Jews from the list (due to the recognition of their high achievement in education and the professions, mostly as a result of the G.I. Bill benefits for European-American male veterans after World War II). This removal was the only change; no more fine-tuning was made. In short, the 1954 parenthetical designation of who exactly are "official minorities" has stuck. In implementing affirmative action programs, federal and state agencies as well as institutions of higher learning have unfortunately relied on the earlier designation. Asians, South Americans, Cubans, and other new *immigrants* were granted eligibility for advancement programs in employment and education, together with the originally intended beneficiaries, domestic African Americans (Skrentny, 2002, pp. 101–02).

The second reason for the inclusion of immigrants is probably this: federal agencies and academic leaders made a *superficial, ahistorical assumption* that these new immigrants had suffered the same stigma and same cultural and economic disadvantages in this country, over a number of generations, as had African Americans. That is, the European-American dominant group had oppressed *every group* here that was not European-American. Every non-European American group was deemed an "oppressed minority group" (it didn't seem to matter that some groups had just arrived and seemed very happy to be welcomed here). Thus, all non-European Americans came to be regarded, ahistorically and sloppily, as oppressed minorities.

The ahistorical and wrong-headed assumption that all "people of color" are oppressed by the dominant European-American group even appears in the report of President Bill Clinton's 1998 "Commission on Race" where the "old religion" is reinforced. That is, the Commission's report "systematically denied that there were salient differences between African Americans, Asian Americans, and Hispanic Americans." David Hollinger's analysis continues:

> *The report offers 53 recommendations for multicultural programs and anti-discrimination remedies, not a single one of which dealt with the historically unique situation of the black Americans whose lives had been affected by centuries of legally sanctioned slavery, violently enforced discrimination, and cataclysmically inadequate educational opportunities.* (2011, p. 179)

The conventional and unexamined assumption—"that all immigrant-based populations from Asia and Central and South American are comparable to descendants of American slavery and Jim Crow"—has done much damage and in fact makes a "mockery" of U.S. history and of the original intentions of affirmative action programs (H. Graham, 2002, p.

192). This assumption led to small business loans being awarded almost exclusively to educated, middle-class Asians who had arrived with English skills and the ability to easily negotiate the paperwork. These new immigrants possessed mercantile expertise and had some capital; they were not penniless farmers or peasants. Affirmative-action educational benefits at colleges and universities likewise were not enjoyed primarily by African Americans and other colonized groups but by recent immigrants who already had educated parents and a middle-class grounding (H. Graham, 2002; also Hollinger, 2011; Skrentny, 2002; Hu-DeHart, 1999).

Further, the new Asian immigrants entered at a fortuitous time. By 1952, Asians could become U.S. citizens. "They were never constitutionally enslaved, nor were they lynched in large numbers in the twentieth century." Miscegenation laws between Asians and Europeans had disappeared. European Americans were embarrassed by the internment of Japanese Americans during WWII and were intent to portray themselves as good citizens of the world. "Hence the new immigrants from Asia were entering the country as a time when anti-Asian prejudice was in decline ... they had vibrant international kinship networks and marketable skills that quickly translated into strong class position." These fortuitous situations "help explain the rapid incorporation of Asian ethnics into American society," their dramatic rise in income and professional standing (their median income in short order surpassed that of European Americans), and their frequent intermarrying with European Americans and other groups (H. Graham, 2002, pp. 169–70; see also Hollinger, 2001, 2011).

Likewise, Central and South Americans entered at an auspicious time: they were often regarded as "White," and in court cases some of them vigorously protested that they were in no way "Black" and subject to the "one-drop rule." Intermarriage between "Latinos" and European-Americans became robust. Therefore, the benefits that these newcomers accrued from affirmation action programs, according to Graham (2002), "never made sense" (p. 191) and would be like offering affirmative action to Middle Easterners (p. 170). Another scholar, after intensively studying this period of social history, concludes: "The distinction between slaves and voluntary, fortune-seeking immigrants (as with the vast majority of Asians and Latinos) could have been [should have been] significant. It was not" (Skrentny, 2002, p. 350). In other words, there was confusion between colonized groups and immigrant groups that led to injustice. And that confusion continues today.

It is simply historically and politically wrong to automatically characterize someone viewed as non-white in this country as a member of yet another group that has suffered from the oppression of the European-American majority. This is broad-brushed, ahistorical silliness. But it is worse than silliness. Hollinger has written several essays that uncover the pernicious effects of the one-drop rule and the one-oppressed-group concept.

The federal officials who specified the list of groups eligible for affirmative action offered few explanations for why they had chosen the Eisenhower language. Nor did they hold public hearings to air the issues. Clearly, according to Hollinger, "they failed to think through the theoretical basis of their decisions. They operated on the basis of an implicit calculus of victimization, but they shrank from the task of following through, of actually developing the calculus and offering it for public scrutiny." Thus, "26 million Asian and Latin American immigrants and their children found themselves eligible [for affirmative action programs] ... simply by virtue of the fact that they had come from Panama or Taiwan or the Philippines rather than from Iraq or Greece or Russia." No efforts were made to fix the flawed eligibility criteria. The entire system "was jerry-built" and a "poorly theorized edifice quite different from what President Lyndon Johnson and his Great Society associates had in mind" (2006, pp. 28–30; see also Hollinger, 2011). In short, global immigration preempted domestic advancement of African Americans despite their having been severely exploited and shortchanged from the beginning of this nation.

Even after the Civil Rights Act of 1964, African Americans continued to be the most colonized group in the U.S. This is still the case, according to Massey, Charles, Lopez, Steele, Wu, Hu-DeHart, Hollinger, H. Graham, Loury, Waters, Lee and Bean; citations in bibliography). African Americans more than any other group still endure "entrenched patterns of poverty, segregation in housing, unemployment, gaps in educational attainment, and negative stereotyping" (Hollinger, 2011, p. 179). Not surprisingly, it is a different story for new immigrant students and new faculty hires from Africa: they now make up 10 percent of all new arrivals. Many African newcomers demonstrate immigrant success and higher status from the very beginning. Colleges and universities are eager to recruit them; in fact, at selective campuses immigrant Africans and immigrant South and Central Americans are shockingly "over-represented" (Charles et al., *Taming the River*, 2009; see also Charles et al, *Chronicle*, 2009; Hollinger, 2011).

Unfortunately African Americans, a colonized group in this country, now face a stunning new terror: a ratcheting up of "punitiveness" in the U.S. criminal justice system (five times stricter than in 1978) which has resulted in the growth of a behemoth prison industry and the "scandalous rise in what is now termed racialized mass incarceration." In the new criminal justice system since 1980, a young African-American male has a one-in-three chance of being imprisoned, a Latino one-in-ten, and a European-American one-in-fifteen (Bobo, 2011, p. 29; also see Loury,

2008). Such outrageous imprisonment rates, it has been argued, far out-weigh any positive effects produced by the Civil Rights Act of 1964. I provide more details on this severe punitiveness and its effects in the Appendix. Also in the Appendix are details about a colonized group living in Japan: Koreans. The abysmal treatment of Koreans at the hands of their conqueror is unfortunately typical for a colonized people.

Asian Americans from China, India, Korea, Japan, Hong Kong, Taiwan (Category: Immigrants)

Are Koreans and other groups of Asian descent—who *choose* to settle in the United States—immigrant or colonized people? The answer is "immigrant." Asian Americans have sometimes endured intense economic, political, and social discrimination at different times in this country's history (including internment of Japanese-Americans in camps during World War II). Nevertheless, those of Asian heritage have usually benefited from being viewed as immigrants and from possessing ambitions and fierce longing to reach the American Dream (Wu, 2002; Takaki, 1989; Hollinger, 2011; Skrentny, 2002). Moreover, the huge numbers of Asian immigrants who arrived after the 1965 Immigration Act was passed (the Hart-Celler Act of 1965) found an unexpected benefit: they were deemed by the federal government and by colleges and universities as eligible for Affirmative Action programs, as I already discussed.

The first Chinese, Koreans, and Japanese to enter the United States did so in small numbers as manual workers, in the middle of the nineteenth century. These male immigrants entered the new land voluntarily and were intent on acquiring money to send back or take back to their relatives. There is no evidence that they were kidnapped and brought here against their will to work in gold mines in the West, on fruit and vegetable farms, or on construction of the transcontinental railroad, according to Professor Ron Takaki, a preeminent scholar on Asians and other U.S. immigrants (1987, 1989, 1993). There is, however, abundant evidence that the first Chinese, Japanese, and Korean workers were not only overworked and mistreated by railroad barons and other employers but also taunted verbally and violently by "nativists" in the majority group and by members of labor unions who resented the new arrivals. Yet the Asian immigrants and their offspring mostly did persist and mostly did succeed economically.

It is important to remember that the first Asian workers were capitalists because they willingly chose to come and they brought money with them (albeit small amounts) to invest and parlay into greater wealth (Takaki, 1993, 1989). In addition, some of them formed among themselves their own rotating credit associations, as they had done in their homelands. This was "their principal device for capitalizing small business" and acquiring real estate, and it worked very well (Light, 1987, p. 84). The Japanese and Chinese newcomers "found themselves free for new associations and new enterprises" in the new country. "Like the immigrants from Europe, many Asians saw America as a place for a fresh start" and a place to realize their dreams (Takaki, 1989, pp. 18, 66) despite at times formidable obstacles and exclusion from earning U.S. citizenship.

In the fascinating study *The Mississippi Chinese: Between Black and White* (1988), author James Loewen traces how the Sze Yap area in South China sent savvy traders and entrepreneurs to South Africa, Southeast Asia, Latin America, and the United States. That part of China was replete with small businesses, enjoyed constant contact with international traders, and had a dense population. Coming to the United States or any other land, these South Chinese immigrants brought sufficient capital and know-how to start small businesses; they had a sponsor in the homeland as well as a mutual aid society in the new land composed of others hailing from the same villages and towns in the home land (more details at the website of the Mississippi Historical Society).

Wasting no time, the Chinese who settled in Mississippi right after the Civil War realized that they had to cross over to the higher white/ European-American caste category and resist being pigeon-holed in the black/African-American, lowest caste. Like the Irish, the Chinese shrewdly and successfully crossed over the color line. When investing and working on small Mississippi farms did not appear to be promising, the new settlers decided to build and operate grocery stores exclusively for African Americans. European-American business people in Mississippi thought it beneath them to serve this group. Most of the new immigrants maintained a wide social distance between themselves and their customers but began to cultivate closer relations with the ruling European Americans. They nurtured ties with European-American sponsors (such as ministers, wholesalers, and so on) who then lobbied for admitting Chinese children to "white" schools, hospitals, and other majority institutions.

Newly arriving male immigrants (from the same part of South China) were brought into the grocery stores as apprentices, where they "accumulated the priceless legacy of business experience, a legacy unavailable to Negroes" (Loewen, 1998, p. 38). Further, the Chinese created revolving credit associations among themselves so that they could access loans at opportune moments. Together they created mutually advantageous partnerships with one another as well as larger trading blocs to get the best deals from wholesalers (business traditions that were of course absent within the lowest-caste position reserved for African Americans). The Chinese forbade marriage or sexual relations between their people and African Americans in order to remain as "pure" as European

Americans. According to Loewen, they "regarded and treated Blacks as inferior 'niggers,' just as Whites did" (p. 87).

Asian immigrants, like Italian, Irish, Jewish, Russian, and other immigrants, benefited socially and economically because they were viewed (or *came* to be viewed) as *higher* on the chain of being than African Americans and other colonized groups. When the number of African Americans migrating to the Western states during and after World War II far surpassed that of the small Asian population, Asians ironically experienced a lessening of discrimination that "facilitated Asian American socioeconomic mobility." Of course, there was a concomitant increase of discrimination *against* African Americans that prohibited their advancement (Yetman, 1999, p. 267; see also Wu, 2002).

Immigrant Status of Asian Americans Has Privileges

The first Asian-American chancellor of a leading U.S. university, Chang-Lin Tien of the University of California-Berkeley, has eloquently described how his immigrant background boosted his self-confidence and professional achievement. He explains, "For me, America is the land of opportunity. This is not merely a dream, but my experience. No other nation in the world has welcomed immigrants like me to its shores, offered us first-rate schooling, and then accepted our professional contributions." Climbing the ladder of academic administration, Tien says he "relied on the grand American tradition of democracy and the extraordinary emphasis on equality among women and men as my foundation." (quoted in Correspondents of the *New York Times,* 2001, p. 360)

Likewise, the first Chinese-American governor of the state of Washington, Gary Locke, habitually stressed the greatness of America where he and his family have thrived despite hardships. "He [the Governor] noted in his inaugural address that his grandfather had worked as a houseboy less than a mile from the Capitol grounds. 'It took a hundred years to go one mile,' he said. 'But it's a journey that could only take place in America'." (quoted in Correspondents, p. 121)

By contrast, Locke's opponent in the gubernatorial election—Seattle Mayor Norm Rice, of African-American ancestry—carefully avoided talking about his origins because he sensed that voters feel guilty and defensive about slavery. Privately and ruefully, he remarked, "I have a great story about how my family came to America. As good as Gary's. *We just happened to have different travel agents* [emphasis added]" (quoted in Correspondents, p. 126). Governor Locke feels sufficiently comfortable to play up his ethnic pride: European-American voters in his state mostly subscribe to the positive stereotype that Asian immigrants are "clever, diligent or shrewd." But the negative stereotypes about African-Americans blocked Seattle Mayor Rice from doing so. In fact, Rice believes he must constantly downplay his background (p. 127), as do "several top-ranked African-American business executives" who refused to be interviewed by the *Times* journalists (p. 330). These two political leaders, Governor Locke and Mayor Rice, illustrate the different cultural contexts inhabited by voluntary, immigrant groups and by involuntary, colonized groups.

Intermarriage: An Immigrant Privilege

In 1980 in California, the rate of marriages to European Americans for Japanese was thirty-two percent, Filipinos twenty-four percent, Asian Indians twenty-three percent, Koreans nineteen percent, Vietnamese fifteen percent, and Chinese fourteen percent" (Takaki, 1989, p. 473). Asian Americans, "more than any other group," are intermarrying with European-Americans (Yetman, 1999, p. 252) and that rate continues to climb. In fact, intermarriage is one major way that *race-to-ethnicity conversion* takes place or at least is signaled: perceived differences due to immutable racial differences get converted to perceived differences due to culturally based (and far less important) ethnic differences (Sanjek, 1994). By contrast, the intermarriage rates for African Americans is still the lowest, as the most recent census data show (Hollinger, 2011; Massey, 2011).

Housing Patterns and College Enrollment

Patterns in housing integration and educational achievement also shore up positive pronouncements about many Asian-Americans' advancement. "In striking numbers," according to *The Boston Globe*'s analysis, "Asian Americans are moving into suburban and affluent neighborhoods where they are being accepted by the European-American majority." Upendra Mishra, a well-educated immigrant from India who owns two successful Indian newspapers, explains the family's residential choice: "When we were looking to move, we looked at SAT scores, the dropout rate, the percentage of graduates who go on to college. When we saw that every kid who graduated from Weston High School went on to college, without exception, we said, 'This is perfect. This is where we are going to live'" (quoted in C. Rodriguez, 2001, p. B3).

Asian-American students—with ancestral roots in India, China, Korea, and Japan—currently are doing exceptionally well in academia and are in fact "over-represented" (Hollinger, 2005, p. 39; Hollinger 2011; Takaki, 1989) relative to their percentage of total U.S. population. In 2011, Asian Americans comprise almost 15 percent of all college and university students and close to *one-half* of student enrollment at Berkeley, UCLA, UCA-Irvine, and several other highly selective public and especially private campuses throughout the country.

What explains this academic and professional success? Attention must be paid to a crucial cultural and political context: most *recent* immigrants with Chinese ancestry, for example, have been middle-class, educated, and highly skilled, according to Brown University History Professor Evelyn Hu-DeHart, herself of Chinese descent. Further, Chinese immigrants arrived during an auspicious political and economic period, as mentioned earlier. They "were perfectly positioned to benefit immediately from affirmative action—originally enacted in the mid-1960s to help African Americans overcome centuries of slavery and racial segregation—because eligibility for the program was extended to all other 'minority' groups just as these Asian immigrants were arriving in large numbers" (1999, pp. 7–8). In other words, the Asian immigrants, given their intellectual resources, business skills, and cultural devotion to education, did not need assistance from affirmative action programs to succeed in business, higher education, and the professions. By contrast, colonized groups did indeed need affirmative action benefits but they did not receive them.

Certain groups of Asian Americans have indeed moved into the "Honorary White" high-status category. "Individuals and communities with the highest levels of acculturation, achievement, and wealth increasingly find themselves functioning as whites, at least as measured by professional integration, residential patterns, and intermarriage rates [with European Americans]." This honorary status is also being enjoyed by those educated and affluent Latinos "who are the most elite and who self-identify with Europe and Spain" and often possess Anglo surnames (Lopez, 2006, p. B8).

Note: One significant exception should be mentioned. Much slower advancement is likely for the newest arrivals from Southeast Asia (the Vietnamese, Laotians, and Cambodians). These are immigrants/refugees, as I will discuss shortly.

Asian Americans' "Model-minority" Problem

Given their relative success in American society, Asians from India, China, Korea, Japan, and Taiwan currently have a rather odd problem: they are held up as the "model minority" group because of their academic and economic success. The positive academic stereotype has considerable downsides. It is true that some Asian Americans often choose quantitative fields of study, such as accounting, computer science, mathematics, and engineering. Such fields especially draw *new* immigrants from other countries because the disciplines require relatively few verbal and written English language skills. But equally important, teachers and guidance counselors channel Asian and Asian-American students into subjects where they assume they can do very well—science and math—and away from those subjects where they assume they will not—humanities and social sciences (Kiang, 1992, p. 107). Although the students ought to be encouraged to have interests and competencies in a variety of subjects, they are frequently pigeon-holed into technical fields.

To remedy this tracking, schools and campuses must help Asian Americans see the richness of academic options they might choose—otherwise, the students' potential is shortchanged. So, too, is the future development of their communities, suggests University of Massachusetts-Boston Professor Peter Kiang: "What are the social consequences, for example, if these students concentrate overwhelmingly in business, science, and engineering, when the communities, in fact, desperately need bilingual lawyers, health care providers, policymakers, writers, filmmakers, teachers, and organizers?" (1992, p. 109).

The erroneous assumption that all Asian-American students are self-sufficient and always succeed translates into their being unable to find tutoring, academic as well as mental health counseling, and other institutional support when they need it. This is particularly troubling for first-generation Southeast Asian refugees (most of whom arrived in this country poor, uneducated, and traumatized). Their needs are just beginning to be recognized and met by communities and campuses (Kiang, 1992, p. 102). In short, the positive stereotype that all Asian Americans are successful "permits the general public, government officials, and the judiciary to ignore or marginalize the contemporary needs of Asian Americans" (Chang, 1993, p. 35).

The model-minority stereotype has a third downside. Princeton University political scientist Jennifer Hochschild points out that "newspapers have a seemingly endless supply of rags-to-riches stories" about Asian Americans but the stories forget to point out that "not all Asians escape poverty, crime, and discrimination." Held up monolithically in this way, Asian Americans are being symbolically and pointedly used to *embarrass African Americans* who have not achieved the American dream to a comparable extent (Hochschild, 1995, p. 34). Takaki agrees that Asian Americans are "again being used to discipline blacks. Shortly after the Civil War, southern planters recruited Chinese immigrants in order to pit them against the newly freed blacks as 'examples' of laborers willing to work hard for low wages." The current argument unfolds this way: "The triumph of Asian Americans affirms the deeply rooted values of the Protestant ethic and self-reliance.... If Asian Americans can make it on their own, conservative pundits like Charles Murray [author of *The*

Bell Curve] are asking, why can't other groups?" (1993, p. 416). Berkeley Professor John McWhorter asks a question very similar to Murray's: Why can't African-Americans perform as well in school as "new immigrants" from Africa or the Caribbean? (2000, p. 115).

First, such a question is built on an unexamined assumption: that there has been the same level playing field for all groups, "without due consideration to varying social origins, unequal degrees of opportunities available in the United States, and different levels of exposure to discrimination" (Martinez, 2001, p. xxiv). Remember that the first Asian workers were capitalists because they willingly chose to come and they brought money with them (albeit small amounts) to invest and parlay into greater wealth (Takaki, 1989, 1993). The second, very large wave of Asian immigrants arriving in the middle of the twentieth century came with numerous assets and were disproportionately welcomed into business and educational programs designed originally for the African-American colonized domestic group. Thus, the direct answer to McWhorten's question, of course, is that the cultural context and status of immigrant minorities are far *more conducive* to academic and economic success than the context inhabited by colonized, caste-like minorities.

The cultural context of colonized minorities *relative* to other groups must be reckoned with. Hochschild (1995) warns that ignoring this all-important cultural context can add "yet another component to the nightmare of a failed American dream." She memorably describes the morass: "Members of a denigrated group are disproportionately likely to fail to achieve their goals; they are blamed as individuals (and perhaps blame themselves) for their failure; and they carry a further stigma as members of a non-virtuous (thus appropriately denigrated) group" that usually fails to succeed (p. 15).

Promulgating the myth of Asian Americans as a model minority also hurts economically poor whites and other groups "who are blamed for not being successful like Asian Americans." This blame is then translated into a justification for less government intervention and social services targeted to these "un-deserving," poor people as well as a justification for eliminating affirmative action measures for such "un-deserving" beneficiaries. "To the extent that Asian Americans accept the model minority myth, we are *complicitous* in the oppression of other racial minorities and poor whites," according to Loyola University Law Professor Robert Chang (1993, p. 361).

Vietnamese, Cambodian, Hmong, and Laotian (Category: Immigrant Refugees)

Southeast Asians, unlike immigrants from Japan and China, did not choose to come to America for a better life. They were forced from their countries of origin. They fled war, famine, and chaos; they endured the intense trauma associated with uprooting, violence, loss of family members, relocation in refugee camps, and then confusing resettlement in strange places. "I'm happier here [in the U.S.] in a way," one Cambodian refugee muses, "because I can look for a better future. But in spirit, no. In Cambodia, I would feel shoulder to shoulder with the people. Even if I were a farmer, I would be proud; I would be qualified. Here, I feel so bad spiritually" (quoted in Kiang, 1992, p. 103).

Indeed, refugees often feel trapped in their new country. "Unlike the Chinese, Japanese, and other Asian immigrants to America, they cannot go home.... More so than the earlier groups of Asian immigrants, the refugees are truly the uprooted" (Takaki, 1989, p. 471; also see Wu, 2002). Nevertheless, refugees are a type of immigrant group because they *do not have a cultural history of oppression with the majority European-American group in this country.* Contrasting the situation they fled from in their home with their new situation here, they often feel gratitude. They can safely believe that the American dream is for them. This point is reinforced by the study *The Boat People and Achievement in America* (Caplan, Whitmore, and Choy, 1989), which reveals how the Vietnamese usually trust public school officials and optimistically believe they can achieve social mobility despite the language and cultural hurdles they encounter. In short, these new people are regarded as immigrants and view themselves in the same way.

* * * * *

Distinctions Between Immigrant Groups and Colonized Groups: A Recap

Colonized people were originally incorporated into this or any other country *against their will*—through slavery, conquest, colonization, possession, or forced labor—and they understandably interpret their presence and status as coerced on them by the dominant group. Colonization depends on two forces: conquest by a more forceful group together with the imposition of new institutions and especially the *denigration* of the conquered people's cultural practices and even humanity. Generation after generation, colonized groups find that their ancestors' violent incorporation into this country continues to undercut their own status and relation with the majority culture and to negatively influence their daily lives. Generation after generation, they feel devalued and see their religions, their native languages, their intellectual abilities, and their substantial contributions to the development of this country underestimated or even scorned.

Take schooling, for example. Claude Steele, as mentioned earlier, maintains that "non-immigrant minorities like blacks and Native Americans have always been here, and thus are entitled, more than new immigrants, to participate in the defining images of the society projected in school." Yet non-immigrants' contributions to the building of this country are usually not part of the positive images found in mainstream schools. Therefore when schools expect these groups to assimilate in the same ways as immigrants assimilate, Steele says this expectation is viewed as "*a primal insult* [emphasis added]: it asks them to join in something that has made them invisible" (1992, p. 121). Because voluntary immigrants lack such an opposing and complex cultural history and context, they usually can approach school and the workplace in a simpler fashion and rightfully expect hard work to pay off in some dependable way (Shimahara; Ogbu; Kain; Gibson; Carter and Seguara; Caplan, Whitmore, and Choy; DeVos; Franklin; citations in bibliography).

Colonized groups routinely measure and compare their own economic and social status with that of majority group members. In this comparison, they find that their status is almost always lower; they find that the American dream—usually regarded as upward social mobility and wealth—is for others but *not* for them. Their reservoir of hope cannot match that of immigrants. Contrary to the U.S. majority group's rhetoric about fair play and equal opportunity, internally colonized groups see ample evidence that the credentials they earn will *not* lead *them* to attractive jobs and accumulation of wealth and status. Generation after generation, they hit a low ceiling which frustrates their advancement in academia and the workplace. While they believe that individual effort, education, and hard work are important, they also believe it is simply not strong enough to overcome built-in discrimination and oppression. Understandably, some children of colonized groups can become depressed and oppositional in their attitude toward the majority group and its schools (Steele, Suskind, Waters, Carter, DeVos, Cummins, Massey and Denton, Gibson, Ogbu, Nieto, M. Suarez-Orozco, Massey, Weis; citations in bibliography).

Yet it is certainly true that some members of colonized groups succeed *extraordinarily* in traditional institutions—despite at times crushing odds—and they bring distinction to educational settings, workplaces, and various musical, religious, cinematic, philanthropic, and community-building arenas. For example, African-American women have narrowed the gap between themselves and European-American women, in the areas of educational attainment, occupation, and earnings (Bobo, 2011). African-American professional Vivian Porche, MD, an anesthesiology professor, captures what her own attainments signify by using poet Maya Angelou's jubilant words: "I am the dream and the hope of the slave. I rise, I rise, I rise" (Porche quoted in Travis, 2009, p. 130).

Other members of colonized groups often channel their opposition and frustration into political leadership and activism: they seek to enlighten, protest, and organize in order to ensure that the United States lives up to its democratic ideals. Past and current examples include: the anti-lynching campaigns mobilized by African-American churches and sorority women; the creation of minority-serving schools and colleges; the establishment and work of the National Association for the Advancement of Colored People and the Urban League; the mutual aid societies organized by Mexican Americans; the Chicano, Native Hawaiian, and American Indian political and student movements; the campaigns for American Indian tribal sovereignty; the struggle to unionize Mexican-American garment workers, miners, and agricultural workers; the mentoring of male youth by members of the numerous "100 Black Men of America" chapters; the political efforts and lawsuits to secure monetary reparations from corporations that benefited from slavery; the Civil Rights Movement of the mid-1960s; and the strong efforts invested in Barack Obama's campaign to become U.S. President. In short, activism and leadership to reduce injustice are always being regenerated.

Is the United States the only country with colonized groups? No. There are others, including: the Burakumin caste in Japan as well as Koreans living in Japan, their former colonizer (see Appendix for more details); also the Catholic Irish in Great Britain; the Maoris aboriginal people in New Zealand; and Maya Indians in Mexico (DeVos, Gibson, C. Lee, Y. Lee, Matute-Bianchi, Ogbu; citations in bibliography).

But to say that colonized groups exist in many parts of the world does not absolve American faculty and administrators of their obligation to understand the differences among the varied historical experiences of colonized groups and immigrant groups in the United States. Why? As power-holders possessing influence, financial resources, and admission and hiring responsibilities, they must exercise their powers wisely and carefully by taking into account the cultural contexts and histories of their colleagues and students. In addition, these power-holders must be on guard—in their thoughts, evaluations, and actions—against *overvaluing* members of the majority group, honorary whites, and visitors and immigrants from other countries. At the same time, leaders in academe must be on guard against *undervaluing* those who are identified with domestic colonized groups. To produce fair evaluations and a level playing-field, academic power-holders must learn to recognize and rise above these *ingrained mind-sets*. I believe that campuses will *not* be able to diversify their faculties until these mind-sets, often operating unconsciously, are understood and then corrected. Countering them may be easier, I believe, when we better understand how positive or negative views and treatment of different groups took shape in this country. That has been my purpose in this chapter.

"Don't know much about history." Some analysts complain that we Americans do not probe deeply enough into our country's political and economic history, in particular the less admirable events in our country's history and these events' pernicious effects on our own people. Our lack of knowledge makes it hard for us to appreciate the challenges that continue to be faced by members of our domestic colonized groups.

Slavery was abominable, we agree, but slavery ended over 150 years ago. Why in the world has the advancement of African Americans been so slow? Similarly, we may regret that American Indians were removed from their native lands and herded to reservations to live, but that too was a long time ago and now look at all the money generated by their gambling casinos. We're puzzled when Mexican Americans say they lost one-half of their homeland in the American Southwest during the middle of the nineteenth century because "the line was forcibly moved." We shake our heads because we think of Mexicans as folks who are trying by whatever means possible to *get into* the United States; we usually don't conceive of them as dispossessed of lands that once were theirs. Thinking about Puerto-Rican Americans, we perhaps visualize East Coast immigrants able to fly back and forth to their sovereign homeland in just a few hours. What's the problem, we wonder: they have equal access to two countries.

Given an unsteady grasp of the histories and contexts of various peoples (as I've just tried to suggest), it should not be surprising when many Americans wonder from time to time: Why in the world are we still offering affirmative action programs in education and economic development, after so many years? Isn't it about time to have affirmative action programs for European Americans?

What I have tried to do in this chapter is to shed some light on our usually shallow comprehension of some very important patterns in U.S. political and economic development. Mistakenly, we may have thought that slavery was over for African Americans once the Emancipation Proclamation was issued. Mistakenly, we may have assumed that *everyone* could participate in the Homestead Acts where American Indian territory was given away to those with the energy and will to settle it. Mistakenly, we may have assumed that the G.I. Bill rewarded and helped to recompense (with low-cost mortgages and educational subsidies) *all* veterans from all groups, including Navaho and Choctaw "code-talkers" and every other veteran who sacrificed for this country during World War II. We were wrong.

I have attempted in this chapter to dispel some of those common but mistaken assumptions about the historical and political histories and the present-day contexts for various groups. It is vital to understand how and why domestic colonized groups (non-immigrants) struggle for full citizenship and fair treatment, generation after generation. And it is vital to grasp that the majority group as well as honorary whites and immigrants find themselves in far more advantageous positions, generation after generation, and to understand how and why this came to be.

SECTION C

Outside the Borders of Academe—Typical Disadvantages Experienced by Faculty Members of Colonized Groups that May Contribute to High Attrition

New faculty hires who are European Americans or "honorary whites" will predictably expect either positive or neutral attitudes from those they interact with immediately beyond their workplaces. But not surprisingly, this gown-town interplay may be troublesome at times for faculty from colonized groups. Attitudes and actions of persons and groups directly outside campus walls can be factors that affect, sometimes profoundly, the *retention or the attrition* of non-immigrant faculty (NIs).

The key question is this: are such faculty being met with hostility and aversion or, on the other hand, acceptance and welcome? It is the job-related duty of provosts, deans, and/or department chairs to inquire about that reception outside the ivy walls and then be ready to applaud or to intervene (subtly or frontally). In particular, NI groups and their families often do *not* find the public deference, social standing, and police protection they deserve. By contrast, members of the favored groups (European Americans and Honorary Whites) usually do find these things. Not to realize and attend to the different contexts enveloping different faculty colleagues in the outside world is a shortcoming, a serious one. Below is discussion to aid academic leaders in understanding and then attending to these different contexts, with the objective being to shore up faculty retention and satisfaction.

Police Harassment and Danger for Certain Faculty and Their Offspring

Racial and ethnic profiling by police has always been widespread in this country. Repeatedly, law enforcement officers in every state are urged to stop such profiling, that is, questioning or arresting certain groups of citizens because of the negative stereotype (a serious cognitive error) that the officers have internalized about these groups. Recall the 2009 outrageous situation sustained by Harvard Professor Henry Louis Gates, Jr. (Director of African-American Studies) *as he was entering his own home.* He was accosted in his affluent neighborhood by a European-

American police officer who suspected Gates (African American) of breaking into the house, by pushing vigorously on the front door that was clearly *stuck*.

Similarly, African-American Studies and Religion Professor Cornel West (at Princeton University) is repeatedly stopped by city police who insist he is driving *too slowly* and in a suspicious way, according to articles in prominent newspapers and magazines. "Driving while black," Harvard Law School Professor Charles Ogletree vigorously complains, is only one danger. There are others, such as "riding while black," "shopping while black," "jogging while black," "walking while black," and indeed "living while black" (quoted in MacQuarrie, 1999, pp. A1, A9). There is also "dying while black," according to law professor Vernellia Randall at the University of Dayton School of Law who has taken an in-depth look at health care disparities (2006).

Numerous local and national studies report that European-American police officers "use ethnicity/race as an independently significant, if not determinative, factor in deciding whom to follow, detain, search, or arrest" (quoted in Reiman, 1998, p. 108). This is bad news, of course, for Mexican Americans, Native Americans, African Americans, and American Indians whether they are minors or highly educated professionals. It is also bad news for faculty members' *vulnerable children* who can be followed, detained, arrested, and terrorized by police for flimsy and illegal reasons.

As a professor at a Southwest majority university complained, "You have to spend so much time thinking about stuff that most white people just don't even have to think about." While the professor legitimately worries when she is pulled over by a traffic cop, she *intensely* worries when she thinks about her partner or her son getting pulled over. "I'm very aware of how many black folks accidentally get shot by cops." She continues: "The freedom to just be yourself" is something that she believes should be guaranteed to all citizens of the country but that freedom is denied to her and her family, despite their professional status and income. Understandably, she "gets resentful" that she must worry about so many things that "even my very close white friends, whose politics are similar to mine, simply don't have to worry about" (quoted in Feagin and Sikes, 1994, p. 398; also see Feagin and Vera, 1995).

Micro-Aggressions on a Daily Basis Committed by Ordinary People

According to Texas A & M Professor Joe Feagin's comprehensive national studies (he was formerly at the University of Florida), NI faculty have to expend enormous emotional energy on a daily basis as they cope with ethnic discrimination—energy that majority group members do not have to draw on. For example, in a segment of the *60 Minutes* television program, Ruth Simmons (President of Brown University and of African-American ancestry) described the shock she felt when she was shadowed by a security guard as soon as she walked into Saks Fifth Avenue in New York City to shop. She has been shadowed a number of times. Corporate lawyer and college professor Lawrence Graham, in his book *Member of the Club*, points out that he, like other African Americans of the middle class, "can shop in the same stores, work in the same firms, and live in the same neighborhoods as our white peers," yet they are still vulnerable to slights and insults on a routine basis. Their status and acceptance are undercut when "we are shadowed by store clerks, passed up by cab-drivers, ignored by bosses who are looking for protégés, and rejected by [social and country] clubs that offer networking opportunities" (1995, p. xiv). Majorities belonging to the same professional class would not have their social standing undermined this way, of course.

In a more ideal world, according to chemical engineering profes-sor Paula Hammond (who possesses African-American ancestry) "you won't have to fight just to be who you are.... When you go places there [will be] an assumption that you too are interested in, say, the education of your child, or you too are interested in investments ... .[and you pos-sess] the same concerns as upper middle-class white folks" (quoted in C. Williams, 2001, p. 973). But enjoying this ideal and positive assumption is still decidedly the exception. In short, middle-class African-Americans and other NI groups find themselves denied the "comfort" that educa-tion, a prestigious job, and money in the bank should be bringing them (Hochschild, 1995, p. 93).

Exclusion from Important Community, Civic, Housing, and Business Networks

To achieve financial, social, and educational advancement, professors and their families must (almost always) become networked with a vari-ety of influential people who can open doors of opportunity for them, help them solve problems, alert them to impending dangers and reorga-nizations, and introduce them to yet more power-holders (Breiger, 1988; Boissevain, 1974). Such accumulation of social capital often happens in *exclusive* places off-campus where disadvantaged groups are not to be found—namely, on corporate boards; at country and golf clubs; and in middle- and top-management positions in professions, businesses, hos-pitals, and so on (Shin, 1996). To remedy this predictable exclusion, provosts as well as deans and chairs can deliberately introduce their NI faculty to various movers and shakers in the community so that net-working can be ensured.

Housing Segregation and Mortgage Finance Difficulties

Housing segregation can severely limit faculty members' access to influential networks. A close connection exists between social mobility and spatial mobility. As a family's assets grow, members usually relocate to a "better" neighborhood where they can "consolidate their own class position and enhance their and their children's prospects for additional social mobility" through better public schooling, higher value of housing, more desirable living conditions, and intermingling and *networking* with neighbors and their children who possess an attractive social standing.

By choosing to move to "successively better neighborhoods," immigrants to this country and their children found a way to consolidate and extend their financial and social gains. Levels of residential segregation "have fallen for each immigrant group as socioeconomic status and generations in the United States have increased." In short, having the freedom and the means to move to a better neighborhood is part of the American dream (Massey and Denton, 1993, p. 150). Yet even in the twenty-first century, there are still affluent neighborhoods where NI professionals and professors are not welcome, as I well know from working with these professors (also see Hochschild, 1995). Only certain Asian-American and Latino/a groups are thus far treated in this nation as "honorary whites" (as discussed earlier) who experience few or no barriers to their residential choices and preferences.

Are redlining practices in residential areas—that is, the blocking of certain groups (almost always NIs) from buying and moving in—a thing of the past? No. New faculty hires from certain groups may still encounter these practices. Newspapers across the country as well as the Federal Reserve Bank continue to unearth discrimination not only by realtors but also by commercial banks that reject applicants from disfavored groups two or three times as often as majority applicants with the same qualifications. Banks in certain cities such as Boston, Philadelphia, Chicago, and Minneapolis are especially culpable (Massey and Denton, 1993; Oliver and Shapiro, 1995). Early in the twenty-first century, *The Boston Globe* newspaper continued to spotlight several New England banks' unscrupulous mortgage practices toward NIs as well as the banks' and realtors' segregation patterns in both rental and residential housing. Such segregation translates into diminished opportunities—financial, educational, psychological, and political—for those who are systematically excluded from living in mostly majority communities (Massey and Denton, 1993; Fischer et al., 1996; Oliver and Shapiro, 1995; Marable, 1995).

A telling example of recent discrimination is provided by Law Professor Patricia Williams. Initiating a home mortgage application over the phone, she found that her loan was approved quickly. "With my credit history, with my job as a law professor, and no doubt with my accent, I am not only middle-class but match the cultural stereotype of a good white person." Because of this, the loan officer of the bank mailed her the contract and he himself checked off her race as "white." She marked through that, wrote in "black," and then mailed back the signed contract. "Suddenly said deal came to a screeching halt," Williams observes. The bank demanded a heftier down payment, more points to be charged for the loan, and a higher rate of interest—because (she was told) the property values in her neighborhood "were suddenly falling" and the bank's risk had thus increased (P. Williams, 1991, pp. 39–40).

More recent discrimination seems to have occurred when banks and mortgage companies exploited Mexican-American and African-American home buyers who had assumed "half of the U.S. *subprime* mortgage loans" between 2004 and 2010. These very-high-cost loans were folded into Wall Street's impossible-to-understand packaging of mortgage derivatives—which then morphed into "weapons of mass destruction," in Warren Buffet's memorable words. A recession resulted, with housing and employment drops producing long-term pain for many people. Those most hurt by these weapons, usually NIs, have suffered a meltdown in the value of their home equity and at times a loss of their homes through foreclosures (for more details, see the website of the Kirnan Institute for the Study of Race and Ethnicity at Ohio State University).

* * * * *

To retain NI faculty, all of us must pay more attention to inequities they may face outside their campus walls: segregation and higher-than-deserved mortgage rates in the housing market; frightening harassment, especially of their children, by police officers and the justice system; social exclusion practiced by community clubs and influential networks. Top leaders at campuses and professional schools can make known the high expectations they hold—for realtors, law and police officers, community clubs, businesses, and other associations—to treat *all* their faculty as first-class citizens. Further, these top leaders can intervene when a violation of courtesy and fair play has clearly taken place. These steps are likely to increase the retention of faculty members: they will realize that their employers care about and will take actions to ensure their families' well-being and safety in the larger community.

To assist deans, chairs, and other academic leaders, a "Welcome Wagon" service could be organized. Several large corporations in the Minneapolis-St. Paul area provide such a service to their mid-level new employees, especially those from non-immigrant groups, in order to accelerate their adjustment to the geographical area. I believe such a Wagon (actually, it is a small, cordial team of experts who specialize in different aspects of the larger community) could be wisely imitated by campuses and professional schools located in predominantly majority settings. This is an example of a small but important step. In addition, I recently learned that the University of Tennessee assigns a community mentor to each under-represented new faculty hire. Easing adjustment to a new area and increasing a sense of well-being for the new recruit and his/her family are the reasons for this strategy (2011 conversation with Theotis Robinson, the Vice President for Equity and Diversity at the University).

Clearly, campus leaders can take feasible steps to inquire about how their faculty are faring in the outside community. Then, leaders can intervene in various ways to make sure inequities and discourtesies in the outside community are not tolerated. With their power and standing, campuses could easily move beyond passive by-standing. If they do not, they are very likely to lose the very faculty whom they are so keen to include within their ranks.

Part 2

REMOVING THE BARRIERS
TO FACULTY DIVERSITY

4

FACULTY RECRUITMENT

Replacing Dysfunctional Practices
with Good Practices

During my ten years as a professor and even in my [current] *role as associate dean and department chairman, I have spent—are you ready—not one hour of formal training in the best practices for hiring in academe.*

(Pomona College Professor Kevin Dettmar, 2004, p. B7)

Our search committees invariably find minority candidates they say are less qualified or less of a "good fit" than majority ones. But those same minority candidates then turn around and land impressive jobs elsewhere. Does this bother us? Not much. We have a regrettable attitude about diversity, if you ask me. What can be done?

(Anonymous associate dean)

I totally agree with the joker who claimed that faculty hiring committees represent academia at its <u>most</u> dysfunctional. Sure, go ahead and throw those committees into that swirling, exhausting process with no assistance or direction. But don't act surprised by the results.

(Anonymous faculty member)

When I express concern to colleagues about the extremely low representation on our campus of minority graduate students and faculty members, the answers I usually get run along the lines of: "But we have a woman from Buenos Aires in the department" or "I have three Chinese students and a Russian" or "I have a post-doc from Nigeria."

(Distinguished Professor Richard Tapia, Computation and Applied
Mathematics, Rice University where he also directs the Center for
Excellence and Equity in Education, *Chronicle*, 2007, p. B35)

Without a doubt, search committees both require and deserve far more coaching and assistance if they are to be effective in helping to diversify the faculty. How to remedy the common dysfunctions and confusions that plague search committees will be the major focus in this chapter. Predictable dysfunctions often compromise careful decision-making of evaluators and in particular block the hiring of under-represented women for traditionally male fields (my shortcut term will be URW) as well as block the hiring of members of non-immigrant, colonized groups for all fields (my shortcut will be NI, which will stand for non-immigrant). As previously stated, non-immigrant, colonized groups include only these five ethnic groups: *African Americans, Mexican Americans, American Indians, Puerto Rican Americans, and Native Hawaiians.*

To recruit new colleagues from these groups, provosts and deans have important roles to play: in guiding search committees, in exerting their own intellectual leadership to advance faculty diversity, and in distributing resources. I will discuss these important roles for provosts and deans in Section C of this chapter. But attention must first be paid to other matters: preparing the campus community for a diversity initiative (Section A) and preparing faculty search committees for their roles in diversifying the faculty (Section B).

Both search committees and key academic leaders at campuses and professional schools must become engaged in thinking through the following questions: Why is faculty diversity desirable for our campus, school, or department? What do we mean by diversity? Are we currently focused on achieving more global diversity (that is, hiring more faculty who are immigrants and international scholars) and less focused on domestic diversity (i.e., hiring NI faculty)? Will the exclusively global or primarily global approach have any likely, predictable impacts on our own citizens and our national economy? What are the barriers that seem to be undermining our efforts to achieve domestic diversity?

Grappling with these questions is essential. I recommend that becoming mindful and ready is a first step for a campus and its leaders. Section A will explore how to promote mindfulness and readiness. In Section B, I will delineate nuts-and-bolts ways to coach search committees and their chairs, and then in Section C, I will outline the important tasks to be undertaken by provosts and deans.

SECTION A

Prepare the Campus Community

Key faculty, administrators, staff, student leaders, and college and university trustees should first understand the importance of recruiting and retaining URW and NI faculty members for their educational enterprises. These key leaders should be coached and practiced *in depth* so that they can defend the diversity campaign and debunk common lines of resistance or confusion. It is insufficient for only a few administrators, a diversity council or more likely only its chair, and perhaps a newly appointed chief diversity officer, to be spearheading the campaign. That number of advocates is just too small to build momentum. A concerted effort is needed by a number of leaders over several months or a year, to dispel myths and inertia which hamper a campus's success.

As a consultant, I have helped campuses jump-start Diversity Dialogues for their faculty leaders or their faculty senates. In fact, several administrators I work with (such as Allegheny College Dean of Faculty Linda DeMeritt) have made participation in Diversity Dialogues mandatory before faculty members can serve on a search or any other powerful committee. Some campuses, sometimes with my help, regularly engage all their department chairs and all their deans in a series of leadership-development workshops dealing with the myths and confusions surrounding faculty diversity. Participating in problem-based workshops, the power-holders have the chance to think these issues with their colleagues, refine their understanding, and then brainstorm with one another about the best ways to construct and execute action plans.

Action-oriented leadership training for chairs and deans may be prompted or reinforced by surveys of campus and department climates, undertaken periodically by outside experts or internal task forces. These workplace surveys often uncover a sometimes chilly climate for URW and NIs (both students and faculty) and a sometimes severe undervaluing of their worth and promise. The University of Michigan, at its website, shares the typical questions it uses in its surveys and interviews. A number of campuses now undertake such climate surveys on an annual or biennial basis because the survey results often motivate remedial actions for the trouble-spots detected.

At yet other places, I have seen less typical approaches. For instance, retired faculty or alumni leaders or business and civic leaders at times become deeply involved, and they spark the impetus and support for faculty diversity. A few campuses' boards of trustees (such as the University of Virginia's and Emerson College's) have taken a very strong role by officially urging its schools to work harder to diversify its faculty ranks and by requesting progress reports. And finally, from time to time student protesters (majority and non-majority) have raised their voices to demand more faculty diversity in order to enrich the educational experiences of all students and to lessen what the protesters view as the European-American clan-like and mono-cultural composition of their campus faculty. However, students' complaints and efforts can be predictably short-lived (after all, they graduate and move on). To build sustainability, some student protesters have wisely built coalitions with alumni, trustee members, faculty, or community leaders. In turn, these coalitions have sponsored campus-wide "teach-ins" designed to spur understanding and incubate action plans.

In short, students, administrators, faculty members, trustees, alumni, and external business leaders can become networked so that they are able to generate and multiply support and momentum. So too can faculty senates, task forces, diversity councils, private donors and foundations, and civic organizations.

Myths and Assumptions

What are the myths and unfounded assumptions that these groups and leaders should be *ready and eager* to discuss and debunk? Here are common ones that I routinely bump into in my consulting practice.

- Few if any domestic, diverse faculty would want to live here. The geographic location—or cultural homogeneity—or weather—or political climate—or pollen count would be lousy for them. They'd see it as a bad fit. We're wasting our time.
- No domestic, under-represented folks would settle for the paltry salary we can offer; Stanford and other well-heeled places will beat us out every time. We'd be wasting our time to assemble a package of non-monetary benefits. They'll get dozens of job offers.
- We already have a sizable number of international faculty (holding non-U.S. doctorates) so why are we concerned about faculty diversity? We already have it.
- No under-represented professors would want to come here because they wouldn't have a critical mass of others like themselves. They are bound to feel isolated. And besides, we wouldn't be able to ensure them mentors from their own backgrounds or gender.
- Why do we need more domestic minority faculty? I don't get it. The great majority of our students, after all, are European Americans, Chinese Americans, and Japanese Americans, with a few students from Turkey, Nigeria, Argentina, Korea, and so on.
- We'll never find qualified candidates for our department; the supply just doesn't exist. That's the reason we have so few Mexican-American and African-American instructors right now.
- Because majority men are having an awful time in the job market, why shouldn't we be giving them extra consideration? We don't need to spend extra time identifying and hiring hard-to-find women and minorities. In this job market, they are having their doors beaten down by recruiters. I myself worry about white men. They need all the help they can get and need it right now.
- Because this campus is already a color-blind and gender-blind meritocracy, we really can't be extra aggressive in our faculty recruiting

106

of under-represented women and minorities. We have to continue to be color-blind and gender-blind in our actions. That's a moral imperative as well as a legal and constitutional one. We are just looking for the best and the brightest. That's always our objective.

These predictable myths and confusions must be met head-on rather than ignored. Disarming them will take a variety of leaders—from campus presidents to students—who have been drilled and practiced so they feel ready for such disarming.

For the past twenty years in my consulting, I have heard variations of these myths and excuses offered as explanations for why a campus or professional school currently possesses only a handful of URW and NI colleagues. Not much has changed, in my view, since the 1997 study funded by the Ford Foundation and undertaken by University of Massachusetts-Boston Education Professor Bernard Harleston and Georgia State University Law Professor Marjorie Knowles.

These researchers uncovered the *biggest myth of all*: the notion that there are no or very few qualified NI and URW available to hire as faculty (the "supply problem"). Visiting eleven major research universities, Harleston and Knowles (1997) interviewed the president, provost, and other key administrators engaged in diversifying the faculty as well as some under-represented, domestic faculty and graduate students on each campus. From the administrators they heard about the supply problem and little else. A further discovery—perhaps not surprising—was that the eleven well-known campuses as a group had granted doctorates to over *one thousand* distinguished Ford Fellowship recipients from non-immigrant groups but in actuality these campuses had astonishingly hired only *seventy* out of that number as faculty for their institutions. Amazing!

Currently, in the top one hundred departments of science and engineering in this country, women and non-immigrants make up a very, very small number, according to University of Oklahoma Chemistry Professor Donna Nelson, despite the increase in doctorates earned at impressive institutions by these groups (see website for Nelson Diversity Surveys; Nelson and Brammer 2010). It is no wonder that faculty diversity is so difficult to achieve, with such persistent myths and what appear to be prejudicial assumptions blocking the enterprise. The first good practice, I maintain, is to vigorously "debunk" the myths and misperceptions (Daryl Smith's apt word; she is a professor at Claremont Graduate University).

Before campuses launch a five- or ten-year action plan to diversify their faculty, I hope leaders and groups over several months will sponsor dialogues and discussions devoted to such debunking of perennial myths, confusions, and excuses just listed. Further, faculty diversity must not be the hobbyhorse or passionate preoccupation of only a few. A large part of the campus must come to realize its importance and recognize the barriers and myths to be resisted. Once that groundwork is laid, intensive attention should be redirected to one of the key actors in faculty diversity: the faculty search committee.

SECTION B

Prepare Faculty Search Committees and their Chairs

Almost a dozen dysfunctions typically plague faculty search committees. After listing the dysfunctional, bad practices, I will outline good practices that make search processes more equitable and, in particular, increase the likelihood of hiring URW and NI colleagues.

Dysfunctional Practices

- Lack of careful preparation for the search committee, despite the utmost importance of the committee's work in helping to add both short-term and long-term faculty members—arguably the most important players at any educational institution.
- Overloading search members; no relief granted to them from other committee assignments; no extra compensation.
- No preparation for the search committee chair, in handling interpersonal dynamics and conflicts among the members and keeping the committee's deliberations on track.
- No serious thought given by the department chair, dean, or other power-holders about which faculty members to choose for the search committee.
- No time spent by the dean or provost to help the hiring department think through its five-year and ten-year programmatic plans and diversity needs, and then construct job criteria and job announcements to address those programmatic needs.
- No coaching so that search members can recognize and rise above cognitive biases, shortcuts, and stereotypes.
- No carefully constructed ground rules to govern the search committee members' tasks and deliberations during the several stages of the search process.
- No antidotes provided to committee members for the infamous one-page document entitled "Illegal Questions to Avoid," usually handed to them by the dean or human resources director. No warning that this sheet has a predictably chilling effect on most committees. No distribution of a document such as "Legal and Fruitful Questions

to Use" that would offer far more options and maneuverability for committees.

- No assistance to the committee in developing legal and effective interview questions to be used in phone and campus interactions with job candidates. By default, the same tired questions are used season after season.
- No outreach resources or strategies suggested to the search committee, so that it can identify and add URW and NI candidates to the pool.

What are the remedies for these standard dysfunctions and omissions? Below is a discussion of good practices that will mitigate the dysfunctions.

Good Practices to Replace the Dysfunctions

Planning by the Hiring Department, with Involvement of the Dean or Provost

Senior administrators sometimes allow a search committee to rush into its tasks using ill-defined job criteria, out-of-date methods, and a slippery grasp of the long-term needs of the department and institution. Far better to have appropriate staff in the provost's or dean's offices assist the entire hiring department (or an appropriate subset of that unit) in taking stock and exploring questions such as the following: What are the anticipated departmental and institutional directions and strategic plans for the next five years or longer? How do the unit's plans fit into the overall plans for the college and campus? What new hiring should be done, in light of those plans, needs, and available financial resources? By grappling with programmatic and institutional needs, hiring departments are less likely to fall into the automatic "cloning" error and more likely to aim for adding diverse new faculty.

Job Descriptions Should Indicate that Diversity Is a Required Criterion that Will Be Counted

The provost, dean, or their representatives should also lead the search committee's process for determining the job criteria for each faculty opening and how to best describe those criteria in the job announcement. In other words, I am recommending that the job description be carefully composed by this larger group, rather than being composed by the smaller search committee itself.

Some campuses still use the vague, lip-service statement: *we are an equal opportunity employer and we encourage women and minorities to apply.* It is time, I suggest, to shelve that tired wording. The provost

109

and dean should make sure that the hiring of URW and NI colleagues is recognized by the hiring department as both an institutional and a departmental need. This "diversity component" should in fact become an *official* and required criterion together with other job criteria set forth in the job advertisement. I typically urge the dean or provost, together with the hiring department, to allot a *specific weighting for this diversity component* (such as 15 or 20 points out of a total of 100). The group should also decide the specific weighting of the other components, such as teaching requirements and applicants' competency to meet them; applicants' research/scholarship achievements to date as well as future promise; publication record; supervision and experience with student interns; and any other categories deemed essential.

Below are excerpts of wording taken from certain campuses' job ads and listserve alerts that are more specific and compelling than the language usually found. I recommend considering alternatives such as these when constructing diversity statements.

- *The university is building a culturally diverse faculty and strongly encourages applications from female and minority candidates.*
- *The college is committed to increasing the diversity of the college community and the curriculum. Candidates should identify their strengths or experiences in this area.*
- *Candidates should describe their experience in mentoring U.S. minorities, women, or members of other under-represented groups.*
- *Successful candidates will demonstrate competency and sensitivity in working in an academic community that is diverse with regard to gender, race, ethnicity, nationality, sexual orientation, and religion.*
- *The college is committed to increasing its faculty diversity and will give individual consideration to qualified applicants with experience in ethnically diverse settings, who possess varied language skills or who have a record of research that supports/benefits diverse communities or a record of teaching a diverse student population.*
- *Given the university's mission and student body composition, the successful applicant will demonstrate experience and effectiveness in teaching, mentoring, and inspiring first-generation-to-college undergraduates, in particular African-American and Mexican-American students.*

These samples are certainly more compelling than the lukewarm statement "women and minorities are encouraged to apply." In addition, I prefer wording that leaves no doubt that the diversity component is a *required* job criterion, such as "the *successful* applicant will *demonstrate* [or the applicant is *required* to present] *a track record* in mentoring, inspiring, and teaching women and U.S. minority students." Indeed, I recommend

110

avoiding the overly broad and often confusing term "minority students" and substituting specifics in this manner: "the successful applicant will demonstrate a track record in the mentoring, inspiring, and teaching of women students and *African-American, Mexican-American, American Indian, Puerto Rican-American students.*" (Chapters 2 and 3 of this book pointed out how the term "minority" has been stretched too far and has come to misleadingly include international visitors and scholars, e.g., Asian Americans with ancestral ties to China, India, Japan, Korea, and so on as well as recent immigrants from Nigeria and other parts of Africa and those from Central and South America and even Spain. The path-breaking scholarship of Hollinger (2011, 2005), Tapia (2009, 2007), Waters (1990, 1999, 2000), Skrentny (1996, 2002), Wu (2002), and Takaki (1989, 1987, 1993) makes clear that the term "minority" unfortunately obfuscates and should be replaced.

Can specific and compelling diversity language in the job postings be viewed as exclusionary and illegal? No. Rather, it is inclusionary and legal. After all, a majority male could certainly demonstrate a track record and could indeed garner a high number of points set aside for the diversity criterion. The specific language in the ad about a *track record* is significant because it signals to majorities and non-majorities that such a record will *actually and meaningfully* be counted during the search committee's deliberations. This goes far beyond lip service; actual and meaningful consideration of the weighted diversity component could indeed affect the decision about hiring.

As I repeatedly explain to various campus leaders, it is unwise near the end of a typical search process for the search chair or anyone else to bring up diversity and insist that one finalist is preferable perhaps because of their own ethnicity or their competency in mentoring under-represented students like themselves or in undertaking undergraduate research especially with women and under-represented students. The diversity component should have been on the agenda and specifically described from the *very beginning* of the committee's work. There should be no surprises when the committee sifts through the evidence it has gathered and decides how many points should be assigned in the diversity category for *each* of the job finalists. This is a methodical, straightforward way to guide the committee's deliberations. I recommend it.

To repeat, requiring a track record for diversity will heighten the likelihood that URW and NIs will apply. Due to their life-long experiences with or observations of negative biases and even stigma, they will probably have developed self-protective strategies to enable them to successfully function in challenging settings. And they probably have discovered ways to shore up others who are subject to the same bias and stigma. But if in fact they do *not* present a solid track record, then in this particular category they would be assigned few if any points. Likewise, if a majority person had built an exceptional track record, then that candidate would be assigned a high number of the possible points allotted for this category.

Composition of the Search Committee—A "Diversity Advocate" or "Good Practices Monitor" Is Important

The dean's and provost's offices should be centrally involved in selecting appropriate members for search committees and especially a competent search chair. In addition, it should be standard procedure for one of these offices to give "the charge" to committee members. Typically, this means outlining the utmost importance of the committee's task and delineating the expectations for all members. Further, the charge often underlines the necessity of: confidentiality regarding the candidates and the committee's work; outreach and actual searching for promising candidates (as opposed to passive screening); valuing evidence and eschewing personal opinion during deliberations; and following a timetable for the search process. Finally, each member is usually asked if they will devote sufficient time and concentration to the process and to committee meetings.

In addition, the dean's or provost's office should ensure that every search committee has within its ranks a designated Diversity Liaison (Washington State University's term). Sometimes this role is called a Diversity Advocate, a Good Practices Monitor, or an Equity Advisor (the term preferred by most ADVANCE-NSF campuses). Duties of the Monitor or Advocate usually include the following: remind other members of the importance of the diversity component, make sure all interviews and conversations with the candidates (and their references) bring up the diversity component, and help the search chair to steer members away from insufficient evidence, cognitive errors, and a rush to judgment. At times, this Advocate or Monitor might be a senior colleague from another department. I have seen this work at several small, liberal arts campuses. At other times, this advocate might be an experienced staff person from the campus's human resources office. I have seen this work at several community colleges, though the staff person's recommendations are at times undervalued by some of the faculty members of the committee.

What I believe is most feasible is this: the dean or provost asks a senior member of the newly formed search committee to serve an additional role as Diversity Advocate/Good Practices Monitor—just as a senior member has been asked to serve as committee chair but also fully participates in the deliberations. Additional coaching should be quickly supplied to the member willing to serve as Advocate or Monitor. Primarily, the person fulfilling this role needs practice in: calling search members' attention to biases and cognitive errors as well as to inadequate attention to ground rules; and to assisting the search chair in dealing with typical lines of resistance and confusion about faculty diversity that may arise from time to time.

Must the committee's Monitor or Advocate be a woman or a non-immigrant? The answer on many campuses is often "yes" because the assumption is that these two "diverse" members not only will be prime movers for identifying and hiring more URW and NIs but also will have a salutary influence on other committee members. This scenario certainly does unfold sometimes, especially if these diversity representatives are comfortable with their special role and are seasoned and *senior* (repeat: *senior*) colleagues. But there are several ways this arrangement can boomerang.

First, the few women or non-immigrants in the school or department can be easily overloaded, with endless requests to serve as the "diversity" committee member. The last thing the school or department should do is spotlight these few and insist that they must carry a much heavier committee burden than other colleagues. Second, these few may feel uncomfortable being placed in the advocacy role because it can be fraught with political repercussions: other members of the search committee may view them as pawns (who have been foisted on the committee) or may regard them as unabashedly self-serving or may even ostracize them and imply that *only they* (and *no one else* on the committee) really care about faculty diversity. Experiencing ostracism and "disregard" from other members can add to what has been called racial or gender fatigue. "By continuing to expect members of our workforce from diverse backgrounds to be responsible for diversity, we risk alienating and losing those employees we have worked to bring to the institution" (excerpt from "Building Diversity Leadership," University of Oregon website).

Far better, I maintain, to choose a senior (not junior) member of the search committee to take on the role of Advocate or Monitor and quickly give that person coaching and practice so he/she feels equipped for the role. Even more ideal, of course, would be to have the *entire* committee itself (whether comprised of all European-American males or of a mixture of members with different backgrounds and perspectives) decide that all members would dedicate themselves to increasing faculty diversity, from the initial charge to the final stage of the search process. In fact, I have seen a few committees proceed in just this manner and successfully reach their goal.

Prepare the Search Committee to Rise Above Cognitive Errors and Negative and Positive Biases

Before a search committee commences its work, all members should be required to participate in at least two workshops on different days (each 1.5 to 2 hours in length), dealing with cognitive errors that predictably contaminate search deliberations and decision-making in general. Search members must be equipped and practiced, so that they can recognize and rise above these contaminants. Self-correction is essential. To recap, those cognitive shortcuts and biases (discussed in Chapters 1 and 2) include:

Typical Cognitive Errors Unwittingly Made by Individuals
1. First impressions
2. Elitism; academic pedigree
3. Raising the bar; shifting standards
4. Premature ranking; Digging in
5. Longing to close
6. Good fit/bad fit & other "trump cards"
7. Provincialism
8. Myths & "psychoanalyzing the candidate"
9. Wishful thinking/personal opinions
10. Self-fulfilling prophecy
11. Seizing a pretext
12. Character over context
13. Yielding to momentum of the group
14. Negative stereotyping/biases
15. Positive stereotyping/biases

Typical Organizational Dysfunctions that Exacerbate Cognitive Errors
1. Overloading and rushing the committee
2. No coaching or practice
3. Failure to consult relevant parties
4. No ground rules
5. Absence of reminders and checklists
6. No monitoring or accountability
7. Lack of debriefing and systematic improvement

In scheduling the two workshops for search members, I recommend two different days so that members have the opportunity to sift through the lessons learned in the first day's session and then incorporate additional ones on the next. (Neuroscientists are finding that learning improves when the brain is given a sleep cycle where it can consolidate new information.)

In Chapters 1 and 2, I have provided ample illustrations of predictable errors and negative and positive biases that all of us often unwittingly rely on. I further discuss such contaminantserrors in my 2010 booklet *Rising Above Cognitive Errors* (2010). In addition, some or all parts of the University of Virginia's on-line Tutorial for all Search Committees could be adapted or adopted and used. It is available at the U.VA. website.

Caveat. If the organizer of the search workshops wishes to cluster together several committees, then I should sound a warning. The number of participants in each session should not exceed fifteen. Why? The facilitator of the sessions must ensure that everyone in the room takes an active part in the analysis and then sorts through feasible ways to prevent or reduce cognitive errors and biases.

Faculty search committees might also be coached by senior colleagues from other units on campus. For instance, the University of Michigan has assembled outstanding faculty advocates for equity and diversity, as a part of its Strategies and Tactics for Recruiting to Improve Diversity and Excellence. The STRIDE advocates, for the most part, are European-American senior male faculty in science, technology, engineering, and mathematics (STEM fields). These Michigan leaders, after some self-reflection and training, help to prep search and tenure-review committees as well as point the committees to resources, check on their progress, and serve as campus-wide overall advocates for faculty diversity. The University of California-Irvine, North Dakota State University, and the University of Maine have followed Michigan's STRIDE example, as have a dozen more campuses that have received grants from the National Science Foundation's ADVANCE program (whose aim is to increase the number and success of women faculty in STEM fields). In the past, Cornell's engineering school, as I recall, used several emeriti professors to help coach search chairs and committees.

Interactive theatre groups can also play a splendid role in search committee preparation, as shown by Michigan, Florida, Cornell, Harvard, and Minnesota Universities as well as Allegheny College and other liberal arts campuses. These campuses' troupes (made up usually of theatre majors and faculty) act out scenarios similar to the ones provided in the Appendix. As you can imagine, the troupes' lively enactments—usually of dysfunctional search committees or tenure review committees at work—spur laughter, tears, reflection, and analysis by those in the audience, whether they are search members, department chairs, deans, future faculty, or visitors from nearby professional schools. Those who have seen an interactive theatre group find it most effective: they remember much about the dysfunctional practices and what good practices were proposed to replace them. (For a short sample of interactive theatre, check Cornell University's and the University of Washington's videos about unconscious gender bias, described at their websites.) When an audience begins to brainstorm good practices to replace the bad ones set forth in the theatre troupe's first enactment, they are engaging in active (very active) learning, practical application, and retelling of the story. Bravo!

In miniature, this is how I run my consulting practice with clients at campuses and professional schools: embed good and bad practices and thorny issues in problem-based "discussion scenarios." Participants in my workshops or retreats are asked to collectively engage in analysis and then problem-solving of these scenarios. Along the way, I summarize what I am hearing as well as compare and contrast participants' insights, sometimes offer caveats about the remedies being proposed, give examples of successful practices invented at other places, and help with the generation of next steps and action plans.

Ground Rules Governing the Search Committee's Work

As another preparatory step, I encourage search committees, before they begin, to construct *ground rules* that will preserve their sanity, prevent assault and battery among committee members, and help them finish their search in a timely fashion. Below are illustrations.

1. **We will concentrate on rising above cognitive biases and errors in our discussions.** Each of us, including the Diversity Advocate and the search chair, will stay alert to the errors, biases, and shortcuts we learned about in our two coaching workshops. To help remind and prompt us, we will verbally review all of the errors from time to time; place abbreviations of them on a banner for taping to the wall of our meeting room(s); and employ other visual aids as reminders, as we go along. Each of us bears responsibility for asking for a "Time Out" if she/he detects a possible error in-the-making. At this point, we will quickly pause to discuss and try to self-correct.
2. **We will adhere to the weighting of each job category, as we agreed when doing our planning with the dean's or provost's office.** There will be no switching or trade-off of points from one category to the other. After deliberating, we will rate all applicants according to the categories and their designated values. A matrix, corresponding to the job categories and their agreed-on value, will be taped to the wall, to assist all of us in staying with the official job criteria and gathering evidence regarding each of those.
3. **Attendance at each search committee meeting will be the norm.** It will undermine the committee's deliberations if one or more members are habitually absent or late. Moreover, no one during a meeting should be multi-tasking (such as texting, phoning, checking email, or whatever) while other colleagues are working and trying to stay on task. Full and courteous concentration is needed. Electronic devices should be put away.
4. **We will present and consider concrete evidence not personal opinion or hearsay about job candidates.**

5. **We will guarantee strict confidentiality regarding job candidates, the committee's procedures, discussions, and deliberations.** First, confidentiality to job applicants is owed, most especially when a candidate does not wish his/her interest in the job opening to be shared with those at his/her current position at their home campus or office. Second, confidentiality is necessary in order to protect the committee proceedings themselves. When members make jokes to non-members about the how the search is progressing, hint at how the applicant pool is measuring up, or confide snippets of the committee's deliberations and internal conflicts, they are in fact compromising the integrity of the process. It is no excuse to explain that the non-member who received the information (or more likely, misinformation) is not a member of the hiring department or resides outside the United States. In order to highlight the importance of confidentiality, some search chairs ask that each committee member plus any secretary or other staff member assisting with the search sign a pledge of confidentiality. Others remind colleagues and staff at the end of each meeting of their confidentiality obligation. All of us together will decide which option we prefer.

6. **We will decide, before the committee commences its work, how we will come to decisions during various stages of our work.** Will we be governed by voting (with a simple majority prevailing), by reaching consensus, or by some other method?

7. **We will undertake outreach to build up the pool of candidates—the searching part of the search process.** Every committee member will undertake pro-active outreach to identify promising job candidates, especially URW or NIs—by means of making personal phone calls to colleagues far and wide; placing info about the job opening on various listserves; contacting appropriate staff at professional societies; asking for nominations of strong candidates from former students, post-docs, outside speakers (who have been on campus and know the hiring department fairly well), and so on. The point is to widen and deepen the pool of possible candidates. The committee chair should at times invite prospects to send in their applications. All this is legal because the committee is trying to enlarge the pool. No prospect will be hired surreptitiously on the spot. On the contrary, everyone invited to apply will be evaluated the same way as those responding on their own to job ads.

8. **All members will have more or less equal "air time" during committee deliberations.** To facilitate this, we will observe the protocol that no one speaks twice until everyone in the room has spoken once. The chair will make sure that no one becomes a monopolizer and undermines the committee's team work.

9. **All members agree to treat every job applicant with cordial respect.** The committee will share essential planning and logistical information with each applicant being interviewed by phone or in person. Even though it may be a buyer's market and applicants seem plentiful, each committee member will be expected to be on their best behavior in interactions with applicants. As a courtesy to all candidates chosen for phone interviews, we agree to provide beforehand to them three sample questions (the same three for all) with one of the three being "How do you see yourself in our geographical area and at our campus?"

Further, as a courtesy, we will provide to every applicant coming for a campus interview essential information so that there are no surprises. The types of information should include:

- the job talk expected of each candidate on campus (length of talk; who will be in the audience; audio-visual equipment that can be provided, etc.)
- interviews of the candidates (length of interview sessions; names and job titles of attendees; format—only questions or also role-playing and simulations; forms used to gather feedback about various interviews, etc.)
- teaching a class or talking with a group of students (length and structure of the interaction, academic level of the students, and so on).

Further, we will ask each on-campus applicant, before their arrival, if there are other groups or individuals on campus whom they would like to privately meet with. Sometimes applicants will request private conversations with other women or other minority faculty on campus or wish to talk with leaders of specific groups on or off campus.

Finally, we will courteously remember to provide a few breaks during the day so that applicants on our campus can have a few moments of silence and a few sips of coffee or water with no one watching. Besides giving the applicants' brain and psyche a short respite, they may also decide during this quiet time that there is something additional that they should add to one of their responses to a question and so on. Wouldn't it be refreshing for candidates to have the chance to refine an answer and demonstrate mindfulness? This is unlikely to happen if candidates are forced to run a marathon and cover new ground every moment of the day.

10. **We will use several behavior-based questions, standard questions, and perhaps simulations during our phone, video, and face-to-face interviews; the same list of questions and simulations will be posed**

to every applicant. Throw-away questions such as "tell us about your research and teaching" should be avoided, if possible. The applicants' materials will have given all of us at least a superficial glimpse of those categories. So let's try to dig deeper and ask questions such as the following.

- Tell us specifically how and why your teaching approaches have evolved over the past few years.
- Tell us specifically why you would be an asset for our department.
- Looking at the courses you've taught, as listed on your *Curriculum Vitae* (C.V.), I wonder which two courses were the most problematic for you and how exactly you dealt with the issues in those courses.
- We are interested in how you have mentored and inspired undergraduates to aspire to graduate studies. This is a requirement we listed in the job announcement. In particular, how have you mentored and inspired women and non-immigrants such as African-American, Mexican-American, and American Indian students? What worked for you and them and what didn't? Why?
- If you encountered this classroom problem (describe a specific situation that a new hire might be expected to deal with), how would you handle it?
- Recall for us a successful collaborative research project that you undertook with others over the past two years. What was your role? What problems came up? How did you resolve them?
- All of us, from time to time, have to deal with colleagues who severely disagree with us. Recall a time when this happened, and explain in detail how you managed the situation. What did you learn from the experience?
- Given our geographical location, how do you see yourself thriving here?
- Given our institutional mission and the needs of our students (or our new cross-disciplinary center or whatever else the committee wishes to focus on), what contributions do you see yourself making?

[Note: more details about behavior-based questions can be found in search guides by Fernández-Aráoz, Groysberg, and Nohria, 2009; Vicker and Royer, 2006.]

11. We will bring up promptly and in a general way that our campus is eager to provide assistance to spouses/significant others in finding jobs in our geographical area. The sooner we bring up this topic,

the better. Many (but, of course, not all) job candidates will appreciate the surfacing of this concern. We can adapt this legal and deft phrasing from the University of Wisconsin: *"If information about dual-career assistance interests you, it's right there in the packet of materials we have sent [or will send] to you. Please let the contact person in the provost's office (who is named in those materials) know of questions you may have."* Or another example: *"Our campus has just joined the Higher Education Recruitment Consortium for our region. Campuses of all types throughout the region now list their current job openings on the HERC data base, which is regularly updated. This is a valuable way to give assistance to spouses and significant others with their own job searches. We are informing all our candidates of this service."*

These eleven ground rules for the search process will certainly help keep the committee on track. Before the committee leaps to its tasks, it should spend time discussing, adopting, and reaching consensus on ground rules. These rules are essential preparation. But do the chairs of search committees require any additional coaching and preparation, especially if they have had limited leadership experience? My answer is yes.

EXTRA COACHING FOR THE SEARCH CHAIR, TO REDUCE OR PREVENT TROUBLESOME DYNAMICS AND SHORTCUTS

The chair deserves and indeed requires special attention, prior to the commencement of the committee's work. The dean's or provost's office (or perhaps a management or communications studies expert on campus) should give the chair real-time practice in dealing with bad behavior and psycho-dramas that can develop (e.g., *Charlie, you and everyone else on this committee needs to know that I will fight to the death for my candidate; the rest of you can go jump*). Practice is also called for so the chair can deal with these familiar situations: one member resorts to bullying or to refusing to yield the floor to others; another seems to withdraw into timidity or indifference; another spends insufficient thought on the homework required for the next committee meeting.

To bolster the chair's preparation, the dean's office could ask senior and retired colleagues who are veteran search chairs to share how they have or would respond to those and other typical problems. The search chair should also be provided by the dean's office with a list of game plans on "dealing with difficult people"; there are several how-to books on this subject. Tips for chairs can also be found in Faculty Recruitment "Toolkits" and guidelines posted at the websites of the Universities of Washington, Wisconsin, Michigan, and others. For instance, the Wisconsin Guidelines for Chairs advises the chair to assign tasks to members at the *end* of each meeting and then ask for a report from *each person* at the beginning of the next. The dean's office should compile a list of pointers for the chair from these and other sources.

Search chairs might consider taping the job-criteria *matrix* on the wall of the meeting room together with a bulleted list of *cognitive errors* to avoid. These two visual aids, as I previously mentioned, will help both the chair and the Diversity Advocate/Monitor keep members on course and avert common mistakes.

Above all, the chair and the Diversity Advocate/Good Practices Monitor together should be given practice "drills" so they are ready to disarm typical lines of resistance and confusion regarding faculty diversity efforts. By assuming the part of devil's advocate and hard-nosed obstructionist in these practice sessions, the associate dean (or chief diversity officer, vice provost for faculty affairs, or some other appropriate person) could act out questions, retorts, bullying, passive aggression, and other actions which both the chair and the advocate/monitor, in real time, might confront. The chair and the advocate should "rehearse the new behavior [and interventions] at every opportunity until it becomes automatic (that is, until mastery has occurred at the level of implicit learning)" (Coleman, Goyatzis, and McKee, 2004).

SECTION C

Roles for Provosts and Deans

While search committees and search chairs are most involved and invested in the myriad tasks associated with hiring new colleagues, provosts and deans have indispensable and broader parts to play in diversifying their faculty. Below are the roles that deans and provosts should assume.

Monitor of Search Committee Process

Ask the search chair from time to time: are committee members' outreach efforts proving fruitful? How could my office or some other office help with outreach? Are there any conflicts within the committee membership that need some problem-solving attention? Are members self-correcting if they find themselves relying on a cognitive error or bias? Are members yielding the floor to one another and observing the "equal air time" ground rule? Are there confusions or problems you want to discuss with me? Are there any snags related to building a diverse pool of candidates? Any snags related to gathering evidence from finalists for the diversity category of the job description?

Participant in the Departmental Recommendation of New Hires

In the final stage of the search process, some hiring departments adhere to this practice: the search committee comes before the entire departmental faculty to present their recommended choices for hiring. Then after the entire department makes its decision, the recommendations are sent on for consideration by the dean and provost. What's wrong with this picture? Often the discussion at the departmental level ends up being dominated by one person or one voting bloc, and the search committee's hard work can be pushed aside or devalued. How can a departmental "free for all" be bypassed? Recommendation: have the search committee explain its recommendations for hire in a *group composed of the department as well as the dean and provost*. With these two officers in the room and actively participating, the departmental power struggles are usually lessened, and higher-order thinking and evaluating can take place.

Some departments and their deans and provosts are asking their search committees to present them with a slate of three "acceptable to be hired" finalists who are not numerically ranked. Then the search members are asked to summarize each finalist's strengths, weaknesses, promise, and so on and to engage in discussion of their findings and insights with the department, the dean, and the provost all together in the room. Blocking the shortcut statement "he's our Number One and she's our Number Two" is usually a wise move because it keeps most people's minds open as well as lessens the likelihood of colleagues obsessing over (and fighting with one another over) the ranking order to which they have publically committed.

Monitor of the Equitable Distribution of Resources to New Hires and Continuing Faculty

Provosts and deans should make sure that departments and divisions are offering equitable salary and benefit packages to new hires. New hires belonging to the favored majority group are likely to start out with better packages and be able to quickly accumulate new successes and advantages. The reverse will hold for those in the less favored group. Virginia Valian (2000 a and b) and others have pointed to research showing that women often not as aggressive as men in negotiating their own salary, benefits, and other forms of support.

Further, deans and especially provosts should make sure that faculty already on board are not being shortchanged (usually due to ethnic or gender differences) in the realms of salary, office and lab space, endowed chairs, campus "bridge" funding for research projects, leadership posts such as department chair, and tenure and promotion, especially to full professor. Inequities in areas such as these are bound to become public information. Whether posted on the Internet or talked about in old-fashioned verbal "grapevines," the effect probably will be that a campus loses the interest of some prospective job candidates. Semi-annual surveys of salaries, office and lab space, bridge funding, and so on are essential so that power-holders can be vigilant about uncovering patterns suggesting inequities. If the MIT dean of science or the provost in 2000, for instance, had activated their equity "radar," then they would have noticed some alarming gender patterns. These patterns were exposed, as already mentioned, by the dozen senior women faculty in the science division (see the *MIT Newsletter* at the campus website). After that exposure and embarrassment, MIT officials did indeed pledge to be alert and to remedy problems as they were discovered.

Those campuses that have received "ADVANCE—Institutional Transformation" grants from the National Science Foundation (the ADVANCE program started in 2000) make it a habit to gather and publish extensive campus data. The review and interpretation of such data can point up various gender and group inequities in: salaries; committee assignments; lab space and other resources from the institution; tenure and promotion rates (especially rates of full professorships); and so on. Distributing such data (called "Indicators" by the ADVANCE program) on an annual or semi-annual basis usually promotes transparency and spurs problem-solving.

Promoter of Faculty Diversity, Using the "Bully Pulpit"

On a daily basis, deans and provosts could seize teachable moments and conversational opportunities to advance support for faculty diversity. After they have received coaching and practice (similar to that provided the search chair and the diversity advocate), they could call attention to cognitive biases. Publicly or privately, they could disclose how *they themselves* are trying to form the habit of recognizing and rising above these cognitive mistakes—in short, forming the habit of self-correction. They *should make it a point* to respond to and disarm typical lines of resistance and confusion about diversity brought up by students, staff, faculty, other administrators, trustees, and so on. Being passive or silent sends the wrong message. Their enthusiastic naming of the benefits accruing to the institution from the hiring of URW and NI faculty is indispensable; the naming should take place in a variety of venues, not just once a year at the opening-day convocation.

Intellectual Leaders

Provosts and deans could spotlight and share key insights from significant publications, in order to add value to their campuses' dialogues about faculty diversity. I often recommend that each year provosts and deans focus on one book that adds a new dimension to their understanding. Often, not only the provost but also the campus president and both their cabinets will decide to devote some group attention to critical reading and in-depth discussion. I always recommend *When Affirmative Action Was White* (2005) by Columbia University historian and political scientist Ira Katznelson (Chapter 3 has additional details about his book).

Using Katznelson's scholarship, provosts and deans can bring stunning insights to the attention of their faculty, students, staff, and trustees about the G.I. Bill after World War II. Most people in academe are very aware that this legislation jumpstarted enormous expansion and construction of colleges and universities in this country right after the war. But most people do not realize that the G.I. Bill was implemented in perniciously *exclusive* ways. Both women veterans and non-majority veterans (that is, non-European-Americans) were blocked from the astounding rewards of the Bill that reached eight of ten European-American male G.I.s. The benefits included: hefty stipends for higher education; preferential hiring in jobs; job-training; small loans for starting new businesses; and substantial home-buying assistance for veterans from the Federal Housing Administration, with its low-interest mortgages, no down payments, and construction and peopling of white (European-American) suburbia.

As a result, G.I.s—many of whom would have been otherwise unable to earn advanced degrees or to become doctors, lawyers, professors, and scientific researchers or to own their own homes—could do all these things, thanks to the largess of the Bill. While the American middle class was primarily built through the G.I. Bill, that middle class was "almost exclusively white" (Katznelson, 2005, p. 114). It became a European-American middle class driven by European-American male professionals and business owners. For Katznelson and other scholars, the G.I. Bill enormously widened the gap in income and status between European Americans and non-immigrant, domestic groups especially African Americans (p. 121). Also see K. Sacks (1997) and C. Harris (1993).

Because women and non-majority veterans were excluded from the bill's largess, they became relatively poorer in various ways after the war (because they could not generate assets and wealth through real estate holdings, business ownership, or high-paying professions of medicine, law, research and university posts). In real ways, women and NIs, according to social psychologist Claude Steele (2009), fell prey to a diminishment of their status because of the Bill's exclusions. Furthermore, the massive influx of former servicemen (16 million) into vocational and especially academic programs *masculinized* both student enrollment in colleges and universities and the make-up of learned professions:

European-American males quickly took up almost *all* the spaces in both these areas (Maher and Tetreault, 2007). One could reasonably suggest that women and NI groups are still trying to catch up in many ways.

Enforcer of Accountability

During their annual job performance reviews, deans and chairs should be penalized or rewarded for the faculty-diversity *outcomes* within their jurisdictions. Such accountability would keep these key leaders centrally involved in the work of their departments' hiring committees. While the search process itself can always be improved (and must be), the real question to answer is: How many under-represented faculty did your department or division actually hire this year? A merit pay increase should hinge on a positive answer. While corporations for years have tied diversifying of personnel to a manager's annual review, colleges and universities are just beginning to do so. Without such accountability for chairs and deans, there will always be easy excuses for why faculty diversity is not being attained. A final caveat: deans and chairs should not be given credit for *activities* (such as their bringing in under-represented minorities as speakers, bringing in woman interns to work in their offices, or going to pizza parties sponsored by minority student groups). Instead, faculty *hiring outcomes* (and, subsequently, *faculty retention*) are the results to be accounted for.

Financial Underwriter

Deans and provosts should provide some or all of the following forms of financial support for faculty diversity.

Sufficient Resources and Skilled Staff Assistance for Search Committees

Extra staff support for search committees is required, beyond that supplied by the usually overworked departmental secretaries. Unfortunately, a dysfunctional practice calls for faculty members to undertake their search duties as an add-on, with no reduction in their other committee assignments or departmental duties. Under these circumstances, committee members often resort to rapid screening and sorting of job candidates. They lack the necessary time as well as staff support to implement outreach campaigns, cultivate potential candidates, and perform genuine *searches* for excellent prospects, especially those from NI groups. Provosts, deans, and chairs should try to reverse this dysfunctional custom.

Targeted Hiring

"Target of opportunity" financial incentives and "bridge" grants from provosts can help those departments that are ready to hire URW and NIs (see Smith, 2009, pp. 150–57). As one example, at the University of North Carolina-Chapel Hill, Executive Associate Provost Ronald Strauss is pleased not only with the recruiting results from such financial incentives but also with the high retention rate of these new colleagues (from NI groups) on his campus. As a safeguard, the Provost's Office *"minutely monitors"* both the hiring and retaining processes (personal conversation, 2011).

But some campuses deem it unwise for provosts to offer special-category funds, and they insist that the hiring department, following standard procedure, provide all the salary and start-up costs for the new non-immigrant or woman hire. If special funds are made available, then I would urge provosts and deans to indeed "minutely monitor" and make sure that hiring departments are not "gaming" the system in order to merely secure extra money for their units. If money is the primary motive, then the hiring department will usually fail to provide support and mentoring to these new hires. Within a few years the department's failure is likely to result in a predictable demoralization of the new hires and derailment of their long-term career advancement.

If targeted funds will be used, should the non-immigrant or woman candidate be informed of this fact before accepting the job offer? In my consulting, I say "definitely, yes" to this question often posed to me by academic leaders. The job applicant should be able to ask informed questions about the duration of the special funding and understand that such funding may be seen as suspect by some colleagues in the hiring department. I maintain that it is the job of the chair and provost to prepare the department for appropriate use of targeted funds, in order to prevent a boomerang effect on the new hire.

Departmental Specialist to do Year-Round Recruiting (like a Talent Scout or an Athletic Coach) and Thereby Assist Search Committees

Recruiting, to be successful, has to occur all the time, not just when an actual job vacancy is in hand and job announcements are distributed. At least one faculty member in each academic department could be dedicated year-round to cultivating relationships with prospective candidates. That faculty member could: invite these prospects to the campus for special events and to interact with departmental faculty; build relationships with possible "sender" doctoral departments that produce a sizable number of Ph.D.s from NI groups; and construct for each department and its search committees what some have called a "Talent Bank" that is continuously expanded with information on possible candidates. To underwrite these extra recruiting efforts will almost always require special funding from the provost or a dean's office. Purdue University's ADVANCE program is experimenting with the use of a senior professor who serves as an overall recruitment specialist for science and engineering fields, with attention to prospective women hires from NI groups (conversation with Professor Chris Sahley, Director of Purdue's Center for Faculty Success, 2011).

When senior faculty attend professional conferences, the departmental specialist should encourage them to visit nearby campuses and meet with URW and NI graduate students who might be persuaded to apply for faculty posts *in the future*. Further, senior faculty should contact their allies at graduate campuses and research institutes throughout the country, to let these allies know their departments are seriously seeking to hire URW and NI faculty. When the allies suggest a promising candidate, that candidate should be personally contacted and invited to come in and meet faculty and students in the department. The departmental specialist should keep records on all such candidates and make sure that follow-up is done. In addition, it is wise to build long-term links to "minority" caucuses within national organizations and to specialized organizations themselves and their web sites. The specialist, together with departmental colleagues, should maintain a productive relationship with various interest groups that are included within professional societies and national educational groups.

This is the advice of Professor Caroline Sotello Viernes Turner in her excellent publication, *Diversifying the Faculty: A Guidebook for Search Committees*, released in 2002 by the Association of American Colleges and Universities (AACU). Examples of such societies include: the American Chemical Society, the American Educational Research Association, the American Psychological Association, AACU, the American Association of University Professors, and so on. By building a network with these societies' caucuses for under-represented graduate students, postdocs, and faculty as well as with important national groups (including the Compact for Faculty Diversity, the Black Physics Students Association, the National Name Exchange, the Mellon and Ford Fellowship Programs, The Faculty for the Future), the departmental specialist will be able to cultivate promising candidates for the future and assist search committees when they have funded faculty posts to fill.

Financial Assistance with Spousal Job-hunting

Central administration must offer genuine assistance to the job candidate's *significant other*—as that partner seeks an attractive job in your geographical area. If the candidate can feel assured that her/his partner will find meaningful employment (at the new hire's school or at a nearby business, civic organization, or another campus or school), then the likelihood of securing that candidate as a faculty member is considerably enhanced. The provost's office should construct an inventory of nearby businesses, non-profit organizations, and other academic institutions in order to be ready to help the spouse reach out to the best contacts, quickly. At larger universities and colleges, the provost's office should be up-to-date not only on current employment opportunities on campus but also on possibilities in the near future which might interest the spouse or significant other. By the way, provosts typically subsidize the salary of a spousal hire if he/she is hired by a department or center on campus.

Spousal hiring has been immeasurably simplified in those regions of the country which now have their own Higher Education Recruitment Consortium (see its website) which posts up-to-date job listings at a wide variety of nearby academic institutions belonging to the Consortium. Having consulted with several HERCS, I have admiration for the void they are filling. Also, the provost's office at the University of Texas-Austin has hired a high-tech business leader, on a part-time basis, to serve as a kind of match-maker for partners (of prospective faculty hires) who express interest in corporate employment in the area. This, too, is an innovation worthy of imitation.

For a splendid study of spousal hiring (both good and bad practices), see Stanford's Clayman Institute for Gender Research and its 2008 report *Dual-Career Academic Couples: What Universities Need to Know.* In Chapter 5 of this book, I again mention spousal hires and *warn* that they must not be abandoned by the provost or dean and left to sink or swim. If the spouse's job satisfaction suffers, the academic couple may quickly decide to go elsewhere and exit through the revolving door.

Housing Assistance to New Hires

Some campuses have built faculty housing units, to offer for sale or rent to new hires. Others have purchased older triple-decker dwellings (very common in Boston) and rented out each floor to a new faculty member. Sometimes, lending institutions and campuses together can offer innovative mortgage loans (or down-payment loans) to faculty. In areas with high-cost real estate, such as San Diego, Boston, San Francisco, and New York, some sort of campus assistance will be essential to enable new faculty to enter the area's housing market.

Cluster Hiring of Under-represented Women or Minorities

Departments and divisions should hire more than one under-represented woman or one non-immigrant faculty member at a time. Clustering is easier on everyone and will help to prevent the "solo" phenomenon that can be excruciating (see Chapter 6 for details on the stresses often sustained by faculty finding themselves in the solo situation). Make sure URW and NI job candidates know that the college is working hard to hire a cluster, in order to prevent the isolation and extra burdens typically faced by solos.

The experience of one Cluster Hiring Initiative program may be instructive. In the early 2000s, the University of Wisconsin-Madison began an initiative that yielded some success in the focused "hiring of African-American and Latino/Latina faculty for tenure-track posts." According to Law Professor Linda Greene (at the time also Associate Vice Chancellor of Academic Affairs), the campus created and funded cross-departmental areas and informal centers to attract intellectuals especially from *non-majority* backgrounds (both emerging and established leaders). Some of the cluster areas included Environmental and Global Security; Urban Ecology and Ecosystem Dynamics; International Gender Policy Studies; Family Policy and Law; Poverty Studies; Visiting Artists; American Indian Studies; and the African Diaspora (personal conversation, 2003).

Visiting Scholars from URW and NI Groups

Visiting or adjunct non-majority professors, on campus for a year or more, will enrich the intellectual enterprise for students and faculty and probably attract additional non-majority faculty and students to the campus. Equally significant, a steady stream of visiting scholars will help to *reduce the novelty* of having non-immigrants and under-represented women on campus. And it may be that the host campus and department will decide to make job offers to some of the visiting scholars.

Women and Non-immigrant Speakers in Every Lecture or Seminar Series

In department and campus lecture series and intellectual forums, deans and provosts should make sure that a sizable—not a token—number of experts from URW and NI groups are featured. Again, reduction of novelty will be hastened by the presence of these speakers. When such scholars visit, extend to them a warm welcome and a meaningful introduction to your departments and campus. Above all, let them know how genuine are the departments' and campus's determination to diversify its faculty and student body. Some of these visitors will become invaluable allies who recommend promising candidates to you from time to time. Such "word of mouth" promotion of your departments' and campus's strengths by a credible authority is highly desirable and will increase the effectiveness of your recruiting.

In addition, why not invite in *junior scholars* from under-represented groups (who are enrolled at the pre-doctoral level at nearby doctorate-granting campuses or working as post-docs at nearby labs or institutes) to speak to one or more classes and to talk with undergraduates outside of class about "tips for succeeding in graduate school"? Gaining such experience will be professionally enriching for junior scholars and bolster their own C.V.—besides earning them a modest honorarium. Having junior scholars from under-represented groups on campus will also please the recruitment specialist (just discussed) who can cultivate these scholars for consideration by future search committees.

Visiting Dissertation Scholars-in-Residence Program on Campus, or a Post-doc Program with Direct Connection to a Tenure-track Job

With funding from the provost, a college or university can play host to one or more members of colonized groups close to receiving their doctorates from other doctoral campuses (their "home" campuses). These advanced graduate students receive a stipend from their hosts, spend twelve months or so completing their dissertations while being visiting scholars-in-residence, and undertake a very light teaching assignment (usually one course in the spring semester) for the host department. The Visiting Scholars typically make three or so presentations about their dissertation work at formal campus forums sponsored by the president's or provost's office. Attending a few informal pizza parties during the year, the Scholar share tips with students on campus on "how to succeed in graduate school," "how to secure financial aid for graduate school," and similar subjects.

The *get-acquainted period* of twelve months often results in the host departments hiring the scholars as assistant professors. Having launched and directed such a residency program since 1994, I find that the Visiting Scholars appreciate not only the financial support while completing their dissertations but also the chance to learn a great deal about the geographic area and the host campus, department, and students. Because the Scholars become adjusted to their new settings over the year of residency and usually develop positive yet realistic perspectives of their hosts, they often become interested in staying and eagerly accept assistant professor appointments when offered. Host campuses in my residency program—especially the University of Rochester and Northeastern University—hire a large percentage of their Visiting Scholars. Similarly, campuses have found it helpful to operate post-doctoral programs for under-represented scholars and researchers. Typically, the post-doctoral post combines research and teaching and gives the host department and the recipient some valuable time to become acquainted.

Conclusion

To increase a campus's or professional school's faculty diversity, a number of recruiting dysfunctions will have to be supplanted with pro-active and long-term good practices. A former campus president has delineated how Canadian universities have changed their business-as-usual. Intent on faculty appointments for women, aboriginal peoples, and international scholars, several Canadian lead campuses have become "much more aggressive and thorough in their approaches to recruitment." For example, the universities identify and ask for candidates to apply, instead of waiting. Faculty members "exploit" personal and professional networks and work the corridors of professional conferences. The universities pay for spouses or significant others to accompany job candidates on the campus visit. Campus leaders "actively sell their locations, lifestyles, and amenities" to job candidates. And university personnel organize focus groups so that they can find out what recent hires view as strengths and weaknesses in the universities' recruitment campaigns. These approaches are reaping success (Farquhar, 2001, p. 16).

Likewise in the United States, recruiting under-represented women and members of non-immigrant groups will take considerable innovation and energy. What must be resisted are these all-too-familiar default behaviors: *Passively waiting for job applications to arrive. Asking an untrained and overloaded search committee to speedily sort through candidates' materials. Continuously reusing a "boilerplate" diversity statement in job ads. Unwittingly allowing cognitive errors to permeate committee deliberations. Rushing to judgment in order to simplify or speed up the decision-making process.* These defaults will almost always ensure that members of the hiring department continue to *clone* themselves.

5

FACULTY RETENTION

Replacing Dysfunctional Practices
with Good Practices

We found [in our Campus Diversity Initiative study of 28 California private campuses] *that, on average, 58 percent of all under-represented minority faculty new hires were replacement hires—nearly three out of every five URM core faculty hired simply took the place of URM faculty who had left the institutions.*

(José Morena, Daryl Smith, Alma Clayton-Pedersen, Sharon Parker,
and Daniel Teraguchi, *The Revolving Door for Underrepresented
Minority Faculty in Higher Education*, 2006, p. 11)

Retention [at MIT] *is challenged by a notably higher loss of minority faculty* [specifically "Black, Hispanic, and Native American faculty"] *in the years before tenure. These results are complemented by the finding that the mentoring experiences of minority faculty are less positive than those in the non-minority group...minority faculty indicate greater concerns about objectivity in tenure and promotion decisions, and in many cases express frustration with regard to isolation and climate.*

(MIT Provost Rafael Reif's Summary Statement for
the comprehensive MIT Report of the Initiative
for Faculty Race and Diversity, 2010)

Poor retention of non-immigrant (NI) faculty can indeed be fairly likened to a "revolving door," as the first quotation suggests. Associate Professor José Morena, at California State University-Long Beach, specializes in Latino/s Education and Policy Studies and edited *The Elusive Quest for Equality: 150 Years of Chicano/a Education* (1999). He and his colleagues named above have brought critical-thinking analysis to retention rates and retention practices for "under-represented minorities," by which they mean "Black, Hispanic, and Native American." As the reader knows by now, I myself prefer and will use the term "non-immigrant" (which means African Americans, Mexican Americans,

Puerto Rican Americans, American Indians, and Native Hawaiians), as I explained in Chapter 3.

A revolving door is an indisputable sign of serious organizational dysfunctions. But notice that Morena and his colleagues highlight something else that is very worrisome: statistics can easily mislead (or *lie*, as Mark Twain insisted). That is, a superficial and misleading interpretation of a campus's numbers for what it calls its "diversity hires" can obscure a shockingly high attrition rate for its NI faculty. Simply talking about bald numbers of "diversity hires" over several years or for a single year is insufficient. Those doing institutional research should track the retention of each individual NI. Only in this way will a campus or department be able to grasp that its fairly new "diversity hires" are quickly exiting—and are being replaced by brand-new "diversity hires."

But replacement hires, of course, "will not increase the net number" (Smith, 2009, p. 159). In short, the actual attrition rate for "diversity hires" on a campus can be far higher than imagined (maybe even 100 percent), since the revolving door is out-of-control, with fairly new arrivals leaving while ever newer ones are entering. The attrition rate is (or can easily be) higher and more worrisome than originally thought. And it is sad to reflect on what the revolving door probably signals to students and other faculty about NI faculty members—and what the revolving door does to undermine continuity within campuses' learning communities.

Note, too, that throughout this discussion, I have placed "diversity hires" in quotations, to remind the reader that this term itself can be misleading, as I explained early in Chapter 3. Are members of Asian-American immigrant groups as well as other immigrants from South and Central America, Africa, and the Caribbean being included in the term? If so, then what is meant by "diversity hires" to me is overly broad and is confusing global with domestic diversity.

Revolving doors are a serious matter. In 2010, MIT forthrightly faced up to its own problem. MIT admitted that its own retention of "Black, Hispanic, and Native American" faculty was acutely faulty and disclosed the comprehensive research and investigation behind that conclusion. The provost, campus president, and a number of others pledged to begin fixing the embarrassing problem rather than ignoring them. Their efforts will be intriguing to follow in the coming years.

In the MIT 2010 report, the authors wryly underline some unique things about MIT that they predict will make the solving of the problem quite challenging as well as interesting. For instance, the authors point out that many at MIT pride themselves on *already* having achieved a campus-wide and admirable meritocracy. Assured that such steady-state perfection already exists, many at MIT will at first express disbelief as well as innovative denial along these lines: How could contaminants—such as "hidden bias" (both negative and positive) and aversive behavior towards non-immigrant faculty (NIs)—be present in any of our MIT peer-review evaluations and mentorship relationships? How could the campus's standards of excellence be criticized as "monolithic" and "narrow"? How could any topic at MIT—including inequities and at times a chilly treatment of some NIs—be ignored for so long or brushed aside when professions such as ours are so committed to rigorous investigation? And exactly when do we start to "harness" some of our most "respected scholars, scientists, and engineers to act as spokespeople on diversity issues" so they can inspire us to reflection and corrective action?

The good news is that with its 2010 Report, MIT has *publicly* placed its poor retention of NI faculty on the table for serious consideration. MIT is to be applauded for its forthrightness. Unfortunately, many, many campuses and professional schools have *similar* blind spots and *similar* denial mechanisms around their exceedingly poor retention of NI faculty but fail to acknowledge the problems. There is more good news: the MIT Report lists several action recommendations that are also included in *this* book. I have added to this list as many helpful nuts-and-bolts suggestions as I can manage—so that the reader possesses a blueprint for action and quality-control. These can be adopted or adapted, given the particular contexts and situations at particular institutions.

Yet other good news is linked to MIT's solid track record: since 2000 this campus, like some others, has done remarkably well at remedying inequities experienced by their women faculty. As mentioned in Chapter 2 (in the section on gender bias), the seriousness of the gender problem at MIT surfaced dramatically in 1999 when the tiny number of tenured women in the science division protested and documented the differentials between men's and women's salaries, lab and office space, MIT bridge funding for researchers, rates of departmental leadership roles (such as chairs), and so on. These inequities, the women asserted, did not come about because obnoxious sexists were conspiring against them. The reasons were more subtle. Many of their male colleagues were habitually and unwittingly viewing them through the *lens of prejudice*. The unintended result was a significant undervaluing and marginalizing of women faculty. Updates by the MIT women (see the campus website) indicate that much progress is being made in correcting those problems.

MIT's new and urgent attention to improving its retention of NI faculty leads us directly into the subject matter of this chapter: Why is the retention rate for NI faculty so low at many professional schools, institutes, colleges, and universities? Are NIs also being viewed by others through a lens of prejudice and being unwittingly mistreated? What changes are needed in order to improve faculty retention and mentorship, especially of under-represented women (URW) and non-immigrant (NI) groups?

Dysfunctions in Faculty Retention

Dysfunctional practices, contributing to high attrition rates, can be readily observed during the early years of a faculty member's employment. Experiences during these first years (and especially the *first* year) will of course determine the answer to "will I go or will I stay"? I have gleaned the following list from an array of publications and my own decades of consulting experience. Typical dysfunctions include:

- Holding the view that new and other early-stage faculty simply have to sink or swim.
- Failing to prompt faculty in the hiring department on ways to offer concrete forms of support to new hires, beyond the chair or dean urging colleagues to play nice and be welcoming.
- Providing only one orientation session for new hires, consisting of a five-hour marathon meeting in late August, where they are saturated with logistical information and administrators' speeches. This is familiarly known as the session from hell!
- Little or no sharing of tricks of the trade in professional-development workshops that would help early-stagers deal with typical challenges and anxieties they face.
- Failing to include *all* faculty in orientations or professional-development sessions, including tenure-track, adjunct, term, clinical, research, and others.
- Assuming that all junior colleagues are having the same experiences and, therefore, everyone should be treated the same.
- Failing to recognize the existence of extra stressors for URW, NIs, or those who find themselves in a solo situation (as the only one or one of a very few—see Chapter 6). Failing to act to reduce these stressors. Failing to immediately frontload these colleagues with support and encouragement, to interrupt the pattern of their leaving in the very first years of their employment.
- Overloading URW and NI faculty members with committee assignments (both departmental and campus-wide); expecting these same individuals to assume obligations for academic advising and even psychological counseling of large numbers of students.
- Ignoring the need for cordial and regular check-ins with new hires and early-stage faculty because the department chair insists "my door is always open."
- Failing to organize annual job-performance reviews by the department chair and senior colleagues. Offering little or no constructive

feedback to early-stage faculty (tenure-track, adjunct, term, clinical, research, and others) about how they can improve.

- Judging teaching competency based solely or primarily on students' evaluations of their courses.
- Not bothering to sponsor formal mentoring programs for early-stage faculty or to organize writing or professional support groups for their benefit.
- Failing to make available clear, detailed guidelines in writing about what is required to secure tenure and promotion.
- Failing to organize venues where pre-tenure faculty can listen to the candid accounts of new associate professors about their recent promotion and tenure-review experiences.
- Ignoring spousal hires and their need for regular check-ins by the chair or dean, to learn about their progress and job satisfaction. Sink or swim is viewed as the wisest doctrine. If the partner sinks, so be it. These things happen.

SECTION A

Good Practices: Demystifying Workshops, Orientation Seminars, Writing and/or Support Groups for All New and Early-Stage Faculty

Professional Development Sessions, on a Constant Basis

Demystifying workshops on important topics—most often organized by the dean's or provost's office—are relatively easy to assemble and to offer on a repeating basis. Medical schools often do this for their faculty and researchers. For early-stagers, workshops usually focus on: typical stressors, challenges, and confusions they are probably experiencing; inside information and *self-help* strategies they should possess; and actual practice and skill-building in writing and publishing, fund-raising, conflict-resolution, time-management, and other fundamentals. Below is a list of sample topics for workshops, aimed at increasing the job satisfaction, success, and retention of early-stage and middle-stage faculty.

While chairs, mentors, and senior colleagues certainly have the expertise to do these professional-development tasks, they hardly ever have the time. One or two specific offices on campus (in particular, the provost's office) should organize a series of practical workshops—and ensure that the standard workshops are *repeated* every year so that some junior colleagues can use them as refreshers when needed. After all, neuroscientists have found that developing new cognitive skills is a slow, cumulative process especially when the learner is preoccupied with dozens of other concerns. Finally, I recommend that workshop organizers take steps to foster the community-building among participants and thereby help to reduce isolation that some early-stagers may be feeling (whether they are adjunct, term, tenure-track, research, clinical/medical, clinical/legal, or something else).

Constructing the workshops and deciding on content are relatively straight-forward tasks. Organizers can download and adapt sound materials from the faculty-development sections of websites belonging to the Universities of Michigan, Washington, and Wisconsin as well as Hunter College and a variety of other campuses, especially ADVANCE-NSF campuses. ADVANCE campuses, I hope, will someday record their workshops (on Proposal-Writing Tips, Managing a Lab, and so on) and share or sell these to other institutions. And wouldn't short DVDs containing testimonials and concrete details from actual early-stagers—about how they are doing their work differently as a result of some specific workshops—be worthwhile and handy? So-called "before-and-after" testimonials are usually compelling. In short, video and audio recordings could prevent some reinvention of the wheel and enrich professional-development and retention-oriented workshops offered to faculty.

Recently, a senior medical school professor at the University of Connecticut argued that, in his view, all new hires in their first year should be *required* to attend several key orientations and workshops. In fact, he thought the requirement should be part of the written job offer and in the newcomer's employment contract. Why? He explained to me that he repeatedly sees new hires become overwhelmed in their new roles and thus decide that they cannot afford to devote time to the workshops. Missing out on some important inside information and some warnings related to the culture of their department and school, they often come across as somewhat naïve or incompetent to senior colleagues. In fact, they can be perceived as downright rude or arrogant when, for instance, they unknowingly violate important local customs (such as, in the surgical wing).

Associate provosts and department chairs likewise express their frustration when some newcomers fail to attend and benefit from the demystifying workshops being offered. The problem, they say, is that *the new folks don't know what they don't know*. Perhaps campuses should require attendance of a few key workshops during a hire's first year and include this condition in the newcomer's contract. I recommend it.

Possible Workshop Topics

Below are sample workshop topics for early-stagers. Probably two or three closely related topics can be interwoven and dealt with in one session.

- Managing Time and Stress
- Dealing with and Surviving Departmental Politics (or Surgery Room Dynamics and so on)
- Dealing with Difficult People (clients, patients, supervisors, students, staff, colleagues)
- Resolving Conflict
- Negotiating and Saying No
- Fine-Tuning Communication and Problem-Solving Skills
- Balancing Work Life and Private Life; Making Use of Family-Friendly Policies
- Managing Dual-Career Families
- Parlaying Small Academic Successes into Larger Ones
- Reducing Gender Bias or Group Bias in Labs, Departments, and Offices
- Surviving as a "Solo" (see Chapter 6 for the stressors experienced by a person who is one of a "numerically few")
- "What I Wish I Had Known as a New Professional" (A few seniors could disclose how they at times muddled through some part of their early careers. Their short stories, each twenty minutes or less, could underscore the importance of resilience. The session can be compelling and at times downright hilarious, as Stanford Medical School's Faculty Fellows Program has found.)
- Cultivating Mentors for Myself
- Setting Up and Managing a Lab
- Starting a Support Group or Writing Group
- Tricks of the Trade in Becoming a More Productive Writer
- Honing Writing Skills and Presentations
- Constructing Successful Fund-Raising Proposals
- Tricks of the Trade in Getting Your Work Published
- Options for Self-Promoting One's Work
- Understanding the Standards Used During Reviews of Job Performance, Contract Renewal, Tenure, and Promotion
- Building a Strong Case for Tenure and Promotion
- My Strategies for Getting Tenure (a panel led by brand-new associate professors)
- Constructing and Implementing a Five-Year Career Plan

Additional Demystifying Sessions and Videotapes from Teaching and Learning Centers on Campuses

I would like to see Teaching and Learning (T/L) Centers create and then post to their campus websites "trigger discussion" scenarios that dramatize good and bad practices in classroom interactions, medical grand rounds, feedback sessions with students, and so on. These could

138

be viewed on early-stagers' smart phones or other electronic devices at any hour. A handful of DVDs have been developed and distributed by the University of Nebraska ("Managing Difficult Situations"), Harvard University ("Managing Difficult Moments in the Classroom"), and a few other campuses, for use in the coaching of teaching assistants and new faculty hires. In addition, T/L Centers could distribute *short* updates and email summaries which could serve as "memory prompts" for faculty members (e.g., circulate a short update about Harvard Professor Eric Mazur and his latest innovation for incorporating peer-assisted learning within large lecture classes). And, of course, when early-stagers have to be absent from a T/L Center workshop, they at least would receive some details of what they missed.

Months before new hires begin their teaching, I wish they would receive from the T/L Center some sample language for their course syllabi which describes *classroom decorum to students* and illustrates uncivil behavior to be avoided. Helpful examples about ground rules for the classroom can be found at the University of Denver's website. Further, faculty newcomers should participate in *mandatory* T/L Center workshops dedicated to finding and practicing ways to become efficient and effective teachers. Countless researchers have shown that most new hires' uneasiness and lack of preparation for their teaching duties put a *tremendous* drain on their time and confidence. Center staff and faculty affairs should intervene *much earlier* than is the custom, to ease the sometimes demoralizing transition and to increase the likelihood that new hires become time-efficient, quick starters (see Moody, 2010, *Demystifying the Profession: Helping Early-Stage Faculty Succeed*; and Boice, 2000).

Additional Professional-development Workshops for Mid-career Professors, Especially Women and Minorities

Studies are confirming that mid-career women as well as non-immigrant groups (NI) often hit a glass ceiling as they attempt to climb from the rank of associate professor to the rank of full professor. In their 2011 article "The Ivory Ceiling of Service Work," Misra and colleagues set forth their findings about the glass ceiling; they also summarize similar findings from studies undertaken by the Modern Language Association, a University of Pennsylvania researcher, and two Georgia Tech professors. On an anecdotal level, I notice in my consulting that invariably a dozen or so mid-career colleagues will wish to speak to me about how they feel stymied in their promotion and advancement plans and also feel cavalierly dismissed or delayed by more senior administrators. As mentioned earlier in Chapter 2, MIT President Vest acknowledged that even "tenured women faculty feel marginalized and excluded from a significant role in their departments," making their jobs at MIT progressively more difficult and less satisfying (see MIT website).

In particular, mid-career professionals who already have won tenured status need demystifying and clear information about how to build their cases for promotion. Many report that the guidelines (or perhaps more correctly described as "sketchy hints") for achieving promotion to full professor are even more vague and tightly guarded than the earlier ones for promotion to associate professor.

Second, women and NIs at the mid-career stage often get overloaded with administrative posts (such as director of undergraduate studies) and most especially with important University-wide committees on shared governance, strategic planning, and the like. While such service is absolutely crucial for the health and evolution of the campus or professional school, it counts little or nothing at the time of promotion review. (In fact, I suspect such service triggers an automatic response in some evaluators that "well, here is another sign that so-and-so is just not as serious a researcher or scholar as we would wish. This has been my suspicion all along.")

Certainly this important service takes time away from research, scholarship, and the generation of publications. Chairs and deans must become far more protective of associate professors, especially URW and NIs and put a stop to the overload. These administrators should examine "teaching, advising, mentoring [of students], and service responsibilities to ensure that all faculty members pull their weight and are rewarded accordingly." Further, chairs and deans must equitably distribute service assignments and then be sure to *enforce* them rather than ignore them (Misra et al., 2011).

Enforcement is necessary because I have personally seen some majority male faculty plead incompetence or deliberately demonstrate incompetence in order to be excused from burdensome tasks such as teaching composition courses; serving on curricular-development, faculty search, or other demanding committees; or overhauling a technology-transfer or research contracts office. Year in and year out, some of these professors ("gold-brickers" is an apt term) successfully slip out of heavy assignments. But as an African-American professor once astutely observed to me, "you know, women and minorities would never risk trying to *finagle* the system in that way because we'd be exposed and royally called on the carpet."

Finally, it is time for campuses and professional schools to readjust their expectations for promotion to full professorship. If critically important mentoring, teaching, administration of programs, and committee work are so essential, then they should be valued and receive credit within the promotion guidelines and processes. Ohio State University has started reexamining what always counts (research) and what is usually discounted (teaching, mentoring, and service) in promotion from associate to full professor. Other campuses should do a similar recalibration.

Misra and her colleagues (2011) call for demystifying workshops for mid-career professors. I agree. The dean's or provost's office, in my view, should undertake annual professional-development sessions on these and other topics.

- Improving Your Negotiation Skills and Conflict-Resolution Skills
- How Associate Professors Can Protect Themselves from Committee-Service Overload
- Constructing and Following a Plan for Promotion from Associate to Full Professor
- How to Add a New Research Thread to Your Work: Full Professors Share their Experiences
- How and Why to Set Up a Support Group (like the group for senior female scientists and administrators depicted in Ellen Daniell's 2006 book *Every Other Thursday*)
- Why Take a Summer Leadership program?
- How to Survive in Solo Situations (details on Solos can be found in Chapter 6)
- How to Build a Mentoring Committee for Yourself. Or Find a Sponsor who Advocates for your Advancement

Indeed, mid-career women and men may need more than mentors. They perhaps need "sponsors" who pull or push them up to the next level. How? A sponsor uses his/her "chips" on behalf of the protégé's behalf and personally advocates for advancement. In addition, a sponsor usually makes it a point to build up the protégé's reputation by boosting others' understanding and appreciation for what the protégé accomplishes. Perhaps the sponsor also helps the protégé make important connections outside the institution or company that will get the attention of those inside who have the power to grant promotion (Hewlett et al., "The Sponsor Effect: Breaking through the Last Glass Ceiling," *Harvard Business Review,* 2011). Admittedly, a pro-active mentor can do all these things.

Finally, it is reassuring to know that Cathy Trower, research director of the national Collaborative on Academic Careers in Higher Education (COACHE) focused on studies of junior faculty experiences, has expanded the program's scope to include associate and full professors in the surveys and interviews conducted by her staff at almost 200 client institutions. In 2010 a small number of these senior colleagues, in a pilot run, were included in the COACHE work performed at seven land-grant campuses. By late 2011 the experiences of more advanced professors will be included in the data and insights typically collected and analyzed by the organization for all its clients (conversation with Trower, 2011; also see the COACHE website).

Orientations for First-Year Faculty Hires

It is amazing that some campuses provide only one bare-bones orientation session for their new hires (full-time or part-time). And often the topics covered in that session are confined merely to logistics: parking areas and permits, access to the athletic club or gym, personnel forms to be completed, and computer passwords and protocols. At other places, far more valuable information is shared—regarding the campus's learning and teaching center, libraries, computer center, mentoring programs, Internet service, research grants office, and family-friendly policies and practices. But two problems usually remain: the rapid power-point delivery of overwhelming mounds of information to newcomers and the missed opportunities to help new arrivals build supportive community and camaraderie with one another.

Over two decades, Professor Robert Boice, an exceptional expert on faculty-development initiatives, has developed an ideal year-long orientation program. The first session for new hires, held prior to their first semester, comprises these components and caveats.

- Hold the orientation to less than one day and keep it relaxed and collegial.
- Include only a few administrators, who are each confined to 10-minute comments after lunch. (My suggestion: use a timer that beeps when 10 minutes is up.)
- Organize small clusters of new faculty who have kindred interests and concerns. Each cluster should have a "guide"—an exemplary early-stager in their second or third year who acts as a peer mentor, answers specific questions, and leads discussion in each cluster.
- After lunch, offer three mini-workshops of 12 minutes each (on Teaching; Obtaining In-House Grants; Being a Productive Scholarly Writer; and several more) that preview a number of *in-depth workshops to be offered during the first and second semesters.*

The special "guides" come to the orientation prepared to facilitate the interaction of their cluster of three to five newcomers, to introduce members of their cluster to all other clusters at lunch and during the day, and to follow up with occasional phone calls to their cluster members after the orientation. These guides say they enjoy being selected as "quick starters" (Boice's term), reflecting on their experiences and sharing them, meeting new colleagues and potential collaborators, and even sitting through the mini-workshops for a second time (Boice, *Advice*, 2000).

At North Carolina State University, an exemplary four-day orientation workshop for all new faculty is held every August by the College of Engineering. Since 2000, NCSU Professor Emeritus of Chemical Engineering Richard Felder and several colleagues have used a highly interactive, active-learning, "mini-clinic" approach to help newcomers become "quick starters," both as time-efficient teachers and researchers. The organizers aim to help participants meet or exceed the College's expectations for research productivity and teaching effectiveness, in their first two years instead of the usual four to five. Due to the success and annual offering of this orientation, NCSU search committees in engineering understandably decided to use this orientation as a recruiting tool: they give details to all prospective job candidates about the substantial investment that will be made to promote their success and satisfaction. The orientation, in fact, has been a deal-*maker* for several job finalists (Brent, Felder, and Rajala, 2006).

At Bristol Community College, Macalester College, Connecticut College, and a number of other campuses, all new faculty hires are welcomed into a semester-long or year-long seminar (one could dub it "New Professor 101"). This seminar promotes better understanding and increased likelihood of succeeding in the roles of assistant professor. Members of the cohort are excused from teaching one course so that they have the time and motivation to invest in this remarkable professional development. As a result of the seminar, newcomers usually develop an increased loyalty to the campus and also a lasting camaraderie that they would otherwise not enjoy. These seminars are an excellent retention strategy.

Writing and Support Groups to Improve the Quality of Life for Early-Stage Faculty

"Professors as Authors" is the name of a University of Virginia program that awards to both junior and senior faculty members relatively small, short-term grants to spend on writing coaches and editors and then distributes a list of dependable experts from various disciplines. As a second bonus, grant recipients participate in several *group retreats* during the year, to share their work-in-progress. Inevitably, these interactions lead to new collaborations, serendipitous mentoring, and supportive networks.

Throughout her career, sociologist Sarah Willie-LeBreton has made it a habit to join or form writing groups. She did so as a graduate student (at Northwestern University), a visiting dissertation scholar-in-residence at a host campus (Colby College), and now as a member of the professoriate (currently Associate Professor at Swarthmore College). Increased productivity and valuable companionship are the happy outcomes, she tells me. I always urge doctoral and dissertation scholars to invest the time and effort to construct such groups for themselves if none already exists or if on-going ones are not accepting additional members. The same advice should be heeded by early-stage faculty. In fact, associate and full professors could make far more use of such groups. A long-term support group is vividly described in Daniell (2005).

At Grinnell College in Iowa, members of the Early-Career Faculty Group provide one another helpful (and tactful) critiquing of manuscripts. By invitation, senior professors visit the group, over lunch at the dean's expense, to share tricks of the trade regarding: research and scholarly writing; advising students; visualizing and preparing for third-year review as well as full review for tenure and promotion; balancing work life and personal life. These exchanges between senior and junior faculty increase transparency about how to succeed at Grinnell and reduce anxiety often felt by juniors.

The early-career group also sponsors potluck dinners for members, monthly weekend getaways, and Friday afternoon "decompress" sessions over pizza or other finger food. Tips on housing are shared with those just arriving in the area. The College wisely regards the leadership provided by the group's two or three key organizers as campus service: their efforts are recognized and documented in their tenure files. In another smart move, leadership of the early-career group is periodically rotated so it does not become the hobbyhorse of only one person or clique (conversations in 2008 with Grinnell Associate Professor Karla Erickson and Associate Dean Jon Chenette whose office provides adequate yet modest funding for the group; Chenette is now dean of the faculty at Vassar College).

SECTION B

Good Practices: Department Chairs Have Key Duties to Perform, Related to Faculty Development and Retention of Junior Colleagues

Department chairs are central "power-holders." Sometimes when I use this phrase, one or two chairs will throw up their hands and bemusedly retort: *Oh, how I wish!* Despite their demurrals, chairs do indeed have large roles to fill (and everyone seems to agree with that statement). To enable chairs to effectively fill these roles, they deserve practical workshops, several per year, where they learn time-efficient and productive strategies and options for fulfilling their obligations. Such workshops are recommended by national higher education experts such as University of Southern California Professors Bill Tierney and Estela Bensimon in their classic book *Promotion and Tenure: Community and*

144

Socialization in Academe (1996). A number of professional societies, higher education associations, and federal funding agencies have recently called for more leadership-development sessions for department chairs, including the National Academy of Sciences in its *Beyond Bias and Barriers* (2006) and the National Research Council in several of its later publications. In fact, a bill introduced in the U.S. Congress outlines a program of *mandatory* workshops for a wide group of leaders—federal agency program officers, peer-review panel reviewers, STEM (science, technology, engineering, and math) department chairs and deans throughout the country, and federally funded researchers—on concrete ways to reduce or prevent gender bias. But chairs, to my mind, should be at the top of the list.

Chairs and other power-holders should engage in practice drills, simulations, brainstorming, retrieval "quizzes," debates, and other active-learning exercises—collectively with other chairs and program directors. Without chairs' sustained practice, workshops and enrichment sessions will prove academic/conceptual rather than practical and problem-based. Above all, beware in these sessions of inflicting *passive* consumption of data and insights on chairs and directors via powerpoint presentations.

Because the faculty-developer role is an absolutely essential role for chairs and directors, I want to make sure these leaders receive straightforward suggestions and caveats as they give early attention to early-stage faculty. Let me repeat: *attention* and *frontloading* of early-stagers in their first semesters and first few years are essential. So let's begin.

Essential Tasks for Chairs and Directors—Reducing Stressors and Helping to Increase Productivity for Early-Stage Colleagues

1. **Chairs, every semester or every year, should do a job-performance review of early-stage colleagues and provide constructive feedback to them.**

If this annual review and feedback are ignored, then the campus's and department's investment is sacrificed. Instead, the chair (and other senior colleagues) should regard it as a fiduciary duty to their units to add value and to coach junior colleagues to become more productive, efficient, and settled in their workplaces. Key concerns for early-stagers are, of course: How am I doing? How can I improve? In answering these, the chair should tap other senior professors to assist. But whoever performs the annual review should be coached by the dean's office on how to give constructive feedback (see Chapter 6).

And whoever performs the annual review should be well aware that URW and NIs can sometimes face student harassment, persistent questioning of their intellectual authority, and lower-than-deserved ratings on course evaluations. These unusual conditions of employment should be discussed to see if the early-stagers are experiencing them and have to expend energy and time to cope. (Ways that evaluators can take corrective measures, in light of these skewed ratings and worrisome working conditions, will be discussed shortly. "Hidden penalties" and skewed ratings were mentioned in Chapters 2 and 3.)

2. Chairs should lobby the dean's or provost's office to guarantee a series of professional-development workshops every year for early-stage and mid-stage faculty.

Career-enhancing and life-enhancing workshops that might be helpful to faculty were discussed earlier in this chapter. Chairs should encourage or *even require* their brand-new hires to attend a certain number of these sessions because "they don't know what they don't know." Insights from some of the workshops would help them adjust and perhaps prevent their sliding into anxiety and workaholic habits.

3. Chairs should ensure that effective mentoring programs (serving all early-stage faculty) are in place and are being monitored for quality-control, in their units or schools.

I refer the reader to Chapter 6, where I give abundant attention to mentoring programs and to ways to ensure quality-control through monitoring. MIT in its 2010 Report pledges to activate formal mentoring programs and to make sure that very early interventions and support mechanisms are put in place for all early-stage faculty, but most especially for NIs.

4. Chairs and senior colleagues should clarify the requirements for tenure and promotion.

One of the biggest complaints from junior faculty around the country is this: the criteria for tenure and promotion review seem vague, slippery, and ever-shifting. This is not their imagination in overdrive! In fact, most administrators, deans, and chairs, interviewed by COACHE staff at almost 200 institutions, did indeed "express hesitancy about spelling out, as part of a contract or memorandum of understanding, the specific requirements for tenure." Vagueness and silence are the preferred approaches. "It is often accepted as *de rigueur* that pre-tenure faculty members should *not* receive concrete definitions of what excellence in teaching, scholarship, and service means" (Trower and Gallagher, "A Call for Clarity," 2008, pp. A37–A40). The COACHE initiative, as well as earlier national programs, repeatedly underscore the double-sided anxiety of early-stage faculty in a variety of professional schools, colleges, and universities: that is, tenure requirements remain vague and ambiguous but they somehow become more stringent every year. This is obviously a crazy-making situation!

5. Chairs should include pre-tenure colleagues on tenure portfolio committees.

In some University of Michigan departments, junior faculty are included in the discussions held by the preparation-of-the-portfolio committees. One early-stage faculty member vividly recalled that experience:

> Well, I was pleased. The tenure portfolio gets put together by the college and then it gets judged by the college. The committees that help the candidates put their portfolios together have tenured members, but they also invite a number of junior members to attend these meetings. And every first year faculty is part of this committee. I wasn't a voting member, but I saw an entire portfolio. I saw how they talked about it. I saw how they chose external reviewers and what the letter looked like that went out to them—and all kinds of details that I never would have even thought of asking.... So you go through every single step, and you get to read the entire portfolio. And they discuss the personal statement: what's good about it, what's not... I know some departments do the kind of mentoring where you see a portfolio of someone who went through and got promoted last year or something. This was even better than that because you actually went through the steps together. (quoted in Waltman and Hollenshead, 2005, p. 7)

Another related demystifying practice would involve having brand-new associate professors candidly and concretely discuss their preparation for tenure review and how they handled the complex process. A number of early-stage faculty have told me how much they learned from such "show and tell" panel sessions sponsored by the department chair.

6. Chairs should request that their provost, diversity officer, or multicultural center organize a community-building reception every fall to include on-campus new faculty hires together with new hires invited from nearby campuses.

Each campus participating in this reception could take a turn at sponsorship. We know that faculty retention is enhanced by newcomers' building of meaningful relationships both within and outside their home campuses. The fall reception would be especially important in the following cases: the campus has only a handful of new hires because of its small size, financial constraints, or other reasons; the campus wishes to help its URW and NIs experience a comforting "critical mass" with similarly-situated newcomers from neighboring campuses; the campus wishes to promote a more cosmopolitan, inclusive, multi-cultural atmosphere for its faculty and the communities where they live. I was pleased to learn that one of the regional HERC programs (Higher Education Research Consortium, as discussed in Chapter 4) sometimes takes a turn at sponsoring a reception for all new hires scattered throughout its member institutions.

7. Chairs, assisted by deans and the provost, should hire knowledgeable part-time counselors to provide a great deal of the academic/course advising for undergraduate students.

Students need assistance and double-checking as they sort through what courses to take, when those are available, how they can manage a double major, and so on. But full-time faculty and term faculty, in my view, should be spared most of this course advising *if* there are trustworthy substitutes and the money to pay them. This is one way to somewhat ease the workload and overload for faculty.

8. Chairs (and other top administrators) should regularly and calmly discuss with early-stage colleagues the *predictable stressors* encountered at their professional level as well as the *extra stressors* encountered by those who are URW, NIs, and "solos."

These discussions can take place during occasional "group pep talks" with early-stage faculty or in one-to-one conversations. Also mentors and senior colleagues should candidly acknowledge (rather than try to hide) the predictable stressors—*both the typical and the extra ones.* (These stressors are fully discussed in Chapter 6.) Some examples are: few or no time-management habits; confusion about how to become an effective and time-efficient teacher; fear of saying "no" to a heavy load of committee assignments; inability to balance work duties with family and private lives; encountering some hostility and aversive behavior from a few members in the department; being viewed as a group or gender stereotype rather than as a complex person.

Further, during these informal or formal talks, senior and junior colleagues should explore feasible steps to mitigate one or more of the stressors. Sometimes mentors and chairs tell me that they don't like to hold these perennial problems and stressors up to the light. Their well-intentioned reasons are that the seniors want to avoid the power of suggestion and prevent these problems from taking center stage. I disagree with this strategy although I understand it. Some early-stage folks, I have found, are wrestling with the predictable stressors but are shy about bringing them up to senior colleagues or sometimes assume they are actually the *only one* struggling so they remain silent.

Moreover, junior colleagues can feel chronically overwhelmed but not be able to disaggregate and name specific symptoms and tasks contributing to their general unease and overload. Thus, I recommend that chairs and early-stage faculty periodically go through the list in Chapter 6, to see which stressors are impinging the most and what possible remedies are being or should be tried. Think of this as a *checklist* to spur discussion and problem-solving and to take stock. In addition, this checklist would also prove handy for a chair to review occasionally in departmental meetings, so that senior associates are reminded to "take serious interest in the conditions of employment" for junior colleagues (Jarvis, 1991, p. 41).

Details about typical stressors as well as extra stressors are primarily taken from Moody (2010) *Demystifying the Profession*, Boice (2000), and Sorcinelli (1992, also see recent articles at Sorcinelli's University of Massachusetts-Amherst website).

9. Chairs should ensure that family-friendly policies are translated into actual practices that benefit early-stage faculty and boost their retention.

Some colleges, universities, and professional schools are actually family-hostile rather than family-friendly: they reinforce extraordinary work expectations (e.g., "to be regarded as a serious professional around here, you must work 15-hour days and every weekend"). They defend rigid tenure policies ("up or out in six years is our rule").

Fortunately, the Sloan Foundation and the National Science Foundation, especially through its ADVANCE gender-equity program, are pressing schools to adopt pro-parenting measures that enhance faculty members' quality of professional and family life (such as automatic family leave for those with newborns, delaying the tenure clock, and assigning extra graduate-student support to help with courses when the instructor is overwhelmed with family duties). These measures can persuade beneficiaries to remain in academe—rather than leaving because the work/life balance seems impossible for those with infants and small children or those trying to cope with ailing elderly parents.

On-site child-care centers are still the exception rather than the rule. Recently, however, MIT and Stanford University built such facilities on campus. These centers, together with several other changes, would make academia far less stressful for those with family and extended family duties. Academic employees should lobby for them. (See the splendid *Mothers on the Fast Track* by Mason and Ekman, 2007. Also go to Professor Mary Ann Mason's website at Berkeley Law School.)

Yet even having pro-family policies on the books of the institution is insufficient. Usually the departmental chair must be the key administrator who transforms family-friendly policies (hard-won but still sitting on the shelf) into actual daily procedures and behaviors affecting departmental colleagues at the microcosmic level. Chairs deserve careful prepping by the provost's or dean's office and in particular interactive, give-and-take practice with more experienced chairs. There are tricks of the trade to be mastered that will allow junior faculty to make use of pro-family structures without being penalized. Protecting beneficiaries is a non-negotiable part of the chair's duties. (For details about family-friendly academic cultures, see Colbeck and Drago, 2005; J. William 2000, 2010; and the website for the Sloan Foundation's Workplace Flexibility Programs.)

Let me give one quick example of a pro-active department chair enforcing family-friendly practices. When Toni P. Miles, M.D., Ph.D. began her faculty career, she recalled that "Paul Levy, the chair, ran interference for me in a number of ways and was very sensitive to my family duties (I was pregnant when I arrived)—by carving out a flexible schedule for me and delaying my tenure clock." Dr. Miles now chairs clinical geriatrics research at the University of Louisville medical school (conversation with Dr. Miles, 2009).

10. Chairs and senior colleagues must take steps to nurture psychologically healthy and collegial departmental cultures.

In their leadership roles, department chairs and lab directors should pro-actively nurture collegiality, respect for others, and a collaborative striving for excellence in their units. Verbal reminders are one very simple step. One law school dean makes it a habit to underscore the following professional behaviors: Focus on self-improvement but also see your own work as intimately connected to your colleagues. Collaborate with them. Don't hold grudges and waste precious energy in personal or factional battles. Appreciate colleagues' diverse approaches and viewpoints. Realize that a collegial departmental culture promotes overall productivity and reduces stress (Matasar, 2000). These reminders should find a place in the repertoire of chairs as well as campus presidents, provosts, deans, and their staffs. (Texas A&M University and its ADVANCE-NSF program have begun a focus on Healthy Academic Workplaces; their website can be periodically checked for pointers and insights.)

Give attention to inequities and isolation. Chairs, directors, and other senior power-holders often fail to realize this fact: not all faculty at the same professional level are having the same experiences within the department's structures and culture. Some may be having a very easy time while others are experiencing very difficult interactions with colleagues. Some may be marginalized and find the departmental climate and culture far less hospitable and productive than others do. We know from dozens of sources, including the National Academy of Sciences and numerous climate surveys annually performed by large and small campuses, that URW and NI faculty often feel shut out of casual but nevertheless important conversations with some of their majority male colleagues. They are left out of important social and professional networks, sense that their careers are not valued as highly, and often find themselves out of the informational loop and not at the table when departmental decisions are being made [see especially *Beyond Bias* (2006) and the MIT Report on women faculty (1999) and the newer one on NI faculty (2010).] In short, not all members in a department may be enjoying a constructive and collegial climate. It is the duty of the chair to activate his/her "radar" and find out if some of the inequities, stressors, and isolation just named are present in the departmental culture. If so, these dysfunctions and omissions need attention.

Second, quality control requires that chairs and others intervene, subtly or frontally, to stop *bullying*, marginalizing, name-calling, or other aggressive behaviors. It is predictable that early-stage colleagues (especially NI and women faculty as well as adjunct instructors) will be most often targeted, most vulnerable, and most hurt by such psychological warfare. Chairs, program directors, and deans should not ignore hostilities and aberrations, with the hope that these will resolve themselves or that no one will be seriously damaged. In my consulting work, I find that chairs and directors are relieved to participate in leadership-development sessions and retreats where they learn time-efficient ways to manage difficult people and antagonistic dynamics and to strengthen or reactivate constructive practices in the department.

The American Physical Society's Committee on the Status of Women has outlined several Good Departmental Practices that are worth reviewing: "postdoctoral and research scientist staff should be welcomed within a department, and made to feel that they are performing a valued role with it." Further, research scientists, adjuncts, postdocs, and others "should be included in departmental social activities" and a "critical mass of female faculty sufficient to impact the climate in your department" should be hired. Both the Committee on Women and the Committee on Minorities organize site visits to member institutions to help them improve their departmental cultures especially for women (see APS website).

Alma Rodriguez, M.D., who is Professor of Lymphoma at the M.D. Anderson Cancer Center in Texas, recalls how fortunate she has been to work in a constructive workplace: "The culture of the Lymphoma section when I joined it was one of collegial and respectful behavior, and I never felt left out or had my opinions disregarded in discussion or planning." She has enjoyed collaborating with several of her co-workers: "together we've done creative and productive work" (quoted in Travis, 2009, p. 147). (As a child, Professor Rodriguez travelled with and helped her parents, who were migrant workers living on the edge of poverty. Because several faculty members at a small college in San Antonio reached out to her as an adolescent, she pursued higher learning and found her life's calling.)

While I maintain that chairs and directors are absolutely central to maintaining a productive and collegial atmosphere (as a number of ADVANCE campuses have come to discover), senior colleagues also play invaluable roles. They should be exceedingly friendly to early-stagers— especially to women, NIs, and new immigrants—and make sure they feel they belong. If chairs or senior faculty, for whatever reasons, feel socially flat-footed and awkward in this role, or feel "aversive" around co-workers whose gender, race/ethnicity, social class, or other background differs from their own, then they should seek coaching to build their social and multi-cultural competence (Gaertner and Dovidio, 1986; updates of Dovidio's work on aversive behavior can be found at the Yale website).

Ways for senior colleagues to help. There are numerous small tasks that senior colleagues can perform. They can informally introduce juniors to other colleagues as well as to information and Internet networks of possible interest. Advanced professors can co-teach and collaborate with early-stagers and/or review their scholarship, research, writing, clinic work, or teaching and make light-handed suggestions. They can appreciate and learn from less advanced colleagues' unique abilities and approaches. They can be alert to junior co-workers' "conditions of employment," as I mentioned earlier. In short, they can be magnanimous associates and, hopefully, stalwart allies. Just as there are productive ways in business organizations to be "one-minute" managers who quickly dispense valuable praise and guidance, there are ways to be one-minute allies. Try this: first remember how you, in your recent or hoary past, have been affected by a positive remark or suggestion, made in passing by a senior person. Now cultivate "mindfulness" of this dynamic so you are ready, in passing, to give similar quick encouragement and pointers to early-stage colleagues at opportune times.

One of my favorite examples of a senior faculty member reaching out is the following. Professor Ronald Wakimoto, in the School of Forestry at the University of Montana, typically asks newcomers in his department to give him very brief advice regarding a troublesome part of a draft manuscript or regarding a teaching or mentoring problem he has encountered. (He deliberately asks the new hires for guidance where they are strong.) By helping the senior professor and knowing that he will return the favor when they have a writing or teaching problem, the newcomers become connected and have the opportunity to participate in a reciprocal, constructive relationship. This has proven to be an effective way to begin valuing and appreciating newcomers' unique abilities, approaches, and competencies (conversation with Professor Wakimoto, 2002). In short, one senior colleague has activated his own retention plan for early-stage faculty.

Chair's Duties Owed to Brand-New Faculty Hires: A Checklist

The department chair has additional duties to fulfill if brand-new hires are to get off to a strong start. Serving as a protector and talent-developer of newcomers, the department chair has a number of practical steps to take, usually with the aid of the departmental secretary and a few senior colleagues. For the sake of convenience, I offer this checklist.

- **Prepare members of the department for the new hire's arrival in several ways.** Prior to *every* new faculty member's arrival, the department as a whole should meet with the dean to decide specifically how the newcomer(s) will be welcomed, professionally supported, introduced to networks and key players, and so on. In addition, the department chair and dean should lead discussion on how diversifying the faculty will enhance (rather than dilute) the excellence of the department and its value to students and the campus. The new colleague (if an URW or NI) must not be undervalued and belittled as a "diversity" hire; it is the department chair's responsibility to be on guard and to preempt any such negativity. How to recognize and rise above unintended gender bias and group bias should be reviewed, together with ways to reduce complex dynamics for those in solo situations. These reminders are necessary for tremendously busy departmental members. Their attention to collegiality and equity should be revived in a tactful but effective manner, prior to the new hire's arrival.
- **Assign short-term (one-semester) allies to new faculty hires.** The chair could ask appropriate senior faculty to make a point of offering *specific* help along these lines: "Do you know much about how the grant process works? I'd be glad to discuss this over lunch. I myself used to be overwhelmed by it." Or "I taught that course last year. Would you like to discuss it? I can dig up my old notes and exams. Feel free to ignore them if they don't help."
- **Disarm those who may be opposed to the new hire.** "Very few faculty appointment decisions are unanimous," observes University of Washington Physics Professor Marjorie Olmstead. "Don't assume that the opposition will evaporate overnight." Take pro-active steps to turn around those likely to undermine the new hire or at least work to neutralize their power (conversation with Professor Olmstead, 2009).
- **Supply a newcomer with essential information about departmental operations *months before* their arrival on campus.** The department chair, aided by other faculty and the departmental secretary, should provide details to the newcomer about course load, anticipated class size, academic level and preparation of students, and expectations

regarding office hours. Details about other duties (as clinical-care provider or museum director, for instance) should obviously be spelled out. Sample course syllabi should be sent, together with sample book lists or case studies that the newcomer may wish to review, plus email addresses of faculty who have taught the courses and are willing to chat with the newcomer. Access should be provided to campus teaching/learning platforms, such as Blackboard, and a schedule of system tutorials should be provided. Texts and case studies previously used in courses and phone numbers or emails for publishers' representatives should be sent to assist the newcomer in selecting course materials. Student advising responsibilities should be outlined, and faculty should be told how student affairs and academic advising staff can support them in their teaching and advising roles. Finally, newcomers should receive a copy of current personnel handbooks. (Bensimon, Ward, and Sanders in their 2000 book provide abundant details and checklists for department chairs wishing to be more effective as faculty developers.) One caveat: a chair should demystify various tasks but *avoid micro-managing* the newcomer.

- **Assign courses carefully to early-stagers and newcomers.** For all new full-time hires, the department and its chair should do their best to arrange a reduced teaching load during the newcomers' first year and also ensure that the courses to be taught are ones that are very familiar. These steps will help newcomers avoid a frenetic launch of their careers (Sorcinelli at the UMass-Amherst website).

- **Double-check to see if equipment and space are ready for the newcomer's arrival.** Several weeks prior to the new faculty member's arrival, find out if their office or clinical space, computer, lab and other equipment and staff are ready. Make sure that all promises made to the new hire during the earlier hiring process are kept. If any of the equipment or support promised fails to materialize or is being delayed, then the chair or a designated senior faculty member should immediately and apologetically inform the newcomer *prior* to his or her arrival. What should be avoided is a lapse or omission that might be construed by either an international or domestic colleague as a *confusing or even insulting slight* which is cultural or personal in nature.

- **Introduce and warmly promote the new faculty member to students (at the very beginning of the semester).** To heighten the newcomer's sense of belonging, the chair or a designated senior faculty member should visit each newcomer's classes on the first day of the semester, to briefly and enthusiastically explain to students why the department is so pleased about its new addition. This courtesy visit will also help students better appreciate the authority of each new faculty member, especially those whose intellectual abilities may be doubted by students unaccustomed to having an URW or NI instructor. In addition, the chair should underscore to the dean and faculty colleagues how valuable the newcomer is to the department. But my caveat is this: perform these courtesies for *all* newcomers; start a new department-friendly tradition for *everyone*. (I am pleased to learn that a senior history professor at Berkeley on the first day of a new lecture class introduces each of his teaching assistants to the students, generously underscores each assistant's qualifications and scholarly interests, and then admonishes students to "do everything these TAs tell you to do.")

- **Acting as a broker,** immediately introduce the new faculty member to each departmental colleague and then, throughout the year, help newcomers make substantive scholarly connections within and outside the department. Merely making casual introductions is insufficient.

- **Protect junior faculty—in particular NIs and URM—from excessive teaching, advising, and service assignments.** This is the responsibility of provosts, deans, and chairs. A chronic overtaxing predictably occurs when URW and NI faculty are asked to serve as the "diversity" member for numerous campus-wide or departmental committees. Prevent an overload not only of committee work but also of student advising. Help early-stage colleagues wisely choose committee assignments and leadership positions that will enhance their standing among their colleagues and boost their career advancement.

- **Ensure that professional-development workshops are being offered** every year for early-stage faculty (including adjunct, term, tenure-track, research-only, clinical, and so on). These workshops were discussed earlier in this chapter.

Conclusion

Deans but especially department chairs must become expert faculty developers. Forming Checklists may be a wise way to organize the professional-advancement and retention tasks to be completed, sometimes with the help of other colleagues and departmental support staff. Mid-career, but especially early-stage, faculty experience predictable frustrations and stressors which should be discussed and addressed rather than dismissed or ignored. Reducing the extra stressors often encountered by URW, NI, and those in solo situations—this is one of the most important retention duties of chairs, program directors, mentors, and deans. And such reduction by these leaders should begin in the very first semester for the new hire. Being passive and adopting this approach—"let's wait and see if any problems develop"—will likely prove disastrous.

The provost's or dean's office as well as the teaching and learning center should annually sponsor a series of demystifying workshops on time- and stress-management, reducing gender and group bias in the workplace, balancing work and private life, and other topics. Well-thought-out orientation sessions for first-year hires are also recommended. Finally, there are self-help steps that junior colleagues should be experimenting with, such as their formation of writing and/or support groups and their rigorous cultivation of mentors and allies (see Chapter 6).

All of these are wise investments in faculty who are after all *assets* to the institution. Helping these human assets deepen their competency, job satisfaction, and professional success makes good management sense. *In fact, bad retention practices can cost the institution a great deal of money.*

One study has estimated that the out-of-pocket costs for a faculty search in a humanities department is $15,000—with even higher costs in other fields. This figure, of course, does not include the intelligence and time invested *gratis* by committee members, academic staff, and the search chair! Once the new person is hired, costs continue to mount as arrangements are made for the early-stagers' office, computer, scientific equipment, materials, and so on (Dettmar, 2004).

In 2006, an official at Cornell University estimated start-up costs to be more than $100,000 for a newcomer in humanities and closer to $1 million for a new hire in engineering (B. Steele, 2006). In 2004, the medical school at the University of California-San Diego figured the start-up costs, excluding salary, to be in the range of $250,000–$400,000 for a junior basic scientist and in the *bargain* range of $150,000–$300,000 for a junior non-bench scientist (Wingard, Garman, and Reznik, 2004). If these studies were to be repeated today, the costs would surely be higher. At a time of severe budget constraints, financial costs such as these due to faculty attrition simply cannot be tolerated.

On a brighter side, *good practices in retention can produce remarkable gains.* These include lowering faculty attrition (concomitant with preventing loss of financial investment in those who leave), improving quality-of-life and collegiality for all members in a department, boosting faculty productivity, and remedying inequities in salary and in distribution of resources and leadership posts. These retention gains were methodically reached by the Johns Hopkins University medical school which in 1990 began a fifteen-year program of comprehensive "interventions"—all of which were *steadfastly* implemented and defended by three successive European-American male chairs.

In 1990, 75 percent of the women faculty reported that most of their male colleagues were unwelcoming and did not treat them and their careers with serious regard. With new attention to departmental culture, to training for mentors and mentees, to annual reviews of job performance, to fixing salary inequities, *both* job satisfaction and success have been demonstrably boosted. The number of women holding tenure at the associate professor rank moved from four in 1990 to twenty-six in 1995, with no changes being made in the criteria for promotion to associate. The proportion of associate professors among women faculty increased from 9 percent in 1990 to 41 percent in 1995, comparable to the proportion for men faculty; and morale and job satisfaction rose substantially among *all* junior faculty (both male and female), according to surveys. By the early 2000s, the department had eleven women full professors and seven women in senior leadership positions. Three times as many women said they expect to stay in academic medicine—this represents a *retention triumph*! (2008 conversation with Professor Linda Fried, a key leader in the interventions program, who is now Dean of the School of Public Health at Columbia University; also Fried et al., 1996).

6

FACULTY MENTORING
Replacing Dysfunctional Practices
With Good Practices

*Their intentions are very good but the reality is that, once somebody
is assigned to be a mentor, there's got to be somebody else who makes
sure that all the mentors are doing their jobs.... I'm not sure I would
call it 'accountability,' but at least they need to be prodded and asked,
'Did you do it?'*

(a pre-tenure faculty member at the University of Michigan, quoted
in Waltman and Hollenshead, 2005, p. 5; Carol Hollenshead is
Emerita Director of the award-winning Center for the Education
of Women at the University and Jean Waltman is the Center's
current Senior Associate for Special Projects and Initiatives)

*African Americans and other under-represented faculty still receive
little or no serendipitous mentoring. That's an unconscionable gap
that I see across the country. Formal mentoring programs, I agree,
are the answer.*

(conversation in 2011 with Christopher K.R.T. Jones, the Bill
Guthridge Distinguished Professor of Mathematics at the University
of North Carolina who was formerly at Brown University; he has
received the annual mentoring award from the national
Compact for Faculty Diversity)

*Our medical school has posted on its website a 75-page Manual for
Mentors and Mentees. Because our folks are very, very busy, we
decided that is the best way for encouraging informal mentoring. That
said, I do admit that some of our senior leaders are far more proficient
at mentoring than others. But that's life, isn't it?*

(Anonymous associate dean)

*Mentors must be attentive to mentees' needs that are not strictly pro-
fessional, such as finding the right balance between work and family
responsibilities; coping with cultural transitions after a move from a*

different part of the world; developing confidence in a culture that
may not be welcoming; or opposing ethnic or gender bias if it arises.

(Lee, Dennis, and Campbell, 2007, p. 792); quotation from
an article in *Nature* on mentoring by authors Adrian Lee, an
Australian professor; Carina Dennis, a science journalist;
and Dennis Campbell, editor-in-chief of *Nature*
and founder of the *Nature* mentoring awards.)

Effective mentoring of early-stage faculty heightens their job satisfaction and success as well as multiplies their institutions' short-term and long-term investment in them. Mentoring is *essential* for under-represented women in male-dominated fields (URW) and *essential* for non-immigrant, colonized group members (NIs), given the extra taxes and stressors that these outsiders often encounter. Mentoring has two dimensions: a senior person in the organization assists and advises a junior colleague regarding his/her career advancement and, secondly, provides to the less advanced colleague social/psychological support to enhance the mentee's sense of well-being.

Unfortunately, systematic mentoring is spotty. This is true despite controlled studies that demonstrate mentorship's substantial value to early-stage colleagues, including their increased productivity in publications and federal grants secured; greater competency in teaching and mentoring students; increased sense of belonging and feeling appreciated; and improved retention in academe and academic medicine (Blau et al., 2010; Wingard, Garman, and Reznik, 2004; National Research Council, 2009, MIT Report on Race and Diversity, 2010; Travis, 2009). Despite these proven results, I hear during my consulting travels far more empty talking and pontificating about mentorship than I see actual relationships taking shape and deepening for senior mentors and junior colleagues.

The clear *lack* of systematic informal and formal mentoring for early-stage faculty repeatedly surfaces in the nation-wide COACHE program that employs comprehensive surveys and interviews (2011 conversation with Director Cathy Trower; also see COACHE website). The omission usually surprises and concerns key leaders at the institutions being studied. Ratcheting up the leaders' concern is the complaint from many early-stagers who feel that their job satisfaction and success are being compromised by this lack of mentorship.

The recommendations in MIT's 2010 Report underscore that formal mentoring programs must be established in all schools and departments, with training given to both mentors and mentees. Further, early-career supports and constructive interventions (what some would call "front-loading") must be put in place for all junior faculty. These steps are certainly essential for NIs who, it was discovered, leave MIT very early, usually in their third through fifth years.

The present chapter will begin with a list of typical myths and unfounded assumptions that undermine the effective mentoring of early-stage colleagues, especially URW and NIs. Then I will underscore good practices that would reverse this situation. Along the way, I will suggest ways to embed pointers, caveats, and practice exercises for mentees and mentors within readiness workshops, workshops they would attend prior to the inauguration of the mentoring relationships. Even though mentoring makes up such an important part of professional-development and can bring measurable benefits to a department and school, rarely are deans' and provosts' offices regularly mounting readiness sessions. To me this is a bad practice.

At the end of this chapter, I spotlight how deans, provosts, and department chairs, in their influential positions, can help sustain mentoring climates and mentoring programs. Parts of this chapter are adapted from Moody (2010) *Mentoring Early-Stage Faculty at Medical, Law, and Business Schools and Colleges and Universities*; see www.diversityon-campus.com for more information.

SECTION A

What are the Typical Dysfunctions and Myths that Block Effective Mentoring?

Myths About the Value of Creating Mentoring Relationships

> *Myth #1.* "We have no problem. Informal mentoring is widespread at this medical school and is being enjoyed by all or almost all of our early-stage faculty/physicians. I'm pretty confident of that. Certainly, as a department chair, I urge senior colleagues to assume their rightful responsibility to the next generation."

This is an example of wishful thinking. What chairs, deans, and provosts almost always mean, when pressed, is that they don't have any evidence, but they certainly hope that non-assigned, ad-hoc mentoring is occurring. Most often, it is not.

Years before the large-scale COACHE study, numerous researchers, faculty developers, and professional organizations had warned that systematic, equitable, and attentive mentoring was just not happening. Red flags and action recommendations were issued by organizational behaviorists, social scientists, law and medical experts; also by several learned societies and national education groups; and even by campuses' and schools' own internal task forces. Yet nothing *really* changed. Wishful thinking and inaction continued at many schools. This much is clear: mentoring is not being amply given and amply received. Recently, the National Institutes of Health and the National Science Foundation have begun insisting that mentoring and mentoring plans be guaranteed for post-doctoral and early-stage faculty involved in all their research and training grants—to protect the agencies' investment and to quicken early-stage colleagues' professional advancement.

> *Myth #2.* "We don't need mentoring because our department chairs are terrific. We maintain that a junior person needs only one mentor—his or her <u>chair</u>. You don't want too many cooks in the kitchen, who could be giving conflicting signals and intervening in maybe random ways. No, it is only the chair who can give consistency and continuity—regarding institutional investment and supervision—to the junior person over the entire period of their employment. That said, chairs sometimes ruefully tell us we will have to clone them in order to get all their duties fulfilled."

A chair does have key duties to perform as a faculty developer of early-stage colleagues. Chapter 5 includes abundant details and a checklist for what a chair should do, assisted by the departmental secretary and others. But should a chair—usually a very busy leader—be the only source of information and guidance for a junior co-worker? No. Less advanced colleagues need constructive attention from a variety of sources, as I explain below. Above all, they need mentors who can be allies and protectors—and *not* sit in judgment on them during evaluations of their job performance or reviews of their cases for tenure and promotion. Maintaining confidentiality, mentors can encourage their mentees to disclose confusions and apprehensions that they may have (perhaps about some part of their own performance as a teacher and scholar, their interactions with a few puzzling colleagues, the school's budget and long-term financial solvency and viability, and so on). Mentees need mentors who are sympathetic, non-judgmental listeners and supporters who are on their side.

For these reasons, chairs can be guides but they cannot be mentors to early-stage colleagues. The chair is the most important steward of the department; that entity is her/his overarching responsibility. Given such a context, a conflict can easily develop. The department chair's best interests are on one side of the counter (you may hear: *oh fine, as chair I've got to lean on somebody to quickly start teaching that course*). On the other side are the best interests of a junior colleague who is relatively powerless (*I'll have a meltdown if I take that extra course but I dare not say "no" to my chair—that's what I'm thinking*).

> *Myth #3.* "Mentoring is not something we do at this university. Most of our departmental faculty insist that mentoring is unacceptable hand-holding. If someone seeks mentoring, then they must be alarmingly deficient in some way. I guess most of us older types faced a 'sink or swim' situation early in our careers so we think this is still a fair test for newcomers. The brilliant ones will swim. That's our view."

Those from the established majority group often do not recall (or wish to recall) how much inside information, encouragement, and protection they did receive and still do receive from others in their "clan." Informal mentoring in various forms usually radiates to clan insiders but not to outsiders (Turner and Myers, 2000; Hu-DeHart, 2000; Gallagher and Trower, 2009). Further, those in the dominant group enjoy and accumulate advantages because of the positive bias widely held about their innate abilities (though they may not have asked for this special treatment and though they have worked very hard in their careers). The positive halo saves beneficiaries some time and energy, guarantees them the benefit of the doubt in ambiguous circumstances, and contributes to their accumulation of advantages, as Chapter 2 delineated.

Those with a positive halo realize a compounding of their small successes. They accumulate advantages at a fast clip (see the National Academy of Sciences' *Beyond Bias and Barriers* 2006 report). This is not the case with URW and NI groups that constantly have to push back against negative societal bias about their capabilities. Having to reestablish their competency, day in and day out, leads these frequently vulnerable faculty to conclude that they are forever on *probation* (see Chapters 2 and 3). To deal with such shortchanging requires extra allies, especially trustworthy mentors.

> *Myth #4.* "We can't do mentoring because we have so few senior professors in our geography department. At this point we don't have enough to pair up with our less advanced faculty. So we're in a demographic bind."

Having only a few senior faculty members is not an acceptable excuse. Mentoring can take different forms and configurations such as: group mentoring, zone, peer, external, transitional, and others. Whatever configurations are finally chosen, both dimensions of mentoring should be present: *social-psychological* support and *career-advancement* interventions. For more details on various mentoring modes, see Section C of this chapter.

> *Myth #5.* "We shy away from formal, organized mentoring programs at this law school: they diminish the spontaneity and chemistry that have to be part of the mentor-mentee interaction. And remember that our mentors and mentees come to the mentoring arrangements voluntarily and obviously with good intentions. Checking on them, especially on the mentors, would be bad form."

Yes, micro-managing mentors and mentees should be avoided. But faculty affairs officers or other academic administrators can facilitate relationships; remind both parties in the relationship of the typical stressors and challenges that confront early-stagers; point to other resources the mentor and mentee might wish to consult; monitor how the relationships and the outcomes are evolving; and help with problem-solving—all without insulting the intelligence of either the mentors or mentees.

Given that an early-stager usually has a limited period in which to shore up her/his competencies and build a solid track record, it is dangerous to wait for a serendipitous mentoring arrangement to somehow miraculously unfold (Wunsch, 1990; Boice, 1992; MIT report, 2010). It is likewise dangerous to depend solely on the good intentions expressed by the mentors and mentees; these cannot ensure quality control. Good intentions but *bad* mentoring can quickly undermine a mentee's morale and optimism. It is wise, therefore, for appropriate campus officials to check light-handedly on progress, to verify that mentors and mentees are investing their time efficiently and building a productive relationship. More details on how to monitor and gather feedback are located in Section C of this chapter.

I agree with veteran faculty-developer Robert Boice that personal chemistry and spontaneity are superficially overvalued in mentoring processes (2000). Also overvalued is the matching of mentors and mentees so they share the same gender, ethnicity and group membership, disciplinary subspecialty, socio-economic upbringing, and zodiac sign (just kidding on that one). If that sort of mirror-matching were strictly observed, then URW, NIs, and those in solo situations would never receive mentoring. What is needed, instead, is coaching for mentors and mentees so they develop confidence about their responsibilities and how to execute them.

163

Myths about the Design of Mentoring Programs

Myth #6. "We just launched a new initiative. Our school of public health now has up on its website a 75-page handbook for prospective mentors and mentees, so that anyone at any time can check on pointers about career advising, mentoring, and succeeding at our institution. This handbook will double or triple the amount of informal mentoring we see."

This is another example of wishful thinking. Certainly a *first* step is to compile for mentors and mentees a handy list of pointers, caveats, feedback forms, and ground rules to consider for guiding their relationship. The mentor and mentee, for instance, should decide:

- how often will we meet each semester?
- will any of our meetings take place in informal settings?
- are there any exceptions to the strict confidentiality rule which is supposed to govern all our conversations and communications?
- What other ground rules should we adopt?

But it is simply unreasonable to expect mentees and mentors to plow through a 75-page mentoring handbook and incorporate all or most segments into their work together. In addition, the authors of these daunting handbooks usually urge mentees to think of barriers and "burning questions" about their career advancement and then bring these to their informal or formally assigned mentor for consultation. Is it realistic to exhort a junior person, especially a brand-new hire, to figure out what they need, what they don't know, what speed-bumps they will probably encounter, and what resources they need to increase their likelihood of success?

Mentors find themselves similarly overloaded by such handbooks' long list of time-consuming and complex tasks. Instead of putting the burden solely on mentors, a variety of major players on the campus should develop and offer the following for junior colleagues:

- substantive orientation sessions organized by provosts, deans, faculty-life offices, and others;
- a series of professional development workshops organized by provosts, deans, faculty developers, or outside consultants;
- demystifying videotapes and sessions as well as email updates circulated by teaching and learning centers;

- helpful assistance and protection from transitional, short-term mentors and allies; and
- faculty-development steps perennially undertaken by department chairs and their staff.

Myth #7. "Our research institute is minimalist. We believe that <u>one</u> senior mentor is the best source of wisdom and answers for each hire. We urge less advanced folks to ask their assigned or informal mentor (rather than their department chair) questions such as: 'where do I pick up my office keys? how do I deal with sticky personnel situations in my lab and with student interns? what can I do to get the equipment promised for my start-up? how do I make sure I secure a positive job evaluation? how do I collaborate on the writing of funding proposals?' We believe this range of questions underscores how essential the mentor is to the junior's orientation and success."

Appealing for help with all these questions is a sure-fire way to overwhelm a single mentor and to send additional prospective mentors scurrying for cover. *Several offices* and leaders should be ready to offer answers and guidance or, even better, they themselves should pro-actively contact the mentee with helpful assistance. Do not expect or portray a mentor to be an omniscient oracle residing on a mountain top. Do not suggest that a junior person rely on the advice and caveats of just one senior person. This can be a dangerous arrangement for both.

In other words, do not overload mentors. Others in the organization have important roles to play: namely, the department chair, a short-term ally or transitional mentor, the departmental secretary or executive assistant, the dean's and provost's offices, the research contracts office, and the teaching/learning center. More information will be provided later in this chapter.

Myth #8. "In our business program, senior faculty and administrators usually express unease about providing social/psychological support to early-stage appointments. So we have to ignore this dimension and specify that the mentors at their one or two meetings per year focus solely on career advising. After all, we can't expect them to be psychiatrists. And if they focus only on career advising, then they will be treating all mentees the same—a kind of generic treatment. That's not only fair to all of our less advanced colleagues but also that behavior saves time and headaches for mentors.

> Besides, we caution mentors against anything that might be construed as 'touchy-feely.' That includes any discussion of special problems for women and minorities or ways, you know, that a mentoring relationship can 'go bad.' Focus on career, be upbeat, and treat everybody the same—that's our motto for mentors."

Embedded in this myth are at least four assumptions:

- mentors need provide only career advice, not psychological support;
- all mentees should be treated the same;
- effective mentoring can be done in only one or two meetings per year; and
- mentors are incapable of helping the mentee prepare for and confront issues concerning inequitable treatment.

I am the first to concede that mentors should not minister to mentees with intense crises nor dispense amateur therapeutic tips. Mentors should be assured that the role of therapist is off limits and that mentees with alarming symptoms should be referred to appropriate professionals for help. But important middle ground exists.

Whether mentors are extroverted or introverted, experienced or inexperienced in mentoring, they can be coached on how to help their mentees feel welcomed and valued; become connected to other peers and leaders; socialized and clued-in so they understand some of the behind-the-scenes dramas (and at times soap operas) in academe. To attain these goals, mentors and mentees must certainly meet several times each semester rather than a perfunctory once or twice a year.

But why not try to treat all mentees the same? In the first place, mentees do *not* have the same personalities and needs. Nor do they have the same generic experiences. Indeed, some receive interpersonal and situational signals within their departments that differ dramatically from those received by other colleagues. Workplace climate is not experienced the same by everyone in a unit—far from it. University of Michigan Professor Abigail Stewart, a splendid leader in the ADVANCE-NSF national program, explains that workplace climate includes subtle but powerful signs and "cues [which] we pick up that tell us we are taken seriously (e.g., included and consulted), valued, and appreciated, in contrast to cues that we are invisible, devalued, and not appreciated" (Michigan's ADVANCE website). In particular, gender as well as group membership can have significant effects on who is valued or devalued, although those in the majority group (regarded as the norm) usually have thought very little about these effects and why they are generated (see Chapters 2 and 3).

Negative gender bias and group bias often create extra problems and taxes for under-represented women in traditionally male fields (URW) and for members of non-immigrant groups (NI) namely, African American, Mexican Americans, Puerto Rican Americans, Native Hawaiians, and American Indians. Hidden penalties for them can include: under-valuing of their intellectual abilities and worthiness; doubting of their serious commitment to their profession; regular questioning of their leadership potential and "good fit" in the workplace. By contrast, members of the European-American majority group, members of "honorary-white" groups (that is, certain Asian-American and South American groups), and international scholars and new immigrant arrivals from around the world—all these are less likely to experience such extra stresses, particularly if they are males. As a result, they preserve both energy and time and enjoy what could be termed "hidden profits" (Rains, 1999) related to their sense of belonging and their steady career-advancement. The points above are dealt with in more depth in Chapters 2 and 3.

In short, while mentors should endeavor to treat each of their mentees *fairly*, they cannot and should not try to treat each of them *the same*. Context and positive or negative bias do matter. Accomplished mentors should try to understand as well as deal with the differing contexts inhabited by their mentees (Lee et al., 2007). Later in the chapter, guidance will be offered about how to make sure that mentors are comfortable and confident in examining and talking about their own contexts and those of their mentees.

> *Myth #9.* "Until about six years ago, I guess the engineering school sponsored a series of professional-development workshops during the year for pre-tenure folks. While this series was ranked as very helpful by participants, we honestly got tired of organizing these sessions year in and year out. Why can't mentees informally get the same info from senior colleagues and their assigned mentor? After all, 'our doors are always open.' Why do we have to keep scheduling workshops?"

I am always disappointed to find schools that are not offering professional-development workshops for their early-stage members. Admittedly, teaching and learning centers usually do an admirable job of offering *teaching*-related workshops (e.g., Preparing for a New Class; Handling Classroom Problems; Leading Class Discussion). But given their restricted mission, such centers rarely organize sessions for early-stage faculty on non-teaching subjects. A gap exists.

It is fundamental for early-stagers to learn about "tricks of the trade" that will increase their job success and satisfaction. And the information, caveats, and testimonials should be derived from a variety of sources, *not just* one senior mentor.

Professional-development sessions (as discussed in Chapter 5) should shed light on the following: Time- and Stress-Management; The Nuts-and-Bolts of Setting Up a Lab; Balancing Work Life and Private Life; Making Use of Family-Friendly Policies at this School; Understanding How Job-Performance Is Evaluated; Dealing with Difficult People (Patients, Clients, Students, Supervisors); Negotiating and Saying "No"; My Strategies for Getting Tenure (a panel led by brand-new associate professors); Honing One's Writing Skills; Supervising Post-Docs, Graduate and Undergraduate Students, and Interns. Some medical schools and some universities (such as the University of Wisconsin) share details about their sessions at their websites. Chapter 5 contains more details about how to organize such sessions.

In a small discipline such as geography, it is possible to run a nation-wide program for beginning assistant professors. From 2002–2007, the Geography Faculty Development Alliance, with funding from the National Science Foundation, ran a summer series of professional-development workshops in Boulder as well as a variety of follow-up seminars and panel discussions at conferences of the Association of American Geographers and the National Council for Geographic Education. A similar program "On the Cutting Edge" is run for current and future geosciences faculty by that discipline's professional societies (Solem and Foote, 2007).

In my experience, professional development workshops are more valuable if they rely on *active* learning and include: collective analysis by all participants of discussion scenarios and videotapes (showing *ineffective* versus *effective* behavior about negotiation, for instance) plus attention devoted to problem-based role-playing, interactive skits, and other active-learning techniques. Beware of power-point presentations and "talking heads" that take up much of the air time and render participants passive and keen to leave. Active learning should be the approach—and that will generate cognitive stretching, laughter, give-and-take, and community-building.

> *Myth #10.* "It is the sole responsibility of the department chair to ensure early-stage colleagues are being effectively mentored by senior members. Quality-control is <u>not</u> the business of the provost, dean, or anyone else."

For several reasons, chairs find it nearly impossible to ensure that the mentoring going on in their shop is of high quality. First, the tradition at many places is for chairs or directors to rotate every three years or so. "Just as I'm finally becoming competent as chair, I rotate out and another amateur comes in" is the way that some have sheepishly captured their experience. A primary reason for the rotation seems to be that the chairs' many duties are an add-on with little or no compensation or relief given. Is it any wonder that most chairs find they have neither the time nor the patience to coax colleagues to become mentors or to verify the quality of mentoring underway?

Inadequate coaching and preparation for chairs add to this already burdensome situation. It is disheartening to find that brand-new chairs and directors sometimes receive only one leadership-improvement workshop organized by the provost's or dean's office. Some get none. Instead, several retreats should be held every year, both for established and new leaders. But in designing such retreats, go lightly on power-point presentations because they can easily use up most or all of the time (as they spotlight new campus or hospital regulations; new data on personnel, patients, clients, and students; and the like). Such sessions tranquilize chairs and directors into quiet passivity.

Wherever I consult, many department chairs and program directors tell me that they are offered very little leadership-development and professional stretching. What do they need? More than anything, they need to actively collaborate and perhaps spar at times with their peers in workshop settings, not passively listen. Collective analysis and problem-solving are critically important. Workshops should prompt chairs to generate new ways of dealing with situations they routinely confront. Through the sharing of successes and failures and through joint practice in solving problems presented to the group, they can develop new perspectives and skills as well as acquire a community of allies to get in touch with in the future, for ideas and commiseration.

Retreats for chairs are even more worthwhile and memorable if deans and provosts (*not* their representatives) lend their support, intellect, and wisdom to the occasions. Moreover, deans and provosts should themselves participate in readiness workshops for mentors, so they are equipped in their words and actions to be advocates for mentoring. Top power-holders are clearly indispensable for sustaining a campus-wide or school-wide mentoring climate. They do this by:

- debunking myths about mentoring;
- including in their public speaking various metaphors and stories about the value of mentoring to the campus community;
- disclosing how they have personally benefitted from giving and receiving mentoring; and
- recognizing and rewarding excellent mentors.

Further, deans and provosts should designate appropriate members of their team to undertake *monitoring* to ensure that effective mentoring at the departmental level is actually taking place (details later in the chapter).

In short, mentors' value-added interactions with adjunct, research, clinical, tenure-track, and other early-stage colleagues cannot be treated in a casual manner. Junior colleagues' productivity, job satisfaction, and retention do matter—and even more so in a time of budget constraints.

SECTION B

Good Practices—Knowledge and Skills that Mentors Need to Help in Overcoming Dysfunctions

In the first section of this chapter, myths about the mentoring process and mentoring programs were interrogated. In the remainder of this publication, I want to focus on elements and approaches that mentors, faculty developers, and others only intermittently consider and employ.

Preparing Mentors to Discuss with Mentees Eight Typical Stressors Facing Early-Stage Colleagues

Sometimes mentors and chairs tell me that they don't like to bring up and discuss typical stressors that their mentees and new hires may be struggling with. The well-intentioned reason is that they don't want the stressors to become a constant preoccupation. Better to keep quiet and keep these from registering on the junior folks' radar screens, they say. I always cordially disagree. Some early-stagers, I point out, feel the predictable stresses but are shy about disclosing them up to senior colleagues. Second, others may feel chronically overwhelmed but not be able to disaggregate and name specific symptoms, tasks, and roles contributing to their general unease and overload.

For these reasons, I recommend that mentors and mentees periodically go through the list below, to see which stressors are impinging the most and what possible remedies should be tried. Think of this as a *checklist* to spur discussion and problem-solving and to take stock. More details about stressors and ways to shrink them can be found in Moody, *Demystifying the Profession: Helping Early-Stage Faculty Succeed* (2010).

1. Not enough time

This is perhaps the major stressor for new and early-stage faculty members. The stressor arises from having to manage the demanding new

170

tasks of *teaching* (e.g., course design, preparation of sessions, evaluation of student performances, unexpected classroom snags, student advising, supervision of interns in the office, lab, or field). A related stressor arises from not having enough time for *research, clinical work, scholarship, or writing* (e.g., setting up a lab or project; hiring and supervising clinical assistants and interns; refining a research plan; starting to work on new publications; establishing a writing routine; raising funds to pay for one's research). Early-stagers often feel pulled and pushed because of the hours taken up by *committee or community work*; because they do not know how to refuse such assignments from deans and chairs; and because they are confused about *what* service will be counted or discounted when their job-performance is evaluated. Almost always, early-stagers expend too much time and anxiety on teaching their courses—primarily because their graduate schools or post-doctoral institutions have not adequately prepared and practiced them for this role. Wrestling with the new teaching role easily drains energy and time from other professional functions and from private life, family, and recreation. In short, imbalance sets in.

2. Confusion and anxiety about job performance and about performance review and promotion

Annual job-performance reviews and constructive feedback from department chairs or a committee of senior colleagues are often lacking, for both part-time and full-time employees. Requirements for contract renewal and for tenure and promotion mostly seem opaque, perhaps in order to jealously preserve the subjective discretionary power held by some senior faculty. The COACHE initiative, as well as earlier national programs, repeatedly underscore this double-sided, anxiety-producing confusion for early-stage faculty in a variety of professional settings: tenure requirements remain ambiguous but they seem to become more stringent year by year.

3. Unrealistic, self-imposed expectations to hit the ground running and be prodigiously competent at all one's roles

Many professionals, when they sense they are not meeting their own standard of excellence and perfectionism, succumb to anxiety and workaholic behavior patterns. The "imposter syndrome" is likely to kick in from time to time in the new professional setting (Clark and Corcoran, 1989; Boyle and Boice, 1998). In a related manner, "stereotype threat" can affect those who have been assigned a negative bias about their innate intellectual capabilities or their innate suitability for high-powered science and engineering tasks (see Claude Steele's website as well as the supremely helpful website www.reducingstereotypethreat.org). By undermining vulnerable faculty members' and students' confidence and prompting them to become preoccupied with the stereotype, this threat can do real damage. The threat can trigger the debilitating, disconcerting behaviors/experiences of "choking" and "clutching" (to use sports analogies), and thus cause faculty and students to do less well than expected during high-stakes situations and tests. Some women and *many* NIs are vulnerable to this threat which can of course overlap with the imposter syndrome (Gonzales, Blanton, and Williams, 2002; Sekaquaptewa and Thompson, 2002). (More details about high-stakes testing in schools and colleges and their unanticipated effects are in the Appendix.)

4. Lack of collegiality

Longing for more intellectual companionship with their colleagues, early-stagers may recall the cocoon-like community they enjoyed as a graduate or professional student, a medical resident, or a post-doctoral researcher. In their old setting they probably had achieved some status—but in the new setting, they are back to being treated as novices. Cultivating relationships with senior colleagues can be frustrating because they seem bound up in their own projects and politicking. To make matters worse, there may be bullying (intellectual or personal) by a few department or institute members.

5. Personal lives suffer

Demanding roles and seemingly non-stop tasks negatively spill over into one's personal life, sometimes severely hurting family life and social and recreational activities. To make matters worse, some old-school male colleagues (whose wives took care of most duties in the home) still believe that family responsibilities are a distraction from the mandatory 24/7 total commitment to professional life and excellence. If such commitment is not displayed, the early-stage member may be regarded as inferior or as not genuinely serious about research and scholarship. We should remember that most universities and professional schools were originally built by and for European-American men of financial means; all others were excluded. The institutional structures and customs established during these exclusionary times no longer suit the lives of today's professionals.

This is why ADVANCE programs throughout the country are intent on encouraging schools to become far more *family-friendly* for female and male faculty, clinicians, and researchers. More insights can be found at the website of Berkeley Law Professor Mary Ann Mason. Also recommended are the thought-provoking publications by Hastings College of Law's Distinguished Professor Joan J. Williams *Unbending Gender: Why Family and Work Conflict and What To Do About It* (2000) and *Reshaping the Work-Family Debate: Why Men and Class Matter* (2010).

6. New pressure on faculty to constantly adopt new technology

A continually changing array of technologies will be a boon to some early-stagers but pose severe difficulties for others. Included in the array are blackboard and other teaching-learning platforms, distance-learning courses, listserves, and rapidly proliferating modes of social networking. These networks and technologies add pressure on faculty members to keep up-to-date and to respond to myriad requests on a moment-by-moment basis. In other words, here is another 24/7 task and urgent demand coming from one's students, co-workers, top administrators, and funding agencies. This out-of-control situation of course compounds one's time-management problems. Preoccupation with more and more *urgent*, immediate concerns can short-circuit one's completion of *important*, less immediate projects and activities. The conflict between urgent and important is a constant one for faculty, according to University of Michigan Associate Professor Naomi André (personal conversation, 2010) and many others with whom I have worked.

7. Increased competition to secure extra-mural funding

Several studies of funding from the National Institutes of Health and the National Science Foundation suggest that proportionally fewer research grants are secured by early-stagers, in contrast to the pattern of two decades ago. Yes, the pool of money for grants is relatively small. But perhaps also the peer-review panels (made up mostly of senior academics) favor seniors' requests for funding or for renewal of funding. Whatever the combination of reasons, early-stagers understandably feel they are in a pressure cooker. They tell me that on an all-too-frequent basis, they must direct enormous cognitive acuity and very long stretches of time to the construction of more and more grant proposals.

8. Visa and immigration complications for international scholars

International faculty and their campuses expend a great deal of energy and worry as they try to satisfy ever more complex government requirements for working and residing in this country. Government bureaucracy—enough said!

Equipping Mentors to Discuss Additional Stressors Faced by Certain Groups or Individuals

The eight stressors above are grappled with by all or almost all early-stage faculty. For this reason, I recommend that department chairs and especially mentors on a regular basis mention these stressors and then discuss with their less advanced colleagues *how exactly* they are coping and what tricks of the trade they are discovering or jerry-rigging.

Mentors, I hope, will also engage in brainstorming with their mentees, in search of yet other coping mechanisms. Such empathetic brainstorming would be invaluable. *Someone is on my side.*

For under-represented women in predominantly male fields (URW), for members of colonized, non-immigrant groups (NIs), and for those who find themselves placed in "solo situations" in their academic settings, there are usually additional pressures to deal with. The discussion below will reemphasize points which I made in Chapters 2 and 3 and will also add several new ones about the solo phenomenon being studied by organizational behaviorists. But before I begin, I want to acknowledge that some mentors are reluctant or nervous to take part in or initiate discussions touching on biases/stereotypes or solo situations, despite the huge impact these can have on some of their mentees or anyone else. By choosing to diligently avoid seeing the "elephant in the room," well-intentioned mentors blunt the positive impact of the social-psychological and career-advancement support they aim to deliver to mentees. This deliberate silence, as mentioned in earlier chapters and in the 2010 MIT report, not only personally confuses and hurts URM and NIs but also lessens the integrity and forthrightness of educational institutions themselves.

My purpose directly below is to help mentors become knowledgeable and comfortable entering into these discussions. With greater conceptual and practical knowledge, mentors would be better equipped to assist their mentees in coping with one or more of the following:

- negative, unintended *gender bias* about their intellectual abilities;
- negative, unintended *group bias* about their abilities;
- the complexities arising in a *"solo" situation* where they are one of a numerically few or indeed the only one, such as the only woman in an engineering department.

Gender Bias Against Women Especially in Science and Engineering Fields

Believing women are innately less competent than men is a pernicious assumption found in many countries and cultures. A man from the majority group is more likely to be regarded as the norm and as a comfortable "good fit" for the department. Gathering unearned advantages and hidden profits (sometimes quite unknowingly), majority males are assumed to be competent until they definitively prove otherwise; they receive the benefit of the doubt from colleagues as well as students (see Chapter 2 and Appendix; also McIntosh, 1989; Delgado, 1998). These advantages for majority males are denied to females, no matter what the women's group membership. Mentors must understand how these advantages and disadvantages play out in academic life and how their own mentees can be impacted.

In 2006, the National Academy of Sciences documented the various ways that under-represented women in science and engineering fields are shortchanged especially during peer-review processes. The Academy's *Beyond Bias and Barriers: Fulfilling the Potential of Women in Academic Science and Engineering* cites hundreds of studies about gender bias. In general, the report reminds us that careers advance when one's accomplishments are appreciated and recognized by various evaluators. But if these evaluators themselves are encased in a time-warp and automatically guided by their in-grained biases, then they will impede or, even worse, derail URM's career advancement. These evaluators will habitually and unwittingly subtract points from women and add extra ones for men. Of course, the extra points and benefits of the doubt go only (or primarily) to men who are European Americans, "honorary whites," and new immigrants from the Caribbean, Africa, Asia, and so on. Not only gender bias but also group bias will influence who receives penalties and who amasses profits (see Chapters 2 and 3).

In short, under-represented women (URW) in academic science and engineering face several cumulative disadvantages, including less mentoring than males, less inside information, less networking and inclusion in influential circles, and less positive evaluations than they deserve. Because they are viewed as outsiders whose worthiness is suspect, they will often be regarded as second-class citizens and treated in aversive, stand offish ways. They will have extra penalties and taxes to deal with, as I highlighted in Chapter 2. Mentors must first grasp these disadvantages and then take steps to help their female mentees overcome them.

Negative Group Bias Against Colonized, Non-immigrant Groups (African Americans, American Indians, Puerto Rican Americans, Mexican Americans, and Native Hawaiians)

Those who self-identify with certain stigmatized "out-groups" in this country (or who are associated by others with these groups) usually have to push against a *severe* negative bias that they are innately inferior, as I explained in Chapter 3. Struggling against the bias, or even at times a stigma, requires the investment of extra intellect and energy. The person marked with the bias will receive little or no mentoring, inside information, and benefits of the doubt; those with the positive bias will reap these things and probably feel entitled to them. Being kept on eternal probation, as opposed to acceptance as a full-fledged member of the club, is another taxing situation. These and other stressors named in Chapter 2 must be understood by mentors. If they do not, then they will mistakenly believe that their NI mentees are somehow flawed and incapable of building impressive professional careers. And the mentors will also make a serious mistake if they fail to notice that those belonging to "in-groups"—namely the European-American majority, "honorary whites," and new immigrants—enjoy a positive group bias that helps them more easily and steadily realize their ambitions.

Because of the stigma and barriers they face, members of colonized, non-immigrant (NI) groups named above clearly need to muster extra resilience and strength on both personal and professional levels (see *Sisters in Science: Conversations with Black Women Scientists* by Diann Jordan, 2006; also Travis, 2009). But besides their own self-help strategies and stamina, it is necessary for mentors, department chairs, and colleagues to take immediate and effective steps to reduce these barriers and stigma. Obviously, the attempt to treat all new hires, early-stagers, and mentees the same is neither feasible nor wise. Instead, each person's context and standing in the academic workplace must be taken into account by mentors, chairs, and colleagues if they wish to be effective coaches.

"Solo Situation" in a Department: Extra Stressors

Solos are those who find themselves in a setting where they are the only one or one of a numerically few of their group—such as a woman professor in a male-dominated business department or a NI member in a majority-dominated setting. Management professor Rosabeth Kanter first described the bewildering and stressful dynamics that numerically few women (whom she called "tokens" in "skewed-ratio" businesses) can find themselves trapped in (1997). Her findings have been verified in academe. Scholars predict that typical organizational dysfunctions will occur and will confuse and harm solo—unless department chairs, senior colleagues, and solos themselves take steps to short-circuit them. Further, solos themselves should be educated about the complexities—if they are not, they may tend to blame themselves. On the contrary, it is the organization itself that needs fixing. The following dysfunctions should be dealt with by mentors, chairs, and deans.

- *Heightened contrast* occurs because the presence of the solo accentuates the differences between the outsider and the majority insiders already established in the unit. Unless mitigated by the department chair and senior faculty, heightened contrast is one contributing cause for the isolation that solos often feel.
- *Being made to represent a stereotype or a group* results in the uncomfortable feeling that "I somehow stand for my whole tribe." Some colleagues and students will be unable or unwilling to treat

the solo as a complex individual. Instead, they will be fixated on the solo's group membership.

- *Heightened visibility* makes solos feel that they're always "in the spotlight." They are allowed little or no anonymity. "If I miss a faculty meeting, at least six people will ask me where I was. No hiding in the woodwork for me." And yet *heightened invisibility* also occurs: "I notice that I'm never included in important decision-making. I'm the last to know what's going on."

- *Unease, aversion, and even hostility are directed at solos* by those faculty and students who feel comfortable with and respect *only* those from their own clans (Gaertner and Dovidio, 1986; also see Yale website for more articles by Dovidio). The solo will predictably have to deal with some micro-aggressions—both intended and unintended.

- *Disrupted colleagueship* is experienced by the solo and arises from the aversion and discomfort that some colleagues feel and express (Yoder, 2002). Being denied the coaching of some colleagues can be serious for the solo: it can lead to an *accumulation of small disadvantages* that mount up and impede one's career advancement.

- *Performance pressures can be intense.* Solos usually have to work harder than their colleagues just to be judged as average—because their intellectual worthiness is suspect from the start. In short, solos are correct when they observe that their accomplishments do not "cohere" in others' consciousness as well as majority colleagues' do.

For additional details about tokens/solos go to: Rains, 1999; Kanter, 1997; Dovidio's articles, Yale website; Sekaquaptewa and Thompson, 2002; Law, 1975; Neimann, 1999; Yoder, 2002.

How Can Mentors Help their Mentees Deal with Negative Bias and/or the Solo Phenomenon?

Some form of disrupted colleagueship or aversive behavior is almost certain to occur. Mentors, therefore, should be alert to the experiences their mentees are having. Consistent slights and undervaluing by some students, patients, clients, or co-workers can be especially unnerving for a new hire. Student ratings of non-majority instructors are likely to be lower, with a few students expressing barbed, hurtful comments (Harlow, 2003; Stanley, 2006; Solem and Foote, 2007). Mentors, whenever possible, should educate their senior colleagues to these stressors and call on appropriate leaders to minimize them and to consider student ratings very carefully. I also recommend that students be prepped before they are allowed to fill out the evaluation forms. They too should be slowed down, so they can reflect on the importance of the task awaiting them.

Protection from service overload is essential. An overload of committee assignments for non-majority colleagues may occur when academic power-holders want at least one "diversity" member symbolically serving on committees (see Chapter 2; Stanley, 2006; also see the American Association of Law Schools website). Second, mentors should realize that scholarship on colonized NI groups (such as critical race theory in law schools, for instance) and on women's issues may be denigrated by some academics who view these subjects as outside the conventional canon and faddish.

Further, some members of the dominant group may believe that women or under-represented colleagues have been hired primarily or solely for the sake of affirmative action (a political reason) and have been underwritten by special funds from the provost's office. Faculty hires such as these, they believe, *must* therefore be insufficiently qualified. Because of their inadequacy, they will make a "poor fit" for the school, department, or campus. And these "poor fits" will undoubtedly pack their bags and leave very shortly (thus, a self-fulfilling prophesy can become activated, as I illustrated in Chapter 1). The 2010 MIT report on NIs verifies that a provost's extra funding is often viewed by departmental members as an enticement for the unit to hire an under-qualified woman or NI. In these cases, the perception will lead to what I call the "boomerang" effect and to severe undervaluing of the new hire. Such a start for a new career must be avoided! As I pointed out in Chapter 4 on Faculty Recruitment, I advise against using targeted funds. The odds are that the boomerang effect will be triggered.

What should mentors do if their mentees are dealing with any of these unfair perceptions or extra taxes and penalties? First, mentors should listen carefully and empathize. Second, mentors should help their mentees cope with these extra pressures and overloads. Brainstorming together by the mentor and mentee usually surfaces some helpful strategies. Third, all mentors and mentees, I maintain, should participate in at least two skill-building, readiness workshops where they will have ample *practice* in sorting through options to shrink special challenges and cumulative disadvantages. (Although I do not have sufficient space in this book, see Moody's booklet *Mentoring Early Stage Faculty in Colleges, Universities, and Professional Schools* (2010) for details about how to construct these two readiness workshops and their agendas. Moody's booklet *Demystifying the Profession: Helping Early-Stage Faculty Succeed* (2010) offers self-help tactics that solos, URM, and NIs themselves could adopt and adapt.)

SECTION C

Missing Elements in the Design of Formal Mentoring Programs

Readiness workshops, of course, are not the only important component of a mentoring program. I have discovered in my consulting visits to dozens of campuses and professional schools that organizers of mentoring programs rarely consider the multiple forms that mentoring might take. Furthermore, many key issues often receive little attention as a mentoring program is instituted. All too often, mentors and mentees are quickly "paired-up" and left to their own devices. To have an effective mentoring program, consideration must be given to overall design, execution, and assessment. Below is discussion of all three.

Experimenting with Various Modes of Mentoring

Many in academe are unaware of mentoring options. The two dimensions of mentoring (career-advancement interventions and social-psychological support) can be activated not just in a one-to-one relationship between a senior and a less advanced colleague *but also* in several other modes. The caveat is this: *Make sure that at least one attentive senior person is functioning as a mentor to one or more juniors.* Despite the benefits, for instance, of peer mentoring and writing groups, these should be treated as supplements not replacements for mentoring provided by senior colleagues.

Transitional "At-Large" Mentor (such as the Faculty Director of a Mentoring Program or an Associate Dean)

This go-to person can fulfill the confidential "buffer" role for several early-stage faculty over several months or a year, until or even after more formal mentors are assigned. In the alternative, one or more senior colleagues could be asked by the department chair to be short-term *allies* who frontload brand-new faculty members with collegial attention and several invitations to lunch with other colleagues. Chief diversity officers on some campuses serve as mentors-at-large to faculty and staff members of NI groups.

Informal or Formal Mentor

If the relationship occurs spontaneously and in an ad-hoc manner, the term used is "informal" mentoring. If the relationship is planned and a mentor is assigned by an appropriate leader or office, then the

179

term used is "formal" mentoring. As mentioned earlier in the chapter, formal mentoring is preferable for several reasons: URM and NIs are unlikely to have serendipitous mentoring offered to them; formal mentors and mentees can be encouraged or required to participate in readiness workshops that will end up saving both parties time and confusion. The workshops will also ensure that both parties are on the same page regarding ground rules, using "I" messages when disagreeing with one another, being aware of dysfunctional behaviors to avoid, and so on.

Internal Mentor or External Mentor

An external mentor is located outside the mentee's department and may even be at another institution. Because of this professional distance, mentees are far more likely to disclose hurtful and confusing "critical incidents" to an external mentor who will not be evaluating them during annual and tenure reviews. In the MIT 2010 report on the high attrition of NI faculty, the authors recommend assigning, far more frequently, an external mentor to every early-stage colleague—together with an internal mentor who is well-versed in departmental expectations. The MentorNet organization creates email-based mentoring relationships using only external mentors. At Boston College, the English Department assigns one senior *internal* mentor and then rotates the assignment *every year* up to tenure-review. While the mentee receives attention from several seniors, the internal mentors gain an in-depth appreciation of the mentee's development (conversation with English Associate Professor Cynthia Young, also Director of African Diaspora Studies, 2009).

Project-Oriented Mentor

With the guidance of faculty affairs or a research grants office, the early-stager chooses a career-advancement project—such as a funding proposal to a federal agency—to undertake over several months or longer. Once the project outline is refined and decided on, the faculty affairs office assigns an appropriate senior mentor (on or off campus) to help with the project and to provide social-psychological support. Utah State University runs such a program. Project-oriented mentoring is used frequently to improve teaching confidence and skills or to refine part of the curriculum. For instance, a teaching and learning center lines up an accomplished teacher to be a mentor for a limited time to a junior person. The two may decide to co-teach together in some manageable way or collaborate on a small project related to incorporating a new issue into an introductory course. Many community colleges routinely assign a friendly senior person to be a hands-on teaching mentor to a brand-new hire.

Group Mentoring

A senior colleague agrees to be a mentor to several mentees. All meet to share experiences, confusions, tips about time-management, and so on. While the mentor also meets one-to-one if a mentee wishes, most of the mentoring takes place in the group setting so that the benefits to the mentee flow from both her/his peers and the senior expert. At Rice University, the ADVANCE program for gender equity lines up two female assistant professors to be mentored by one tenured faculty woman (see Rice's website). The mentoring program at Michigan State's School of Human Medicine likewise employs group mentoring, with one group headed up by two seniors specializing in clinical, two in basic sciences, and two in behavioral (conversation with mentoring program director William Anderson, Professor of Medical Education, 2008). The University of Illinois-Chicago, according to its website, has begun experimenting with group mentoring.

Mentoring Networks, including Peer Mentors

Several ADVANCE campuses (that is, recipients of large institutional-transformation grants from NSF, to advance gender equity in science fields) have reaped success by combining group activities with mentoring attention for female science faculty. Typical components include: informal get-togethers and brown-bag lunches for junior faculty where senior allies sometimes speak and lead discussion; peer support groups solely for junior faculty; career counseling sessions run by experts; modest financial assistance so that junior faculty are in the enviable position of identifying and then bringing to campus one or two senior experts (and prospective mentors for themselves) to speak at forums. For more details about similar mentoring initiatives see Sorcinelli and Yun (2007). At Connecticut College, a productive year-long seminar for incoming tenure-track faculty is provided by peer facilitators (second- and third-year faculty) as well as by both the director and faculty fellow of the teaching and learning center (Reder and Gallagher, 2007).

Groups for Writing Support and Peer Mentoring

As mentioned earlier in this book, the University of Virginia's "Professors as Authors" program enables both junior and senior faculty to hire writing and editing coaches. Grant recipients participate in several retreats during the year, to share their work-in-progress. Inevitably, these interactions lead to new collaborations, serendipitous mentoring, and supportive networks. Grinnell College has an Early-Career Faculty Group that features: peers' helpful and tactful critiquing of one another's

181

manuscripts; conversations at times with senior professors about key milestones toward tenure review; assistance to adjunct faculty colleagues who wish to position themselves for tenure-track posts; and monthly weekend getaways (with rotation of kid-sitting), frequent pot-luck dinners, and Friday-afternoon "decompress" sessions. A long-term support group is vividly described in Daniell (2005).

Zone Mentors

Michigan Tech Graduate School Dean Jacqueline Huntoon (also a geology professor) recalls that three key faculty in her department informally "took me under their wings when I arrived, and each of them spent time chatting with me on a regular basis about what I was doing and how it would either contribute to or detract from my efforts to get tenure." One mentor was the research guru and included Huntoon as a co-Principal Investigator on a project. A second focused on teaching, and the third (a woman professor) gave her political advice about succeeding as one of a very few women on campus (conversation, 2008).

Search Committee Evolves into a Mentoring Committee for the New Hire

Because a search committee often will know the new hire better than others in the department, it makes sense for committee members (if circumstances permit) to continue on as the first-year mentors, either informally or formally. While newly recruited provosts and campus presidents have routinely benefitted from such year-one support, I notice that hiring departments increasingly ask their search committees if they would undertake this role for new colleagues.

Enhancing the Quality of the Mentoring Relationship: Pointers for Mentors and Mentees

Whatever particular form(s) mentoring takes within a department or campus, I have often found in my consulting practice that certain potentially useful strategies and practices are often missing. Those designing mentoring programs as well as mentors and mentees themselves might take heed.

Frontloading—Start Early; Avoid Keeping a Mentee on Probation

Frontloading brings dividends for the future. From the beginning, mentors should convey positive signals and high expectations for success. Avoid the temptation to keep mentees on probation until they prove themselves worthy of attention. Instead, take the initiative in the relationship and resist the inner voice that whispers, "Wait, I might be seen as patronizing if I offer to do that for/with my mentee." Do not wait for a major problem to occur before engaging with your mentee. As a mentor, you possess the experience to help mentees put disturbing problems-in-the-making in perspective as well as engage in brainstorming about options and remedies. Remember that early-stage faculty, especially NIs, decide relatively *early* to move on, if they meet a series of hurtful incidents in their workplace. You, as a mentor, can help stop the revolving door (Morena et al., 2006). In Chapter 5 on Retention, I gave the same advice to department chairs: get in the habit of "frontloading" new hires and early-stagers so you can short-circuit the operation of the revolving door.

Ask about Hurtful or Confusing "Critical Incidents"

It would be amazing if an early-stage co-worker did not hit some snags—in the classroom, clinic, lab, or field and in interactions with colleagues, patients, students, or clients. A mentor, especially an external one who will not be evaluating the mentee for contract renewal or tenure, can light-handedly ask about these incidents from time to time (or together, the mentor and mentee can review the typical challenges for early-stagers in Section B). When some new colleagues experience a series of hurtful incidents (as I already mentioned), they decide pre-maturely—sometimes even in the *first* semester or *first* year—that their department or campus is not a place where they will be able to thrive.

To prevent this rush to judgment, an empathic mentor can encourage the mentee to talk about difficulties and thereby reduce their hurt and significance (see Boice "Turning Points," 1991). It is important for the mentor to be calm when hearing about these incidents and not rush to dismiss, deny, or solve them. Instead, help the mentee process them. And finally, the mentor should resist the habit of soliciting only good news from the mentee such as "I bet you're doing really well, right? No big problems, right? I'm guessing that you've got smooth sailing."

Disclosure by the Mentor Can Build Trust

I always recommend that mentors, by the third or so meeting with a mentee, disclose a painful and/or hilarious incident they lived through as an early-stage professional. Remember the epigram "Experience is what we call our mistakes"? It would be surprising if mentors themselves did not have bruises and scrapes from earlier stumbles and confusions. But they have grown stronger. This lesson of building resilience is, of course, vital for mentees. In addition, candid disclosures will show mentees that you trust them and that you do *not* live high on Mt. Olympus where inspiration (rather than perspiration) flows freely and easily.

When Arguing, Use "I" Messages

At times, mentors and mentees will disagree, perhaps fiercely. At these moments, it is wise for both of them to switch to using sentences that begin with "I" rather than "You." For instance, *"I don't quite follow what you're saying"* is far better than *"You're being obtuse again."* "I *feel uneasy when you call me dear"* is likely to be more productive than *"You're way outa line!"* And *"I'm puzzled when you show up late for our coffee meetings"* is preferable to *"You're always late and making me wait."* In this society, "you" messages are usually provocative and lead to blows, verbal or otherwise. Stay centered with careful expression of your feelings by starting with "I."

Give Constructive Feedback

Many mentors find it difficult to critique the work of their mentee, being fearful of embarrassing the mentee or creating defensiveness that might damage their relationship. Many mentees, on the other hand, have difficulty asking for feedback or, when it is offered, accepting feedback as part of their learning process. The suggestions provided below are intended to assist mentors in critiquing the work in progress of their mentees as well as to identify issues for both parties to consider as they accept and provide feedback in the mentoring relationship. (This section has been generously adapted by organizational psychologist and retired Management Professor Joan Tonn from her "Tips for Asking Questions About and Critiquing Each Others' Work" used in a graduate course at the University of Massachusetts-Boston, Spring 2004.)

- Before you begin your analysis of the mentee's work, *review the goals or objectives that the mentee was to have accomplished.* This will give you a *shared baseline* against which the work at hand can be measured. As a result, comments can be presented in the form of: "This work does not yet seem to meet Objective X. Are you still working on that part? Or have you decided that the project needs some changes?" or "Does this paper meet all the objectives you laid out for me? Let's review them again."
- *Avoid personally attacking your mentee.* All questions or criticism should be directed at the work in question; the motives of the person should not be questioned. When framing your question or statement, take the burden of responsibility upon yourself to reduce your mentee's defensiveness. For example, you could say, "I'm a

little fuzzy about what you were trying to say about that case study. Could you explain it to me in another way?" If the mentee's verbal explanation clarifies the issue at hand, you might then suggest that he/she consider using some of that language to rewrite the point to make the section clearer.

- *Avoid asking questions with a demeaning tone or intent.* Your goal is to improve the mentee's work, not to damage that person's confidence with sarcastic comments or "put-downs." Never use language such as, "Why in the world would you want to do that?"

- When formulating your questions, *tell the mentee about other people and resources* that might be helpful in his/her work. The critiquing process is intended to be a joint effort to improve the work of the mentee, not an attack that makes the mentee hunker down and blindly defend what he/she has already done. You might say, "Let's take ten minutes right now and brainstorm about how to strengthen your draft."

- *If the mentee's work includes an idea or approach that you think might be unwise, you could elicit a discussion* of whether or not to include it by asking, "What do you see as the major advantages and disadvantages of this approach?" You may find that the mentee's response causes you to change your mind about the issue at hand. Or the mentee may decide, after setting out the advantages and disadvantages in response to your question, that the approach should be changed. Or you might say, "If you focus so strongly on self-awareness variables, I'm afraid you may overlook the importance of the group. Or do you already have in mind a way to handle that problem?"

- *If your mentee seems to be doing only a portion of what he/she is responsible for* (e.g., as a team member in a lab setting), it is important for you to point out the problem in order to *hold the mentee accountable,* help the mentee develop new skills to better contribute to the team, and ensure the quality of the team's final product. You can ask questions that avoid personal attack while still raising concern about the quality of the work.

Gauging the Effectiveness of Mentor-Mentee Relationships and Overall Mentoring Programs

Regardless of how much attention is paid to the design of the program, readiness workshops, and additional skill development for mentors and for mentees, program implementers must periodically *assess* how things are going. A hands-off approach will work neither for informal mentoring arrangements nor for formal mentoring programs (Boyle and Boice, 1998). Below are some concrete suggestions for directors of mentoring program directors and for key academic staff in provosts' and deans' offices.

Secure Systematic Feedback and Help Mentors
and Mentees Stay On Course

Regularly and cordially, an appropriate person should check by phone, email, or in person to see that mentors and mentees are meeting with one another and having productive interactions. An expert on mentoring programs, Professor Felder observes, "Keep track of how the mentoring is going and make sure that it is going—most mentorships that fail do so because the mentor and mentee simply stop meeting" (conversation, 2011). It is wise to assign someone whose authority is respected to do the light-handed monitoring as well as to give assistance with speed-bumps encountered at times by mentors and mentees.

Obvious choices for providing quality-control are: the mentoring program director; the already established faculty "equity advisors" on some campuses; or an appropriate academic leader in the provost's or dean's office. Another monitoring option might be a faculty "mentoring coordinator" in each department who oversees and nurtures the development of mentoring in that unit and serves on a school-wide mentoring committee, as happens at the University of Minnesota's school of medicine (personal email from Professor Carole Bland, 2007). If minor adjustments do not succeed, then another mentor may have to be assigned in a careful, face-saving manner by the quality-controller. Do not leave such regrouping to the mentee because of his/her vulnerability in the power structure and the danger of creating bad feelings with senior colleagues.

In pursuit of feedback, perhaps ask mentors and mentees to periodically respond to questions about the two dimensions of mentoring. For instance, one expert suggests compiling five or so questions about Colleagueship, Assistance with Networking, Time-Management, and so on and asking mentors and mentees to give detailed short answers (merely checking a box can sometimes prompt misleading interpretations). Pose these feedback questions on a regular basis, beginning no later than the first two weeks of the relationship (Johnson, 2007).

As another approach, submit these questions to mentors and mentees: "What words or phrases so far capture the quality of your mentoring relationship? What is going particularly well in the relationship thus far? What needs improvement? What are you learning about yourself?" (Zackary, 2000, p. 123). Such queries spur both parties to reflect and perhaps engage with one another about their evolving relationship. A few campuses and schools ask the mentor and mentee to keep a private journal or send progress reports to the program director about the substance and personal dimensions of their meetings. Of course, strict confidentiality would have to be observed; these reports should have a narrow audience.

In short, regular feedback is necessary in order to gain a sense of three dimensions: "*process* (clear objectives and regular, purposeful meetings), *communication* (feedback, mentees being able to challenge mentors), and *outcomes* (sense of progress and development, improved networks, etc.). Such periodic evaluations are valuable tools to help ensure ongoing honesty," according to medical experts Detsky and Baerlocher (2007, pp. 2134–5). A helpful Mentorship Effectiveness Scale can be downloaded from the website of Ronald Berk, Emeritus Professor at the Johns Hopkins University School of Nursing. This scale consists of twelve items to rate from strongly disagree to strongly agree, such as: "my mentor is approachable"; "my mentor challenges me to extend my abilities."

Also essential is realistic scrutiny of a formal mentoring program in its earliest stages. "Build into the development process the expectation (and the resources for it) that an evaluation of the program within its first year will lead to changes ... there may be small or large ways that the program as designed doesn't work in the real world of your institution" (2010 conversation with sociologist Laura Kramer, former Director of NSF's National ADVANCE Program and now an independent consultant). Additionally, scaling-up should be done cautiously. Before expanding its Excellence in Diversity Fellows Program, the University of Virginia brought in external consultants who helped prevent inadvertent loss of program strengths during the scale-up stage (see Bach and Sorcinelli, 2010).

Outcomes Evaluation: Consistently Document Mentoring Program Outcomes

There are two typical avenues for structuring such evaluation: administering pre-tests and post-tests; or comparing outcome patterns of non-participants (the control group) with those of program participants.

For instance, the Sponsorship Program at Hunter College uses a pre-test to measure participants' productivity rates and self-help strategies (such as funding proposals they have submitted, articles or books published, conversations with department chairs and colleagues about their own career advancement). Measurements are done before the participants begin working with their sponsors on a funded project and benefitting from professional-development workshops. Similar measures occur throughout the program, with post-tests coming at several intervals after their "graduation." Go to Hunter's ADVANCE-Gender Equity Project website for more details as well as for updates on how Distinguished Professor Virginia Valian and her Hunter team are uncovering and remedying gender bias. New Mexico State University's ADVANCE program as well as several other NSF-assisted programs have also devoted much care to evaluation of the mentoring process.

Outcomes evaluation is done particularly well at the University of California-San Diego where its School of Medicine (SOM) started a professional-development and mentoring program for full-time, salaried SOM junior faculty in 1998. Each year, before sixteen to eighteen participants enter into the activities of the seven-month program, they rank themselves on "self-efficacy" items dealing with research, teaching, professional development, and understanding of administrative and bureaucratic functions within their SOM and clinical workplaces.

At the end of the seven months, the UCSD participants do a second self-ranking as well as another in two to four years. The SOM program directors have routinely published their findings about: the short-term, project-based mentoring provided to each participant by a carefully chosen senior SOM colleague; the orientation and professional-development workshops where attendance is required; participants' growing self-efficacy in the dimensions outlined by Bland; their improved rates for remaining at UCSD and in academic medicine (as compared with non-participants and with national attrition figures about junior faculty in SOMs); and the cost-effectiveness of the interventions from the 1998 program's founding until the present. The directors have also published the heartening short-term outcomes for under-represented NIs who have been enrolled in the program.

Now being collected are long-term data that contrast UCSD non-participants' and participants' outcomes regarding rates of promotion, publications, funding grants secured, retention in academic medicine, and so on. Those data too, in preliminary form, underscore both the program's success and its cost-effectiveness. The program was co-founded and is co-directed by SOM Professor and faculty affairs administrator Vivian Reznik and Professor Deborah Wingard, with key assistance from SOM Professor Sandra Daley who also serves as Associate Chancellor and Chief Diversity Officer of the University. (Source of details: conversations 2005-2011 with Professors Reznik, Wingard, and Daley; various articles about the UCSD exemplary program at the program website www.nclam.ucsd.edu; also regular updates posted at this website.)

SECTION D

An Effective Mentoring Program Requires Significant Roles to be Played by Provosts, Deans, and Other Academic Staff

I want to shift to the key roles that must be assumed by provosts, deans, department chairs, and other academic staff. These leaders are indispensable to promoting constructive mentoring attitudes and behaviors within departments and divisions. To do this, they must be pro-active and invest sufficient resources, staffing, and *their own* social capital. Failing to do so will mean that informal mentoring as well as formal mentoring programs are likely to fade away in just a few years. The following steps are recommended.

Special Roles for Provosts, Deans and Department Chairs

Before discussing how these leaders might be particularly helpful in creating and sustaining an effective mentoring program, let me first respond to a question often posed to me: *Should a dean, provost, or department chair attempt to be a mentor to an early-stage colleague?* As previously mentioned, my answer is: *No, they should be faculty developers but not mentors.* As stewards of their departments, divisions, and schools, these power-holders have enormous responsibilities. At times, a conflict of interest between the best interests of their units and the best interest of the junior colleague (mentee) could predictably arise—such as one school desperately needs a faculty member to write and make an elaborate presentation to the trustees next week while the mentee, though swamped with other assignments, is loath to say *no* to the chair and dean. Further, these power-holders are likely to sit in judgment on the junior person/ mentee during reviews of their job performance, tenure, and promotion. What mentees need *instead* are non-judgmental, supportive mentors in whom they can *confide* not only confusions and apprehensions but also career opportunities that may have been privately proffered to them

If their role isn't as mentors, how can these senior academic leaders be helpful to a mentoring program? Illustrations include:

- Provide assistance and training to organizers of mentoring programs so they are able to shore up and sustain formal mentoring programs already built by their predecessors. Do not appoint amateurs to do this job nor to build brand-new programs.
- To promote a mentoring climate, make sure key power-holders (deans, provosts, and chairs) have in their repertoire compelling words, metaphors, and anecdotes about mentoring (for use in their bully pulpit or in personal conversations with colleagues). New as well as established leaders should be practiced so they are able to puncture the myths about mentoring (such as "sink or swim" is the best policy; all mentees should receive the same treatment). Practice increases effectiveness.
- Remind colleagues across campus of how mentoring (both formal and informal) is aligned with the missions and core values of the department, division, and school.

189

- As a *safety valve*, maintain an ombuds office on campus that is a safe, neutral, *confidential* place where complaints and disputes involving staff and faculty can be informally discussed. Some conflicts are best handled by ombuds officials who are highly trained in conflict-resolution.
- Urge both mentors and mentees to participate in readiness workshops, whether they are entering into formal or informal relationships. In fact, provosts, deans, and chairs *themselves* should participate in readiness workshops organized solely for them and other power-holders, so they can become knowledgeable and convincing advocates for mentoring.
- Initiate discussion with colleagues and departments about how to guard against unintended gender bias and group bias which negatively affect the mentoring of under-represented women and non-immigrant colleagues as well as their job success and satisfaction. Also lead discussion about the solo phenomenon and how to resolve complex dynamics facing faculty who find themselves in this situation. Make sure to activate extra protections and extra advocates for those faculty who find themselves in vulnerable spots because of negative bias or the solo phenomenon. Don't procrastinate. Instead frontload quickly.
- Check periodically to see that there are no disparities and inequities in salaries and other resources related to gender and ethnic background in various faculty ranks. Johns Hopkins School of Medicine Dean Ed Miller admits that he has to remain vigilant: "In some departments we've had to do an acute fix" (quoted in Swingle, 2002, p. 3).
- Protect junior faculty—in particular NIs and URW—from excessive teaching, advising, service and committee assignments. At the American Association of Law Schools website, several deans share how they block overloads for vulnerable colleagues.
- Make sure a series of professional development workshops are taking place every year for early-stage faculty as well as comprehensive orientations for brand-new hires (see Chapter 5). Don't expect mentors alone to have all the answers and insights. Without these orientations and on-going workshops, the mentors will be overloaded with mentees' concerns, many of which could have been addressed in the group workshops.
- Provosts should seek evidence-based documentation (as opposed to broad assurances and lip-service) from chairs and deans in their annual job-performance reports: How are you *specifically* cultivating a mentoring climate and verifying effective and widespread mentoring?

- Provosts' or deans' offices should be substantially involved in *monitoring* the existence and effectiveness of mentoring relationships. Because mentoring is an investment that appreciably strengthens and enriches an institution, the highest academic officers must make sure that quality-control is a key element in the mentoring enterprise.
- Further, consistency of mentoring should be the goal for all divisions and subdivisions on campus. It is unjust for provosts and deans to look the other way and allow a few units to do little or nothing. The early-stage faculty members in those do-nothing departments are put at a serious disadvantage. I maintain that *all departments, with the assistance and enforcement of provosts and deans, can and must reach a minimum level of mentoring effectiveness.* No excuses accepted.

* * * * *

We know that effective mentoring of early-stage faculty heightens their job satisfaction and success. We know that mentoring is *essential* for under-represented women in male-dominated fields (URW) and *essential* for non-immigrant, colonized group members (NIs), given the extra taxes and stressors that these "outsiders" often encounter. Campuses and professional schools will reap benefits for their faculty and students, justify their considerable investment in faculty hiring, and advance their long-term institutional interests by making sure that mentoring is being done—and being done effectively.

CONCLUSION AND NEXT STEPS

In closing I want to make several action recommendations, although, of course, I have taken the liberty of doing this throughout the book.

1. Practice Makes Stronger Leaders

As a consultant, I increasingly give campus leaders realistic exercises regarding what they might do and say when they hear a line of resistance or confusion regarding faculty diversity. Then we sort through ways to strengthen and enrich their responses. By engaging in practice drills and readiness exercises/quizzes/demonstrations, campus leaders should be able to *quickly* push back and *disarm* typical lines of resistance and confusion (see below). Participants in these practice sessions might include: campus presidents, deans, provosts, department chairs, faculty affairs specialists, chairs of trustee boards, diversity officers, and faculty senate presidents.

I recommend such readiness. Others on campus could assist by constructing relevant exercises and guiding practice drills; those assisting might include the chief diversity officer, communications experts from the management school, and hard-nosed cross-examiners borrowed from the law school. The Discussion Scenarios included in the Appendix should prove useful for structuring drills and exercises.

2. Prepare to Disarm Typical Resistances and Push-Backs

Leaders should gird themselves so they are ready to wrestle with typical myths and forms of resistance that arise during efforts to diversify the faculty. Below are ones I often encounter. They must be confronted and disarmed by a wide variety of student, faculty, and administrative leaders.

- Diversifying means we'll just have to lower our standards (Excellence vs. Diversity).
- Being color-blind and gender-blind—that's the only fair way to be. We shouldn't be conscious of someone's gender, race, or ethnicity.

- Treating everyone the same—that's the only fair way to behave.
- Counting immigrants and international faculty—they're diversity hires too.
- Arguing the "supply problem"—women as well as domestic, under-represented "minorities" are few and far between in our fields.
- Maintaining that the bad old days are over—neither I, my colleagues, nor anyone I know are bigoted, biased, and prone to saying mean things.
- Fostering elitism—our hires have to possess degrees from a special list of credentialing campuses.
- Striving for the "best and brightest"—we must always strive to hire the very best we can.
- Defining "good fit" as being sure the new hire fits into "the way things currently are." What's wrong with that? We want to feel comfortable with the new person and want him/her to feel comfortable with us.
- Contending that diversifying the faculty will violate the U.S. Constitution or several laws—many strategies we will have to use are "illegal, pure and simple."
- Insisting that group bias/group stereotype is irrelevant and ignoring extra privileges accruing to certain groups. In the United States, *every* individual must work hard in order to succeed. Rugged individualism is what brings success, and it's what built this nation.
- Maintaining that there are no contaminants in our search and evaluation processes. All of us pride ourselves on being critical thinkers I don't notice any biases or errors or shortcuts that would disadvantage people from certain groups. Of course, I admit that our committees are always rushed.

Learning to respond quickly and substantively to these lines of confusion and resistance would be a step forward. Some parts of this book, I trust, have given power-holders useful ideas and strategies to ponder and enact.

Other publications can also be mined for ideas. Below are several examples. Any of the following could also be collectively discussed by a campus president's cabinet or included in faculty reading circles.

- Allan Johnson, 2006, especially Chapter 9 where he shows how resistors can choose to blame the victim, deny and dismiss, or profess to being "sick and tired" of hearing about the problem.
- Ira Katznelson, 2005, for his unforgettable discussions of how the G.I. Bill and other affirmative action programs were reserved exclusively for European Americans and thereby immeasurably deepened the plight of non-immigrant groups.

- Richard Tapia, 2007, especially where he explains why immigrant and international faculty at times have low regard for non-immigrant faculty and students; disassociate from them; and discount their hardships in this country.
- Frances Kendall, 2006, especially where she explains how the protest that "I'm colorblind" can be viewed as a majority person playing the "white-supremacy card."
- Jeff Hitchcock, 2002, for numerous insights on the color-blind concept.
- Tim Wise, 2008, for lively history lessons and personal anecdotes about the treatment of different groups in this country.
- Karen Brodkin, 1999, on how immigrant Jews became "white" and part of the U.S. mainstream.
- Eduardo Bonilla-Silva, 2006, on how group inequalities can be reproduced even though there are no overt racists leading the charge.
- Beverly Tatum, 1997, especially on how silence about the separation of ethnic groups (especially the shunning of non-immigrants) makes the problem worse.
- John Humphrey, 2002, especially on ways that a majority business manager can light-handedly insist that customers accept the professional validity of a non-immigrant employee.
- Claude Fischer et al., 1996, where the reader is shown how caste-like inequalities in this country are sustained.
- In the Appendix to this book are excerpts and insights from other authors, which explain how several caste-like features still unfortunately characterize American life.

3. Can We Talk? Interrupt the Silence

I recommend avoidance of the words "minorities," "Hispanic," "race," and a few others, and I explained why in the beginning of Chapter 3. Using hyphenated terms such as European-American, Mexican-American, Chinese-American, and so on can keep our focus on ethnicity and group membership. Am I saying that we should avoid talking about race? No. But I am saying that hyphenated terms seem to allow us to talk with more clarity and ease about certain groups' advantages and other groups' disadvantages, generation after generation.

Trying to be color-blind is the wrong way to proceed. I believe that becoming *more* conscious and *more* informed about various ethnic groups is the better avenue. For instance, what are the political and historical inequities that have been endured by non-immigrant groups, namely African Americans, Mexican Americans, Puerto Rican Americans, Native Hawaiians, and American Indians? How are these groups, in varying degrees, under-represented in some areas of society and over-represented in others? How are *immigrant* groups similar and dissimilar to one another—namely European Americans; "honorary whites" (certain educated Asian American subgroups; educated newcomers from Central and South America as well as Africa); and finally brand-new arrivals from the Middle East and elsewhere.

Are some groups *over*-represented relative to their share of the population in the following areas: higher education (in the roles of students, faculty, and administrators), in high-paying business posts, in the learned professions, in conventionally desirable occupations? If so, then we should try to find out what the reasons are rather than choose silence (perhaps silence means we secretly assume genetics and innate intelligence are the major reason). On the contrary, the reasons for over-representation are centrally related to the possession of social capital (Stanton-Salazar, 1997, 2001), marketable skills, business know-how, tightly-knit support networks and mutual aid societies, literacy and education, strong allies who can pull you up the ladder, and so forth. I totally agree with Hollinger that more of us should study *why* certain groups are *over*-represented—it will teach us a great deal ("Rich, Powerful, and Smart," 2004; also 2011). Probing and cross-examining only those groups *under*-represented in the learned professions, for instance, seems intellectually lop-sided. Perhaps this pattern of scrutiny signals academia's deferential protection of the "haves" as well as its comfortable indifference towards the "have-nots" as subjects for study.

Spelman College President Beverly Tatum encourages educators across the country to talk with their students about group relations and power dynamics. Many times, Tatum has observed, both faculty and students try to gloss over systemic injustices based on group membership and social position. This widespread denial stems from being taught to regard this country as a fair, free, and equal-opportunity society filled with rugged individualists (*Why*, 1997, p. 16). Yes, the faculty and students will admit that there have been a few mean bigots from time to time, especially in the Southern states, but they find it hard to understand that a "system of advantage" can seemingly operate on its own, without the intervention and manipulation of ugly bigots. The concept of an interlocked system of disadvantages/advantages is *exactly* what that we need to *make clearer* to our students and our faculty colleagues.

Unfortunately, those who assert that color-blindness is the best way are usually the same people who want to silence talk about such an interlocked system. Their view is that the injustices of such a system are long gone—so let's stop talking about all this. Remember the defense strategy mentioned earlier: "look, I am so sick and tired of hearing and talking about these problems. Can we just move on?" At the University of Pennsylvania, Professor John Jackson observes: "I teach quite a bit about race and religion, both of which are hot-button topics, growing more and more controversial by the semester." When he talks about race issues, he repeatedly notices that "for many people, any talk about race at all is [itself] an example of racism." In other words, let's move on. "This idea," continues Jackson, "that race talk is an instantiation of racism (nothing more) can mean that a curricular offering on the topic is only ever a venue for preaching to the choir and supposedly damning the unbelievers" (2010, p. B2).

The push to be silent about a system of advantages/disadvantages is disappointing and even dangerous. What should instead happen is a breaking of the loud silence. As I described in Chapter 5, several medical society leaders are urging that teaching hospitals and medical schools organize forums where group and gender stereotypes can be candidly discussed. Further, these forums should help participants grasp in detail how positive and negative stereotypes, on a 24/7 schedule, influence who receives hidden profits and who hidden penalties in various venues and work settings. Finally, the forums should underscore that acting as if we don't see the elephant in the room is dishonest. Closing our eyes and minds to the entire subject sets up a crazy-making situation for those pushing against a negative group bias every day in the surgical room, the classroom, the corner office, the lab, or elsewhere.

4. Change Agents

Creating what I call a "cadre" of faculty advocates for campus diversity is another move I recommend. As mentioned in an earlier chapter, several ADVANCE-NSF campuses form cadres of equity advisors to assist with preparation of search and tenure-promotion committees and to be advocates for group and especially gender equity. The University of Michigan's STRIDE group—a cadre made up of senior STEM professors, most of whom are European American—has proved especially effective and influential on their campus.

This group "harnesses the knowledge and social capital of individuals with a track record for effective problem solving." After these savvy insiders undergo training to become effective as change agents (or "organizational catalysts"), they are ready to promote greater gender equity on a routine basis. They do this in private conversations (and perhaps arguments) with colleagues and also in formal sessions where they help educate committees, deans, chairs and others not only from their campus but also at times from other places (Strum, 2007, p. 265).

5. Chief Diversity Officers on Campuses: Build a Faculty Cadre

At many campuses where I consult, I meet with new diversity officers. I learn of their myriad duties in interacting and problem-solving with students, staff, faculty, top administrators, college and university trustees, and even community and political leaders. Not surprisingly, I sometimes brainstorm with them and their Diversity Council advisors about campus problems (both omissions and commissions) that seem thorny and at times intractable. What I always recommend to the diversity officer is this: build and continue to enlarge a *cadre* of faculty advocates for diversity. One way to do this is to invite in two or three preferably *senior* faculty per year (on a rotating basis) to work part-time with you and the provost on diversity issues. Then rotate out these leaders and bring in fresh ones. The greater the number of faculty who hone their skills and get practice at disarming lines of confusion and resistance (mentioned above), the better for the short and long term. The National Association of Diversity Officers in Higher Education at its website provides more information on the several types of officers and the varying scope of their duties.

6. Keep Peer Review on the Hot Seat and Push Against False Precision

Analyzing peer-review practices should continue at federal funding agencies and especially be *launched and methodically pursued* at educational institutions. Thanks to cognitive scientists, we now know that evaluators are not as even-handed and opinion-free as they imagine themselves to be. We know that search and other evaluation processes can be rushed and contaminated with errors and biases, as I showed in Chapters 1, 2, and 4. Non-immigrants and under-represented women can be easily and disproportionately shortchanged. Antidotes for these biases and contaminants do exist; they should be prescribed and taken at campuses and professional schools.

While the ritual of peer review in académe is familiar, it is not necessarily benign. Professors, researchers, and administrators possess distinctive cultural backgrounds, specialized training, diverse motivations, varying degrees of gender and group bias, some blind spots, probably deeply felt values, and undoubtedly one or two quirks. They do not leave these intellectual and psychological possessions behind when a handful of them enter the peer-review chamber. While regarded by many in society as objective seekers of knowledge and of new solutions to problems, scientists actually are not geniuses dressed in white coats who sequester themselves and work in sterile confines (Chubin and Hacket, 1990). Agreeing with this, medical expert Groopman has warned that we are misguided to think of doctors as dispassionate and all-knowing seers. Ambiguity and complexity can be vexing for them; medical diagnoses and decision-making can be flawed by their shortcuts and preventable errors (2007).

Underway are several studies to determine how "prestige affiliation" threads through peer reviews in numerous fields. Let me mention two recent studies. From 2000 to 2005, several collaborators studied the acceptance rates for abstracts of conference presentations that, if chosen, would be granted formal space and time at the annual meeting of the American Heart Association. In 2002, totally blind peer review was adopted: *no names and no information about institutional affiliations appeared on the applications.* The switch immediately allowed the acceptance of far more abstracts "from [authors located at] non-American institutions and [from authors at] less prestigious U.S. ones" (Guterman, 2005, p. A19). Totally blind review would also predictably increase journal publications of worthy articles written by community college faculty, adjunct faculty, and anyone else located in a non-university setting.

Prestige is very important in peer review. A letter of support for a candidate—if written by someone affiliated with a high-status institution—can carry enormous weight for humanities and social science peer review panels. "Quality by association" means the letter-writer's prestige is used as a proxy for the candidate's worthiness. Not bothering to read the letter, some panelists quickly focus on what they most value: prestige (Lamont, 2009, pp. 164–65).

The results of other blind-review analyses, as mentioned earlier in this book, suggest that positive and negative biases have been lurking in many past evaluations. If peer reviewers are told the group membership or gender of an applicant, they are very likely to grade the *same* article or grant proposal as "higher quality" if they believe the author is a male and a European American or an "honorary white." There have to be blocks to prevent corrupt decision-making and automatic excluding of some and welcoming of others. Gender, group, and prestige-affiliation biases need to be arrested.

We academics must be cautious about ratings based on peer-review processes. Deliberations can be riddled with opinion and likes and dislikes. For instance, looking for "elegant" or "excellent" grant proposals, journal articles, and fellowship applications usually depends on an evaluator's intellectual tastes and preferences. Indeed the term "excellence" and exactly what that means to different people in the same discipline (let alone in different disciplines) is usually *slippery and amorphous.* These topics are astutely discussed by Professor Michèle Lamont in her 2009 publication *How Professors Think: Inside the Curious World of Academic Judgment* (the title is close to *How Doctors Think,* Groopman, 2007). Concentrating on peer review committees in humanities and social sciences, Lamont found the deliberations of panelists to be at times worrisome and very subjective. Clearly, the evaluators are not "holy spirits" who can perfectly rise above their own self-interest and ties to friends and professional networks they hold dear. Further, Lamont shows how nebulous and personally subjective are panelists and most of us when we insist, over and over again, that *excellence*—pure and simple—is our goal.

In short, during academic processes of peer review, evaluation, and decision-making, there is much room for immediate improvement. We need checks-and-balances, ground rules, process monitors, checklists, and cognitive training for all involved, as I outlined in Chapter 4. Faculty diversity will benefit from these protocols. This is because "the" meritocracy at our institutions is in flux. What is meant by academic excellence and "the" meritocracy will depend on the speaker and her/his personal opinions, intellectual bents, and professional context and standing in the institution. Meritocracy and excellence are in a state of becoming. So too is faculty diversity.

False Precision

In academia, false precision based on numbers worries me a great deal. In Chapter 1, I suggested that pre-mature ranking of candidates, applicants, students, and colleagues is the major avenue for arriving at false precision. Moreover, many college and graduate school admissions officers perennially deal in false precision. These officers continue, decade after decade, to use pseudo-objective standardized test scores (SAT, GRE, and so on) despite the dozens of studies demonstrating the invalidity of those rushed, paper-and-pencil tests. In the Appendix is further discussion of how these tests do great harm to many women, low-income students, and non-immigrants. But the tests do in fact succeed in rewarding those already advantaged (just as legacy admissions do). I totally agree with computation and applied mathematics professor Richard Tapia who says that numerous campus officials are reckless when they use test scores to make decisions about admissions, financial aid, and so on. "The misuse of standardized tests, in particular the SAT and GRE, is the under-represented minority's *worst enemy* in gaining admission to college" (2009, p. A72).

7. Let's Worry—Then Act

Finally, I recommend that more faculty, administrators, trustees, students and student leaders, faculty senates, and other bodies come to worry (as I do)—about the caste-like elements existing in this imperfect but beloved country of ours as well as in our varied academic communities.

This book has shown that members of non-immigrant groups often struggle against being labeled and treated as stunted in intellect. Their contributions to academe could be so much greater—if they were invited to sit at the table as full participants. We must do something about this state of affairs. I recommend: first worry about the issues raised here. Then act.

APPENDIX

The first four entries in this Appendix amplify conceptual points made in Chapters 1–3, primarily points on how caste-like elements have been and are *currently* being reproduced. Non-immigrant colonized groups are the subjects of these four entries.

The last and largest part of this Appendix contains several Discussion Scenarios which are designed to serve as Practice Exercises for readers and groups. More information about how to use these Scenarios will be provided at the beginning of Appendix E.

A. A Colonized Group in Another Country: The Same Caste-Like Pattern
B. Imprisonment of African-American Men: A New Caste-System Invented in 1980
C. Caste Systems
D. Reproduction of Group Inequalities through Standardized and High-Stakes Testing
E. Discussion Scenarios—Practice Exercises for Readers and Groups

APPENDIX A

A Colonized Group in Another Country: The Same Caste-Like Pattern

Are we the only country where colonized, non-immigrant groups can be found? Unfortunately, no. Looking to another part of the world will give us valuable cross-cultural insights. It may be surprising to learn that Koreans are treated as involuntary, *colonized* people within Japan, despite the popular notion that the two Asian cultures and peoples are physically similar in many ways. While Koreans who choose to settle in the United States, China, or elsewhere enjoy *immigrant* status, in Japan they have a far more difficult status. They are stigmatized and viewed as inferior because of their past history as conquered subjects, at the hands of the dominant Japanese. Their treatment in Japan parallels that of African Americans and other non-immigrant groups in this country.

In 1910 Japan colonized Korea and quickly and systematically began to suppress the Korean language and culture. Hundreds of thousands of Korean men "were dragooned to work in mines and factories" in Japan; Korean women and girls were kidnapped to work as "sex slaves" for the Japanese military (Brender, 2001, p. A40). While that sad time is past, the Japanese are still brought up to treat Koreans living among them as *outcasts*. In schools in Japan, Korean students face low expectations and discrimination from Japanese teachers and contempt from Japanese students. The Korean culture is portrayed as unremittingly inferior in Japanese textbooks. As adults, Koreans face the same discrimination and negative mind-sets from the majority group: They cannot complete for desirable jobs in Japan on the basis of their training and abilities and have an almost impossible task in economically advancing themselves. In fact, in order to get jobs or rental housing, many Koreans adopt Japanese names with the hope that they will "pass" for Japanese (Y. Lee, 1991, p. 155; also Brender, 2001).

The following summary captures the essence of what a *colonized* group and its succeeding generations must deal with:

> *Members of a minority, many of whom were brought to the country as slave labor, are at the bottom of the social ladder. They do the dirty work, when they have work. The rest of the society considers them violent and stupid and discriminates against them. Over the years, tension between minority and majority has occasionally broken out in deadly riots. In the past, minority children were compelled to go to segregated schools and did poorly academically. Even now, minority children drop out of school relatively early and often get into trouble with the law. Schools with many minority children are seen as problem-ridden, so majority parents sometimes move out of the school district or send their children to private schools. And, as might be expected, the minority children do worse on standardized tests than majority children do.* (Fischer et al., 1996, p. 172)

Most readers would guess that the group being described in this passage are African Americans who were brutally dragged to the United States as slaves. In fact, the above details prototypically describe *any* colonized group in any society. The passage, actually a composite portrait of *Koreans living in Japan*, appears in a book written by several Berkeley sociologists (Fischer et al., 1996) and arises from studies by Y. Lee

(1991), C. Lee and DeVos (1981), and Rohlen (1981). The passage could be applied, in general, to involuntary groups wherever they are found.

To this day, Koreans attending Japanese schools are treated as a conquered and despised people. The educational credentials they manage to earn do not bring them proportionately rewarding jobs (Bruner, 1996). In fact, the higher the Koreans' educational attainment, the less their financial pay-off. Less than 10 percent of Korean college graduates manage to find employment in Japanese companies because the discrimination barrier against them is so impenetrable. About 50 percent are employed in financially shaky and small companies owned by Koreans. The remaining 40 percent work as laborers, inherit their families' modest businesses, are self-employed, or unemployed (Y. Lee, 1991). In short, Koreans are trapped in inequality, not only educationally but also socially and financially, in the land of their colonizer. This is the *prototypical* situation for caste-like groups, including African Americans, Native Americans, Puerto Rican Americans, Native Hawaiians, and Mexican Americans in this country. But immigrants from Asia are not within that caste-like group.

APPENDIX B

Imprisonment of African-American Men: A New Caste-System Invented in 1980

In this country another tragic barrier for colonized groups, especially African Americans, arose in earnest in 1980. The U.S. criminal justice system began to "put record numbers of African Americans behind bars" (the ratio in 2006 had reached eight African Americans to one European American, with more than two million total prisoners). These prisoners are now being kept behind bars for exceptionally long sentences.

Concomitantly, the construction and running of new prisons has become a behemoth, out-of-control industry. The War on Crime (in the Nixon administration) and the War on Drugs (in the Reagan years) brought much harsher and mandatory sentences, the federalizing of formerly state-level crimes, and very severe penalties for nonviolent drug offenses, most notably for the use and sale of crack cocaine. "Criminal possession became the principal legal instrument used by white authorities to regulate the behavior of poor African Americans, despite the fact that rates of drug use are much lower in the black community compared to the white ... The U.S. achieved the highest incarceration rate in the world" (Massey, 2011, p. 46). Our incarceration rate is almost 40 percent greater than our nearest competitors (the Bahamas, Belarus, and

Russia). With only 5 percent of the world's population, the U.S. astoundingly houses 25 percent of inmates worldwide (Loury, 2008, p. 5).

Another way to view these numbers: "a young white male in this nation has a one-in-fifteen chance of being incarcerated; a Latino, one-in-ten; a black, one-in-three." While hundreds of studies show that the drug use of blacks is slightly smaller than that of whites, it is blacks by a huge ratio who are arrested for drug offenses, convicted, and jailed. This is clearly a manifestation of an apartheid system. This injustice probably stems from "our failure as a country to deal honestly with the crimes of slavery and racial prejudice and our unwillingness as a society to confront these evils directly...and to engage in a transformative type of restorative justice" (Frampton, Lopez, and Simon, 2008, p. 207).

Metaphorically speaking, prisons today are used "as a kind of reservation" where many poor African American males are removed. These men permanently occupy the lowest and most stigmatized rung of the caste system. But are these reservations necessary because the U.S. has more serious crimes within its borders than do almost all other places in the world? No. "The criminal-justice researcher Alfred Blumstein has argued that *none* of the growth in incarceration between 1980 and 1996 [in the U.S.] can be attributed to more crime" (Loury, 2008, p. 80). Loury postulates that the exceptionally elevated punitiveness (five times more punitive in 2008 than three decades ago) is perhaps a backlash against the Civil Rights Movement and the Black Power Movement and yet another expression of Jim Crow segregation (p. 13; also Frampton et al., 2008; also Alexander, 2010). Certainly the mass incarceration seems to be another manifestation of the caste-like system in this country, where colonized groups are kept at the bottom.

APPENDIX C

Caste Systems

Caste systems not only psychologically stigmatize members of the lower castes but also structurally segregate them and economically exploit them. For those at the bottom, there is no social and economic mobility but instead rigidity. Those in the majority group take steps to protect themselves from association by raising high barriers to intermarriage, integrated housing and education, and co-equal participation in the professions and businesses, especially at the middle and top levels, according to social anthropologist Gerald Berreman (1960, 1967).

In a caste system, the "superior" group has decidedly greater protection from imprisonment and far greater access to goods, services, and other valued commodities and relationships. Berreman offers a chilling summary of how broadly a caste system reaches: "The ability to influence the behavior of others, the source of one's livelihood, the kind and amount of food, shelter, and medical care, of education, justice, esteem, and pleasure—all of these things which an individual will receive during his life—and the very length of life itself, are determined in large measure by caste status." The explanation continues: "Who may be one's friend, one's wife, one's neighbor, one's master, one's servant, one's client, one's competitor, is largely a matter of caste" (Berreman, 1967, p. 50).

The majority group, according to sociologist George DeVos, predictably insists that colonized groups are innately flawed and possess "some unalterable biological, religious, social, or cultural inferiority." Conquerors probably rationalize their oppression of others in this way to somehow lessen their own culpability and cruelty. What is even worse, the dominant group sees the conquered group as contaminated. In fact, "the pollution barrier is the most distinguishing feature of any caste society," according to DeVos, who defines a caste society as a "system of institutionalized inequality." The pariah groups are considered innately polluted (the "one-drop rule" holds that one drop can be ruinous). These groups are prone to moral depravity and intellectual dullness; they can contaminate any "pure" blood line they marry into. By contrast, the superior group supposedly has purity; enormous capacity for intellectual, aesthetic, and moral pursuits; and must diligently "protect itself" from the inferior group (1967, pp. 266–67).

APPENDIX D

Reproduction of Group Inequalities through Standardized and High-Stakes Testing

Disadvantage: Due to stereotype threat, stigmatized non-immigrant (NI) groups underperform and are unfairly evaluated by high-stakes, standardized, timed tests (such as the SAT and GRE). To make matters worse, these high-stakes tests can trigger NI students' self-screening and "dis-identification" with school.

Advantage: Majorities are aided in taking these high-stakes tests by the stereotypical expectation that they will do well. Their success on such tests usually builds self-confidence for the long term, instead of triggering self-screening.

Scholastic Aptitude Test

"What did *you* make on the SAT?" This question permeates American culture, obsesses families and students, and in a real way holds hostage the entire academic enterprise, from high school on. In fact, perhaps the obsession stretches into the Beyond. A wonderful story makes it clear that one's SAT scores could be everlasting. Here are the setting and punch line, as I remember them: An old (Christian) guy, recently deceased, is stopped at the gates of heaven by St. Peter. St. Peter is quickly checking his ledger book to see if the deceased's tally of good deeds will get him admitted to heaven. The recently deceased man happens to glance down at the ledger book and incredulously says to St. Peter: *"You're kidding! You count SATs?"* SAT scores not only preoccupy gate-keepers such as St. Peter but also college admissions and financial aid committees and some employers such as McKinsey Management and Consulting Company (Lemann, 1999). (McKinsey, it should be remembered, was the primary consultant to Enron Corporation, a prominent exemplar of corporate fraud and greed of the last century.)

But the fact is that SAT, according to a score of statisticians, undergraduate and graduate deans, and psychologists including testing specialist Richard Atkinson, former president of the University of California System, has virtually *no predictive value*. In his book, Peter Sacks (1999) names more than a dozen key studies showing this failure. Even the mammoth Educational Testing Service—administering the test to two million students in 2000 (almost one-half of all high school graduates that year)—regularly issues disclaimers, albeit in tiny print, to campuses about the test's predictive limitations and the inadvisability of setting a rigid cut-off score in the admissions process. The sole scientific claim of the SAT-makers is that their test will predict a narrow target—*first year* grades for college students—but in fact it does *not* even do that. "The SAT measures only about 18 percent, an estimate range from 7 percent to 25 percent, of the things that it takes to do well" during the first year of college. An analogy would be to choose only those basketball players getting the highest number of *free throws* out of ten throws to comprise a team. This would be silly because much more is involved in playing basketball. Likewise, much more is involved in succeeding in the first and all other years of college and, of course, after graduation, according to Claude Steele, Stanford psychology professor (see the "Frontline" interview of Steele at his website).

SAT is especially unreliable in one area: The test consistently *underestimates* the ability of women and non-immigrant groups who typically succeed in college at higher rates than the tests say they "should," according to testing experts as well as practitioners such as college deans. In other words, the test is not actually a standardized test that is fair to everyone. Far from it. The underestimation of women and NI groups causes admission committees to make enormous mistakes and often prompts students themselves to lower their sails: "The evidence [from national studies] strongly suggests that students adjust their college expectations" based on their tests scores and that those receiving disappointing scores "apply to less competitive colleges and universities than their grades [and abilities] would warrant" (Connor and Vargyas, 1992, p. 20). In other words, tragic conclusions and actions flow from the test scores. "The misuse of standardized tests has been the worst enemy of minorities," maintains Rice University Applied Mathematics Professor Richard Tapia. Tapia points out that his university has established broader admissions criteria and finds that undergraduate and graduate minority and women students on his campus, despite their low standardized tests scores, do as well in their grade point averages and retention rates as those with much higher scores (2009, p. A72). (By the way, most women and colonized groups seem to be *spooked* by high-stakes testing *situations* because of the stereotypical threats and stigma looming over them, as I will discuss a bit later.)

Like dozens of other colleges, Bates College in Maine since 1969 has chosen the optional-SAT route. Doing so has made its applicant pool far more inclusive: Twice as many women as men choose not to submit their scores to the college; 60 percent of African-American students do not; *economically poor students* in Maine do not. Bates has found that it can now draw in a diverse and highly qualified group of students who do *unquestionably well* during their college careers and thereafter.

In various public forums while she was president of Mt. Holyoke College, Joanne Creighton characterized SAT scores as unnecessary "affirmative action" for affluent white students who typically score the highest (1997, p. A15), usually because in their suburban or private high schools they have taken Advanced Placement courses that help them on the test, because they have also enrolled in costly SAT-prep courses offered by private corporations, and because the stereotype of competence surrounds them during the testing situation. Someone else has observed that the *"Volvo principle"* manifests itself: every increase of $10,000 in a white applicant's parental income correlates with an additional thirty points in the SAT score. While majority students can expect to do well on the SAT, stigmatized NI students can expect to do poorly.

Graduate Record Examination

Drawing on his own professional experience in teaching and supervising doctoral graduate students, Brown University physicist Robert Brandenberger observes: "There is little correlation between GRE scores and later success as a scientist. Those being tested by the GRE must race against the clock, decide on pat answers, and do this in isolation." These test conditions differ radically from scholarly and research conditions: "Real research, by contrast, requires imagination, in-depth working and thinking with others, and grappling with questions that have no answers" (personal correspondence, 2002). The GRE is "virtually useless from a prediction standpoint," according to a meta-analysis (in the highly regarded journal, *Educational and Psychological Measurement*) of over twenty-two studies covering more than 5,000 test takers from 1955 through 1992. "When this finding is coupled with studies suggesting that performance on the GRE is age-, gender-, and race-specific ... the use of this test as a determinant of graduate admission becomes even more questionable," the authors conclude (quoted in Sacks, 1999, p. 277). National Academy of Sciences President Bruce Albert likewise disparages standardized, multiple-choice, timed tests because the tests measure nothing important and because they spoil the enjoyment and thrill of science and critical thinking for countless students, majority and non-majority (Alberts, 1997).

Tests Serve the Interests of America's Elite

Law professors Lani Guinier and Susan Sturm worry that American power-holders continue to confuse a paper-and-pencil "testocracy" with a true meritocracy. They are especially concerned about non-immigrants (NIs) and low-income majority students who predictably get low scores on standardized tests and then suffer the penalties—in academia, social life, and the workplace—as well as diminishment in their self-esteem and ambitions. The two convincingly argue that these tests function as old-fashioned *poll taxes* because of their chilling and undemocratic purpose and effect: to exclude certain stigmatized groups (Guinier and Sturm, 2001; Sturm and Guinier, 1996). Like poll taxes, standardized tests are used as a very effective—but nonetheless very unfair—screen.

Standardized tests are the foundation on which the pseudo-meritocracy of U.S. schools is built, according to Nicholas Lemann's *The Big Test, The Secret History of the American Meritocracy* (1999) and David Berliner and Bruce Normally's *The Manufactured Crisis: Myths, Fraud and the Attack on America's Public Schools* (1995). The ubiquitous testing in this country serves "the interests of America's elite, further stratifying the society by race and socioeconomic class; second, the companies that produce, administer, score, and coach for standardized tests of all types have gotten rich off the nation's testing habit," argues Peter Sacks in *Standardized Minds, The High Price of American's Testing Culture and What We Can Do to Change It* (1999, pp. 2–3).

Yet foes of affirmative action in education want the opposite: they trust in the test scores. They demand even greater reliance on standardized tests scores because they believe they are the true measure of "merit." In their view, the academic meritocracy must be built on two objective numbers and two numbers only: a student's grade point average earned from the previous educational institution and especially the student's standardized test score. In their view, the student receiving the higher number should win admission. If a student with a lower number, such as a woman or non-immigrant, wins admission, then they claim to have evidence of "reverse discrimination" against majority students. Significantly, reliance on numbers undergirds lawsuits brought by the national Center for Individual Rights and other conservative organizations on behalf of several majority students. These anti-affirmative-action cases hinge on a flawed assumption—that standardized tests are sound and tell us something important and reliable.

The All-Important Cultural Context of Tests

Stanford psychologist Claude Steele has brilliantly identified the "cloud of suspicion" and the "stereotype threat" that make African-American and other stigmatized groups *panic and slow down* as they take timed, standardized, multiple-choice tests. This panic is the very opposite of how they should proceed in order to maximize their test scores, but they typically cannot help clutching and becoming overly careful. Steele theorizes that stigmatized non-immigrants (NIs) are dealing with a *debilitating cultural context* that majority students do not have to deal with. They are all aware of the widespread belief that they are inferior in intelligence and academic abilities. Thus, as they take the high-stakes, timed tests, they fear that they will *reinforce* the negative stereotype. Laboring under such a psychological overload, they clutch and stumble and do indeed fulfill the prophecy.

As a further illustration, University of Connecticut Law Professor Angel Oquendo recalls how intimidated he felt as he took the SAT as a high school senior in Puerto Rico. In the first place, "a test that measures aptitude can make you feel insecure and challenged" (notice the *common* and tragic misperception that SAT is measuring innate worthiness). But for a Puerto Rican student, the test had another kind of psychological significance: "It symbolized America's continuing dominion and control over Puerto Rico." He realized that he "was being tested by the people who kept us [Puerto Rico] afloat with their massive economic support, who from afar made important decisions for us, and who generally were successful where we had failed" (Oquendo, 1998, p. 61; also see chapter 3 of this book). Oquendo's sensitivity about this cultural domination was heightened when he was required to complete a racial profile before the test could officially begin.

Self-Screening Because of Standardized Tests

According to school reformer Deborah Meier, the low SAT scores almost inevitably earned by stigmatized students in high school do long-term damage: "The wound to children's confidence and self-respect is enormous.... Attacking the testmakers doesn't relieve the [youths'] burden of self-doubt" (1995, p. 159). In my own work, I have observed that most non-immigrant students are predictably frustrated and demoralized because they have done poorly on GRE and other such tests. (Yet they highly motivated and gifted students.) Very few have the *chutzpah* to quickly shrug off the wound. In fact, many dramatically scale back their academic and professional ambitions, in the face of poor performance on the tests believed by most in U.S. society to be trustworthy and objective. In Steele's words, these students come to "dis-identify" with the academic domain (1995, p. 809). Physicist Howard Georgi in several public forums has explained why he too believes the GRE does enormous damage. Georgi observes that many of his talented women students at Harvard shelve the idea of going to graduate school because they both fear and despise the multiple-choice, race-against-time, "macho" character of GRE. Rather than submit to the GRE, the students choose a career path that does not involve GRE—this is another example of self-screening. Such self-screening will predictably happen at a much *earlier* age because of a new development on the horizon.

Now High-Stakes Tests for Younger Students

Throughout the country, states have been requiring high-stakes, standardized, paper-and-pencil, timed tests for all students in elementary and high school; a number of states hold back the high school diploma until the test is passed. In the face of doing poorly or even *before* they do poorly on the tests, some non-immigrant students will predictably drop out of school—a very drastic form of self-screening and self-protection. In fact, this is happening. Author of *Subtractive Schooling: U.S. Mexican Youth and the Politics of Caring* (1999), University of Texas Professor Angela Valenzuela deflates the "Texas miracle." That state's approach to testing (which is serving as a model for the nation) has caused the *drop-out rate of minorities to increase.* Valenzuela, in *Hispanic Outlook*, explains that the Houston test scores are improving largely because schools often "switch" low-performing students to special education or bilingual education tracks or use other test-exempting diversions. In the meantime, the city's drop-out rate—one of the absolute worst of the nation's one-hundred largest school systems—steadily rises (quoted in Alicea, 2001, pp. 7–10).

To use high-stakes, multiple-choice, timed tests is a *bad practice.* Such tests, purporting to measure students' intellectual worth, thicken the cloud of inferiority and stigma over certain students—and will quicken their self-screening and dropping out of high school. Misguided state legislators and school officials should find other ways to hold *schools* accountable and improve all students' learning outcomes.

APPENDIX E

Discussion Scenarios—Practice Exercises for Readers and Groups

The following scenarios are designed to help readers review and recall key points set forth in this book. Secondly, the scenarios offer practice to readers in applying some of their learning as potential remedies to problems and dysfunctions embedded in the scenarios. These practice exercises can also be used in *group settings*, such as in leadership-development workshops, in preparatory sessions for various evaluation committees, and in readiness-coaching for mentors and mentees.

Scenario #1: Faculty Search—Some Good and Bad Practices

As you read the following scenario, think about key points made in this book. Now think about how you would respond to the following questions:

1. What Good Practices (at the individual and organizational levels) do you see/infer?
2. What Bad Practices and Dysfunctions do you see or can you infer?
3. What Remedies—by whom, when, how, what—would address the Bad Practices and Dysfunctions? Be as specific as possible.
4. How effective is the Search Committee Chair in this scenario? How could he improve?

Below is a glimpse of a search committee in its early stage of work. The committee, formed by the department chair and dean, has the following members, all of whom are European-American in background: Full Professor A as well as Associate Professors B and C (men); Full Professor D (woman). The search chair is a Full Professor (man) and a veteran of search processes.

Chair: *All right, we've had two eye-opening sessions this spring on how to recognize and rise above typical cognitive errors and biases that often creep into faculty searches and other evaluations. The dean's office worked hard to make our prepping succinct and efficient. And they underscored that these cognitive errors are made unwittingly unless we are on guard.*

Professor A: *I'm not sure I'd call four hours of so-called 'prepping' efficient. Besides, I still resent that anyone thinks we would bring biases to the table or take shortcuts—or that we don't know what good practices to follow in the fall as we winnow down, interview, weigh candidates' strengths, weaknesses, usefulness to our program, and so on and so on. After all, faculty searches are not rocket science! We are simply looking for the best and brightest researcher and grant-producer. We are looking for excellence, pure and simple. I certainly know it when I see it!*

Professor B: *Well, I for one really appreciate the coaching we received. At my last institution, the three searches I served on were mostly chaotic. Our work often got clogged with personal opinions about the candidates. Plus, we were always feeling pressed for time. Being overloaded, we'd often drop back and choose the candidate with the most prestigious pedigree. You know, Cal Tech, Harvard, whatever.*

Professor A: *What was wrong with that? That's exactly what you should do. And that strategy would bolster your own department's reputation.*

Professor B: *I respectfully disagree. Most of the time the candidate we picked when we were feeling rushed didn't pan out. We decided it was a mistake to assume that pedigree would automatically insure competency, you know, in all the roles that a junior colleague has to fill. Life is not that simple.*

Chair: *I agree. Search processes are more complex than we've ever recognized. We want to be careful and deliberate and keep our work grounded in evidence. Remember what medical expert Jerome Groopman said in his lecture last week: in many occupations, including medicine, evaluators are susceptible to preventable and predictable cognitive errors. Self-correction is the name of the game.*

Professor D: *Yes, I've been thinking about what Groopman said. It was sobering.*

Chair: *Well, to enable us do our search in a different way, the dean and department chair have finally given each of us official release from one committee assignment of our choice in the fall semester. So the expectation is that we will do an above-average job, we'll be able to cast a wider net, and so on.*

Professor C: *Does 'wider net' mean that we track down women and minorities and beg them to apply? That's my translation of what the dean is urging us to do. I say we put out our standard ad and anyone can come forward and apply. No barriers there. But what I'm confused about: I thought the U.S. Supreme Court recently said 'hands off' in identifying racial minorities and bringing them into our net.*

Chair: *We discussed this topic earlier with the dean and the campus's legal counsel. Recall that we academics always do pro-active outreach to identify candidates who might not be considering us. That's why we're doing a search process rather than merely screening applications we passively receive. So why is it okay to do searching for white men and not okay to do searching for under-represented minorities or women or anyone else? Please remember that we are not making anyone an offer; we are merely contacting folks who interest us and encouraging them to apply. Everyone will have to be scrutinized and evaluated fully, as we always do. There's no guarantee of a job offer.*

Professor A: *All this talk about being 'inclusive' makes me weary. Listen, our department and campus are not discriminating against any group and or anyone. There are no bigots among us. It's just that women and minorities don't seem very interested in us. That's the bottom line. I want to stay passive and impartial so don't expect me to do any outreach.*

Chair: *I understand. Not all of us will be expected to do that. I know that two of you have already started the outreach we agreed on. All of us will be looking forward to having your reports and some C.V.s in front of us, beginning perhaps in several weeks.*

Professor C: *On another matter, I'd like to surface one problem that I had with the dean's preparation sessions. Too bad this problem didn't occur to me in the moment. I've been thinking about what I would call 'hand-holding' of final job candidates. A few months from now, we're supposed to get assistance from our department chair and then create a custom-made 'professional-development plan' for every one of our job finalists. First question: did any of us get such a plan and such attention as a new hire? Oh no. No way. Second, let's say we end up with five finalists in the home stretch. Who has the time to be signing up appropriate mentors and including perks in those plans for five people—as the dean urges?*

Professor A: *Yeah, who's going to have that kind of time?*

Professor C: *My gosh, whoever we eventually hire will have to sink or swim just like all of us had to do. You could say that I'm opposed on principle to this extra step—this 'coddling'—for any new person we bring on board. He or she will surely be an adult who can figure out what sort of professional development they need. Succeeding as a junior colleague rightfully demands rugged individualism.*

Professor B: *Wait a minute. I hear you saying that you yourself didn't have any attentive mentoring from senior colleagues. Or that you yourself didn't get any inside info about how the department worked and where the landmines were hidden.*

Professor C: *Exactly right. Sure, I went out for beers with some of the senior guys. Sure, some of them were very friendly and sometimes helpful. But I didn't have one official mentor or anything resembling an official development plan. I didn't need such things.*

Professor B: *Well, nor did I. But let's be honest. Because you and I are majority males, we got some doors opened automatically for us by our senior colleagues. Remember? We got some tips and encouragement. We got to sometimes collaborate with a heavy-hitter. Remember? Don't we want that sort of professional attention—call it what you will—for all new hires and not just for majority male insiders like you and me.*

Professor D: *I have to agree. Most majority males, I've noticed, receive demystifying info and buddy-buddy encouragement from some senior males—but they just take all this for granted and don't even think it's unusual. But if you were a woman and didn't receive this automatically, then you're be in a tougher spot. I say this as a solo woman who still feels a lot of the time like I'm an outsider looking in.*

Professor B: *Yeah, that's exactly what I was driving at. I often take for granted the benefits I get as an insider and being just one of the boys. And how about the daily energy I save, too? Back in my youth, I used to assume that everyone with drive and intelligence would get these benefits—but when my niece took a managerial job at a major airline, I quickly and sadly learned otherwise.*

Professor D: *I want to make a few more points about why a professional-development plan is a worthy experiment for us. I believe that most job candidates—but certainly not all—will be favorably impressed that our department would construct a specific plan of action for each of the finalists. Certainly, as the dean explained, we will discuss the proposed plan with each finalist and get his/her input. So when our department and dean get ready to make the hire of the one and only, we'll already have a plan designed to increase our new colleague's likelihood of success and job satisfaction.*

Professor A: *I suggest that this is totally unnecessary. Surely anyone we hire will be the best and the brightest and will not need anything resembling a professional development 'net.'*

Professor D: *Let me say that I myself would have been very impressed if a hiring department had said they would carefully construct a plan for me. Let me also suggest that many other women, minorities, and even majority male candidates would sit up and take notice. I'm not saying all job candidates will care—but most will. And this plan—this new strategy—should give us a competitive edge with our finalists because we sometimes end up frustrated when we run out of money in bidding wars.*

Chair: *Yes, I agree. The plan is an experiment, and we will construct it with our department chair's guidance and then find out the results. Let me ask: does anyone object if we take a 10-minute break?*

Now we're listening in on the <u>final stage</u> of deliberations by the same committee.

Chair: *Yes, let's look at the matrix taped up on the wall. Let's fully discuss our final candidates, one by one, and outline concretely what they bring to each category of our matrix.*

Professor B: *I wonder if we could take a moment and quickly but tentatively rank the five finalists? I guess I always feel better when I'm dealing with numbers. You know, we could finally move into the realm of objectivity. I guess my early training as an economist is showing.*

Chair: *Well, my view is just the opposite. Remember at the beginning of our committee's formation, when we adopted those dozen ground rules to guide our deliberations? One of those rules was that we'd avoid pre-mature ranking. Given that we haven't done a full discussion based on the matrix, I suggest we do this exercise first. Yes, it will take several hours but this may be the most important part of our work. We don't want to downgrade or upgrade a candidate too quickly.*

Professor A: *Okay, I have an item for discussion. Did anyone else notice how nervous and unsteady Lucia was during her first interview? I mean, it was painful. We don't need a newcomer who's scared of her own shadow. If she's timid, then she's just not going to succeed here. Let's be frank.*

Professor D: *Whoa. Wait a minute, please. Lucia was nervous only for the first six minutes of that first interview. I timed it! No kidding. And two other finalists started out very nervously. Want to see the objective numbers in my notes?*

Professor A: *Fine. Fine. Listen, I have nothing against Lucia. Let me be clear. It's just that I don't see her fitting in very well and feeling very comfortable here. Remember that one of her references, both in his letter and in our phone conversation with him, kept describing Lucia as a 'gracious colleague' and a 'steady researcher.' My gosh, that makes her sound like a lightweight!*

Professor C: *Well, I picked up on those same adjectives about Lucia. I think we're seeing a gender-bound perspective here. Here's what I mean: the referee, without intending to do so, probably underscores the personality of women candidates but he underscores the research projects and brilliance of men candidates. There are studies of recommendation letters that show this pattern clearly and* *distinctly. So I suggest that we not take these characterizations of Lucia at face value. We have abundant evidence that she is not a lightweight.*

Professor A: *Well, it's helpful to know that this pattern has been documented. For me, a very important question is: Would Lucia be happy here and succeed here? I think we are obligated to ask ourselves that question. I say probably not. Wait, wait, I see some eyebrows being raised. Let me remind you that I try to be color-blind and gender-blind in my dealings with people. I could care less if Lucia or anyone else is black, purple, brown, polka-dotted, striped, male, female, or whatever. I'm just saying that Lucia unfortunately seems to be a bad fit for us.*

Chair: *Remember our much earlier discussions about 'good fit/bad fit'? We have to give one another solid evidence about why Lucia (or any other finalist) would not be a good fit for our intellectual and departmental needs and for our students. Let's stick with the matrix in front of us and offer evidence as we walk through each category. Let's avoid playing 'bad fit' or 'good fit' as a trump card.*

Professor D: *Yes, I would appreciate our putting off the 'good fit/bad fit' weighing for a while. I have one concern about Lucia and wonder what the rest of you think about this concern. Because Lucia is very, very strong, won't she be in high demand? I mean, she told us she was Puerto Rican American in background. Because she's a non-international, under-represented U.S. minority (or whatever the phraseology is), I suspect that she'll have other places vigorously courting her. I wonder if we have even a remote chance. So maybe we should save ourselves some pain by setting aside her application? I hate to say that ...*

Chair: *Well, I certainly don't want to give up before we try. And hasn't some professor at Claremont Graduate University shown that it's a myth that domestic minorities are showered with academic job offers? Well, whatever the case, I suggest that Lucia be kept in the finalist pool. We could be a very attractive place for her, especially if we have that professional-development plan ready to roll out.*

Professor B: *Listen, is it important that Lucia would be the first and only Puerto Rican American in our department? I've been wondering about this. Remember that we have so few domestic minority faculty in the entire school. And we certainly don't have other colleagues with her ethnic background.*

Professor A: *Now that you mention it, that should probably be a concern. After all, we can't provide her with a mentor from her own background. That is a disservice, in my book.*

Professor B: *Well, we certainly don't want her to feel like a lonely 'solo' and not receive a proper welcome and support. That would be unfortunate.*

Chair: *So many items have been introduced in the past few minutes. Let's take a coffee break and return to our business here at 3 p.m. sharp.*

Scenario #2: Third Week as a New Assistant Professor

As you read the following scenario, think about how you would respond to the following questions:

1. What Good Practices (at the individual and organizational levels) do you see or can you infer?
2. What Bad Practices and Dysfunctions do you see or can you infer?
3. What Specific Remedies would resolve or at least diminish the dysfunctions?
4. If *you* had agreed to become the chair of Wade's and Chris's department, what steps would you take to help Chris? How would you handle the situation with the two disgruntled senior colleagues? Please be specific about what words and actions you might employ.
5. Let's imagine that as the new chair, you are able to assign to Chris (for his first year) a very competent mentor from *another* department. What would you want or expect this mentor to do?
6. What self-help strategies should Chris be considering?

Here is a conversation between Christopher Miller (a new assistant professor in biology with African-American ancestry) and Wade Smith (a senior faculty member in the department who has been assigned as Dr. Miller's mentor; Wade has European-American ancestry).

Wade: *Good to see you, Chris. I'm glad you waved to me this morning, as we were both heading towards the coffee shop. Sit down, please. How are things going during this third week? I've had you on my mind but I've just been overwhelmed, what with the departmental secretary ill now for a month and I myself—as interim chair—trying to resolve all the room mix-ups, delays in book deliveries, and a dozen other things, plus help the new dean set up some committees. Having this leadership role thrust upon me was a big surprise! I'm bushed right now, I have to admit. Here, please: let's try to relax. Have some coffee with me.*

Chris: *Oh, thanks. Yea, I can see that discovering you had become the designated interim chair—just four weeks ago—could be stunning.*

Wade: *Please. Enough about me. I want to hear about you.*

Chris: *Well, I'm very busy, of course, with my new lab and courses. A few colleagues have dropped by to say a quick "hi," and sometime soon I hope I'll be invited to lunch by some of them. I do have one big technical problem. I hate to keep mentioning it, given that you're so overloaded in this busiest season of the year.*

Wade: *No, tell me, please! I want to be truly supportive and help you adjust.*

Chris: *Well, I am wondering when the new computer for my office will be installed. Not having it up and running is a real problem, as I explained to you in person during the first week and then again in a follow-up phone message. I really need my e-mail connection here in the office. Should I be getting paranoid about this? I asked around and some of the other faculty said that their office equipment was totally ready when they arrived on the first day.*

Wade: *Oh, my gosh. I was told last week that your computer was all taken care of. I apologize. I promise that by the end of the week the computer center will have it ready for you. This is embarrassing. Listen.... I want to focus on another subject. Look, Chris, I need to say something. Huh, well, in our department there seem to be—no, there are—two full professors who are still unhappy that we did not recruit a computer specialist when we finally were given money for a new hire. What I mean, sorta, is that they are still unhappy we hired you—a terrific addition, no doubt about it—instead of going far afield and bringing in a computer guru who would shake up this department.*

Chris: *Well, now that you mention this, two senior colleagues seem to find it hard—if not impossible—to speak to me in the hallway. I wondered what that was about. Sooner or later, I would have begun to worry about it.*

Wade: *Well, I have no idea how to handle this situation. I think the only thing to do is let their anger wear out. So I say that we ignore the problem. I'm sure you know that many departments, from east to west and north to south, have internal spats and quarrels at times. This is academia so you just have to cope with it. I've seen it many times during my career.*

Chris: *No, I guess I don't know much about such situations. I wonder if I should have picked up on this during my campus visit and all my interviews.*

Wade: *And one more thing. If anyone grumbles about your being an affirmative-action hire, just ignore them. Listen, let's move on to something more pleasant. Have you found a colleague to collaborate with, on a research or teaching project? I know I said that would be an easy thing to here or at some of our neighboring campuses.*

Chris: *Wait. Can we come back to what you said about affirmative action?*

Wade: *Of course. Let's talk about that a bit later in our visit. But right now, tell me about any joint projects you've been able to join.*

Chris: *So far no one has expressed much interest. I mean, I myself feel sheepish about broaching the topic and sort of pushing myself on a senior person. But I really want to get into a collaborative project with one or more senior folks, because my doctoral supervisor said that all new faculty can learn so much from experienced teachers and scholars. Can you help me meet a few? What advice do you have?*

Wade: *Listen, I'll do some thinking about how I might help you with some introductions. If I can't find time this semester, then I will do it next semester. O.K.?*

Chris: *Yea. That would be great. And remember, during my interviews, the search committee said that as a new hire I would have a mentoring committee, with at least two faculty from outside my department? This, too, is something that would really get me connected to this campus and help me thrive. When might that committee be set up?*

Wade: *Well, didn't you think the campus's orientation for all new faculty was helpful?*

Chris: *Yes, but it was short and sweet and mostly about the intricacies of the pension fund. But what I really feel I need is coaching in professional development. A friend of mine in Atlanta says his mentoring committee is great— they don't shy away from tough issues and they give him handy pointers about the tenure process. I guess the committee meets with him once a month for lunch. Oh yeah, then twice a year, all the mentoring committees and their mentees—from all over campus—get together. My friend says this is really helpful and enlarges his network of allies. That's what I had in mind.*

Wade: *I think it's a great idea, as I said before. But when I talked to our new dean about it, he said that the smallness of this campus and school prohibits us—you know, from having a sufficient number of interested senior faculty to serve as mentors to new faculty. I guess this would be a lot easier at a huge university.*

Chris: *Gee, I don't know. But I do know that being a brand-new hire has its challenges. I really want to thrive here and do an outstanding job. So I will continue to hope that a mentoring committee materializes.*

Wade: *Well, Chris, I feel the same about being a department chair. I could use some mentors myself. I'm still hoping that some help will be forthcoming from the dean's office. Listen, tell me how your classes are going.*

Chris: *Well, as you know, I am keen about teaching. That's why I'm so happy to be here. My classes are going pretty well. But I did hit one big speed-bump last week.*

Wade: *Tell me. What happened?*

Chris: *Well, in the big lecture class, I guess I had assigned too much homework— compared to what other instructors have required. So maybe five students had a royal meltdown and really complained. But you know, I saw their point. In retrospect, I guess it would have been handy for me to get tuned into the typical load of homework in the department. If I had, I wouldn't have started off with unrealistic expectations.*

Wade: *Gee, I'm not sure I could have done anything to prepare you. But to tell you the truth, I'm not sure what the previous chair did regarding preparation of new hires. With the departmental secretary being ill, I am rudderless in a way.*

Chris: *Well, the good news is that I righted the ship in that class, adjusted my homework assignments, and the class and I have happily moved on.*

Wade: *Glad to hear it! A less competent teacher might have frozen or gotten defensive. I'm glad you avoided that. You're very self-sufficient. I like that! Let's have more coffee.*

Scenario #3: Conversation Between a Mentor and Mentee During the Mentee's Second Week as a New Assistant Professor

As you read the following scenario, think about how you would respond to the following questions:

1. What Good Practices (at the individual and organizational levels) do you see or can you infer?
2. What Bad Practices and Dysfunctions do you see or can you infer?
3. What Remedies would resolve or at least diminish the dysfunctions? Be specific.
4. If you were the Mentor, how would *you* propose to help the Mentee? What precautions should be taken? Please be specific.
5. What self-help strategies should the Mentee be considering? How could you as the Mentor assist in activating those self-help strategies?

Below is a conversation between a brand-new faculty hire and his assigned senior mentor from another department. Both the mentor and mentee have European-American ancestry.

Mentor: *Well, Todd, it's great to meet you. I enjoyed our brief email conversation in the summer.*

Mentee: *Susan, I just want to say that I'm very grateful that you have agreed to serve as my external mentor for a year. And getting that email greeting from you in the summer was terrific.*

Mentor: *Glad to hear that. You know, I could have used an external mentor when I started my academic career. So I was happy when the provost's office started this new mentoring program. Oh, before I forget: how's that 'zone' mentor in your department working out—the one, I think you wrote about to me, who's going to help junior folks improve their proposal-writing for research grants? That's another kind of mentor I myself could have used.*

Mentee: *Well, the zone mentoring started up last week. As I understand it, I will get some one-on-one coaching from that mentor but primarily I guess I'll be part of a group coaching situation. You know, all new hires and junior faculty will be invited to meet sometimes with the zone mentor. So I'm guessing that this arrangement will enable me to get to know most of the junior faculty in my department pretty well.*

Mentor: *Hey, that's handy. Good to hear all this.*

Mentee: *And I want to say that it's great to have you in my corner. I really mean that. But I do have one request. Because I'm sort of frenetic in meeting all my obligations during this first semester and I'm guessing it will only get worse, I wonder if it would be wiser for us to start meeting regularly next semester. I don't know how focused I'm going to be for these first few months. I'd hate to be a drag on you. And I know the provost's office is going to do some monitoring of how our mentoring relationship is going. What I'm saying is that I'd hate to be pre-occupied or whatever and cause us to look bad.*

Mentor: *Oh well, I think almost all new hires experience a kind of dizzy, out-of-control sensation. I guess I'd worry if you didn't feel some of that! But this first semester is exactly the time we should meet conscientiously. I'll have some tricks of the trade to share that should help you deal with the overload you're experiencing. I personally think that every new hire should have a reduced teaching load in their first year. But this campus is not yet that enlightened… and lately we just can't afford it!*

Mentee: *Yes, a reduced teaching assignment would have really helped. But thank goodness, my department chair did assign me two sections of the same course. That saves me considerable time. And during the summer, he and the departmental secretary sent me some materials (you know, sample syllabi, student grading guidelines agreed on by the whole department, and so on). Those really reduced the mystery for me and helped me plot out my own plans for the year.*

Mentor: *That's good to hear. Listen, have you started building some sort of working relationship with your chair? Let's talk about that for a few minutes.*

Mentee: *Oh yes, he and I met briefly for the first time last week. He was very cordial. But, well, I am a bit puzzled by one thing. At the end of our meeting, he mentioned to me that there's some sort of 'storm cloud brewing.' Those were his words. And it seems that maybe I'm in the middle of that storm or something like that.*

Mentor: *Really? Okay, let's hear some details. Confidentially, of course. Remember that this summer we agreed to the ground rules that will guide our mentoring relationship this year? Confidentiality is a key one.*

Mentee: *Of course. I agree that ground rules are indispensable. To tell you the truth, I've never had a formal mentor so it's good to know what some good practices are and what we should avoid.*

Mentor: *Agreed. Now, what about that storm?*

Mentee: *Well, my chair and I talked for maybe 15 minutes. And right near the end of the conversation, he said something along these lines: 'Well, Todd, there are a few cross-currents in the department that you need to know about. I doubt that you're picked up on them. But you need to be clued in.'*

Mentor: *Then what did he say?*

Mentee: *He told me that during the past hiring season, two senior colleagues had really wanted to hire a biostats person who would intellectually stretch this department and open up a new curriculum area. But their arguments didn't carry the day. Instead, the chair said: 'We hired you: someone who has exceptional promise and will help us maintain our core departmental expertise. But unfortunately,' he continued, 'the two contrarians still seem to be licking their wounds. And they express their displeasure whenever possible—saying that we made a serious error in judgment.'*

Mentor: *Go on …*

Mentee: *Well, then my chair asked me: 'Say, I hope those two aren't harassing you in any way. Are they?' I answered that without a doubt I knew the two colleagues he meant. I pointed out that they certainly behave uncomfortably around me. They seem to find it hard to greet me in the hall. And I get the sense that they'd like to avoid me as much as possible.*

Mentor: *Okay, keep going. I'm all ears.*

Mentee: *So I then asked the department chair what we should do, to alleviate this situation. He pondered that for a moment and then answered: 'Oh, I don't think we can do anything. I'm pretty confident that those two will finally abandon their grievance. So you and I should just ride this out and try to ignore it.'*

Mentor: *Then what?*

Mentee: *I gently pressed the chair and said something like 'Well, um, maybe there's something we can do or ought to do.' His response was that academe is often marred by such cross-currents within departmental units. It's nothing new, he said. You're nodding in agreement, I see. And then the chair's final words to me were: 'I see no option for us except the passage of time. So I advise you to just keep your head down.' Those were his exact words. I don't have any trouble remembering them verbatim.*

Mentor: *Well, you did the right thing in asking the chair for details. And you and I certainly have some brainstorming to do, to strategize about how you can handle this.*

Mentee: *Listen, I am so grateful that I could confidentially disclose this issue to you. Just telling you about it has lifted some weight off me. And, you know, I am puzzled that the chair claims he can't be part of the solution. But I know I can be. And must be. So I'm ready to strategize with you.*

Scenario #4: A Glimpse of a Medical School Mentoring Relationship in its Third Year

As you read the following scenario, think about how you would respond to the following questions:

1. What Good Practices (at the individual and organizational levels) do you see or can you infer?
2. What Bad Practices and Dysfunctions do you see or can you infer?
3. What Remedies would resolve or at least diminish the dysfunctions? Be specific.
4. If you were the Mentor, how would *you* propose to help the Mentee? What precautions should be taken? Please be specific.
5. What self-help strategies should the Mentee be considering? How could you as the Mentor assist in activating those self-help strategies?

Here is a conversation between an internal mentor and his mentee (both are in the same department). The mentor has European-American heritage and the mentee Mexican-American heritage.

Mentor: *Good to see you, Mercedes. By the way, thanks for the article you sent me. It really helped. One of my hunches, generated last week in my research project, seems to taking shape nicely. The article you shared with me goes directly to that hunch.*

223

Mentee: *Glad to hear that, Joe. Glad to hear the article is proving to be relevant. You know, I'm pleased that every so often I can be helpful to you.*

Mentor: *Listen, I've had a chance to review your grant proposal. Of course, I have some criticisms. After three years here as my mentee, I'm sure you're accustomed to my hard-nosed approach.*

Mentee: *Okay. I'm braced. I'm ready.*

Mentor: *Well ... the section where you offer your rationale for the project is way too vague. I don't think a peer review committee will buy it. You've got to be a lot more convincing about the value of your approach. I surely wouldn't fund this!*

Mentee: *Wow. Guess I'll have to go back to the drawing board. Any suggestions on what would be more convincing?*

Mentor: *Gosh, I don't have time to go into all that. I wish I did. Of course, your proposal also has some strengths, but dwelling on those won't help you, will it?*

Mentee: *Well, I'll revisit the rationale section. Would you be willing to look it over after the revisions?*

Mentor: *Sure. Sure. I can spare a few minutes for that.*

Mentee: *Well, on another matter ... Well, this is a bit awkward but I feel I should bring it up to you. Um. Professor Smith in the last meeting of the curriculum review committee said something about me that I found really shocking ... and I couldn't believe that nobody objected or tried to defend me.*

Mentor: *What happened? What did Smithy say?*

Mentee: *Well, in our committee discussion, I brought up that we didn't have even one history of medicine course on the books. I then went on to give a few reasons why a few such courses would strengthen our departmental offerings. At that point, Professor Smith interrupted me in mid-sentence and said 'Well, surely you are not proposing to teach any of those courses, are you, Mercedes? After all, you're our affirmative action hire. You're qualified to teach only health-disparities courses. Isn't that right?'*

Mentor: *Oh my gosh. That's vintage Smithy for you ... shooting off his mouth. He can be outrageous sometimes, but don't worry. Nobody pays much attention to him.*

Mentee: *Well, Joe, I've tried not to worry about it, but it's pretty hard for me to ignore what happened. It certainly wasn't funny from my point of view. He belittled me—and in front of five senior colleagues and one junior one on the committee. The committee chair seemed embarrassed but said absolutely nothing. Not a word. The icy silence in the room went on and on. Finally, the chair said something to the effect of 'Well, let's take a coffee break and then get*

back to our agenda.' I myself was stunned for the rest of the meet-
ing. And I still keep going over and over it in my mind.

Mentor: *Look. I don't doubt that Smithy would say something like*
that. But honestly, you'll have to grow a thicker skin. He's just
teasing you. I mean, he's not a bigot. We don't have any bigots in
this department—we never have, I'm proud to say. So I'd recom-
mend that you just put this little episode behind you. And just avoid
Smithy from now on.

Mentee: *What I'm wondering is this: if his behavior keeps up, isn't there*
something more that I should do? Or the department chair? Smith
can do me real harm at tenure time and at various places along the
way.

Mentor: *Well, every one of us has enemies. No one is immune. This is*
just part of being in academe. The academic domain is often nasty,
but one shouldn't take it personally.

Mentee: *The thing is... I'm the only Mexican American in the depart-*
ment—and, for that matter, in the whole college. As a matter of
fact, there are only a handful of U.S. domestic faculty at this entire
university. Yes, we've got plenty of international and immigrant
faculty—from South America, Asia, the Caribbean, Africa, India,
and so on—but only a handful of homegrown U.S. folks like me.
My people helped to build this country. They've been in this coun-
try for generations. I mean, I resent being treated as a second-class
citizen or worse!

Mentor: *Look, Mercedes, calm down, please. Calm down. This is a*
very minor episode. Don't blow it out of proportion. And further-
more, I'm uncomfortable with all this talk about race or ethnicity
or whatever. We've never talked much about my 'ancestral roots' or
about yours. That's surely as it should be. My philosophy is to be
truly color-blind in my dealings with people. That is how I try to
live my life.

Mentee: *Well, someone with my ancestry and my group membership*
finds it very hard to understand color-blindness—or to believe that
anyone can actually do that. Saying it, yes. Members of the majority
group often say it. But doing it? I don't think anyone can or should
do that.

Mentor: *Well, Mercedes, I should clarify. What I mean is that I try to*
treat everyone the same. Here, let me give you an example. I have
three mentees. I try to treat all of you the exact same way and not
play favorites. That's the only fair way to proceed.

Mentee: *Yes, but I bet the other two mentees are from the majority*
group. You're nodding 'yes.' Okay, those two wouldn't have to deal
with Smith's belittling comments, would they?

Mentor: *Point taken. Maybe not.*

Mentee: *And how about this example from last year? Would the other two mentees have had to deal with a few harassing students who made it clear that they didn't believe a woman—and a Mexican-American woman, to boot—could possibly be intellectually qualified to teach them? I really doubt that your other two mentees bump into negative gender bias and group bias. No way. If they're lucky, they benefit from a positive bias about their competency, because of their gender and their group membership. I'd guess that they're automatically viewed as a 'good fit' in the department because they represent the norm. You know, I'd prefer such a positive assumption for everyone or at least a neutral assumption for everyone. That would constitute a level playing field, in my book.*

Mentor: *Okay, Mercedes, I'm hearing you about the positive bias. I'm remembering that episode last year when you were coping with a handful of smart-alecks in the big lecture class. You and I together went over to the teaching and learning center, to see what ideas they had about solving that problem.*

Mentee: *Yes, I really appreciated your coming with me, Joe. And of course the coaching I got helped me resolve that problem and establish my authority in that class.*

Mentor: *Well, that was the first time, I guess, that a light bulb went off in my head about my own gender and group membership. You know, how these things bring me 'unearned benefits' (or whatever the director of the center called them). By contrast, your gender and group identity bring you the opposite, at times.*

Mentee: *Yes, both of us learned a lot last year.*

Mentor: *That's for sure. Listen, here's what I'm thinking at this point. You and I should get some more coffee. And then we should start brainstorming about various ways to handle Smithy and minimize the damage he might cause. I'm with you. I may be slow on the uptake, but I'm ready now!*

BIBLIOGRAPHY

ADVANCE (Institutional Transformation) Program, launched in 1990 and funded by the National Science Foundation, is dedicated to advancing women faculty in academic science and engineering. For details about each campus recipient's grant activities, go to: www.portal.advance.vt.edu.

Acuna, R. *Occupied America: A History of Chicanos*. Reading, MA: Addison Wesley Longman, 2000.

Aguirre, A. *Women and Minority Faculty in the Academic Workplace*. San Francisco: Jossey-Bass, 2000.

Aguirre, A., Jr., and R. Martinez. *Chicanos in Higher Education: Issues and Dilemmas for the Twenty-First Century*. ASHE-ERIC Higher Education Report, No. 3. Washington, DC: George Washington University, 1993.

Akerlof, G., and R. Shiller. *Animal Spirits: How Human Psychology Drives the Economy and Why It Matters for Global Capitalism*. Princeton: Princeton University Press, 2009.

Alberts, B. "A Scientist Assaults the Science of Testing." *Business Week* (Oct. 6, 1997) (www.businessweek.com).

Alexander, M. *The New Jim Crow: Mass Incarceration in the Age of Colorblindness*. New York: New Press, 2010.

Alicea, I. "Latino Perspectives on Paige, New Secretary of Education." *Hispanic Outlook*, (Feb. 26, 2001), 7–10.

Allen, B. "Learning the [Academic] Ropes: A Black Feminist Standpoint Analysis." In *Rethinking Organizational and Managerial Communication from Feminist Perspectives*, edited by P. Buzzanell. New York: Sage, 2000.

Allen, B. *Difference Matters: Communicating Social Identity* (2nd edition). Long Groves, IL: Waveland Press, 2011.

Alvarez, R. "The Psycho-Historical Socioeconomic Development of the Chicano Community in the United States." *Social Science Quarterly* 53 (March 1973), 920–942.

Astin, H., A. Antonio, C. Cress, and A. Astin. *Race and Ethnicity in the American Professoriate, 1995–96*. Los Angeles: Higher Education Research Institute, University of California-Los Angeles, 1997.

Aviles, R. "How to Recruit and Retain Latino Faculty." *Hispanic Outlook* (Feb. 12, 1999), 64.

Bach, D., and M. Sorcinelli. "The Case for Excellence in Diversity: Lessons from an Assessment of an Early-Career Faculty Program." *To Improve the Academy* 28 (2010), 310–326.

Bell, D. *Faces at the Bottom of the Well.* New York: Basic Books, 1992.

Bell, E., and S. Nkomo. *Our Separate Ways: Black and White Women and the Struggle for Professional Identity.* Boston: Harvard Business School Press, 2001.

Benjamin, L. *The Black Elite: Facing the Color Line in the Twilight of the Twentieth Century.* Chicago: Nelson-Hall, 1998.

Bensimon, E., K. Ward, and K. Sanders. *The Department Chair's Role in Developing New Faculty into Teachers and Scholars.* Bolton, MA: Anker, 2000.

Berger, T. *A Long and Terrible Shadow: White Values, Native Rights in the Americas.* Seattle: University of Washington Press, 1991.

Berk, R., J. Berg, R. Mortimer, B. Walton-Moss, and T. Yeo. "Measuring the Effectiveness of Faculty Mentoring Relationships." *Academic Medicine* 80 (2005), 66–71.

Berliner, D., and B. Normally. *The Manufactured Crisis: Myths, Fraud and the Attack on America's Public Schools.* Boston: Addison-Wesley, 1995.

Berreman, G. "Caste in India and the United States." *The American Journal of Sociology* 66 (1960), 120–127.

Berreman, G. "Stratification, Pluralism and Interaction: A Comparative Analysis of Caste." In *Caste and Race: Comparative Approaches*, edited by A. DeReuck and J. Knight. London: J. & A. Churchill Ltd., 1967.

Betancourt, J., and A. Reid. "Black Physicians' Experience with Race: Should We Be Surprised?" *Annals of Internal Medicine* 146.1 (2007), 68–70.

Beyond Bias and Barriers: Fulfilling the Potential of Women in Academic Science and Engineering. Washington, D.C.: National Academy of Sciences, 2006.

Biernat, M. "Toward a Broader View of Social Stereotyping." *American Psychologist* 58 (2003), 1019–1027.

Blackmon, D. *Slavery by Another Name: The Re-Enslavement of Black People in America from the Civil War to World War II.* New York: Doubleday, 2008.

Blackshire-Belay, C. "The Status of Minority Faculty Members in the Academy." *Academe* (July-August 1998), 30–36.

Blair, I., and M. Banaji. "Automatic and Controlled Processes in Stereotype Priming." *Journal of Personality and Social Psychology* 70.6 (1996), 1142–1163.

Bland, C. *Successful Faculty in Academic Medicine: Essential Skills and How to Acquire Them.* New York: Springer, 1990.

Blau, R., R. Croson, J. Currie, and D. Ginther. "Can Mentoring Help Female Assistant Professors? An Evaluation of a Randomized Trial." *American Economic Review* 100.2 (2010), 348–352.

Blauner, R. *Racial Oppression in America.* New York: Harper and Row, 1972. [Chapter Two of this book is entitled "Colonized and Immigrant Minorities." This path-breaking article has been widely anthologized and was republished in Blauner, R. *Still the Big News: Racial Oppression in America.* Philadelphia: Temple University Press, 2001.]

Bobo, L. "Somewhere Between Jim Crow and Post-Racialism: Reflections on the Racial Divide in American Today." *Daedalus* 140.2 (2011), 11–36.

Boice, R. *The New Faculty Member: Supporting and Fostering Professional Development.* San Francisco: Jossey Bass, 1992.

Boice, R. "Early Turning Points in Professional Careers of Women and Minorities." In *Building a Diverse Faculty*, edited by J. Gainen and R. Boice. San Francisco: Jossey Bass, 1993.

Boice, R. "New Faculty Involvement for Women and Minorities." *Research in Higher Education* 34.3 (1993), 291–341.

Boice, R. *Advice for New Faculty Members.* Boston: Allyn and Bacon, 2000.

Boissevain, J. *Friends of Friends: Networks, Manipulators, and Coalitions.* Oxford: Basil Blackwell, 1974.

Bond, W. "Using Simulation to Instruct Emergency Medicine Residents in Cognitive Forcing Strategies." *Academic Medicine* 79 (2004), 438–446.

Bond, W., L. Deitrick, M. Eberhardt, G. Barr, B. Kane, C. Worrilow, D. Arnold, and P. Croskerry. "Cognitive Versus Technical Debriefings." *Academic Emergency Medicine* 13.3 (2006), 276–283.

Bonilla, J., C. Pickeron, and T. Tatum. "Peer Mentoring Among Graduate Students of Color: Expanding the Mentoring Relationship." In *Mentoring Revisited: Making an Impact on Individuals and Institutions*, edited by Marie Wunsch. San Francisco: Jossey-Bass, 1994, pp. 101–114.

Bonilla-Silva. E. *Racism Without Racists: Color-Blind Racism and the Persistence of Racial Inequality in the U.S.* New York: Rowman and Littlefield, 2006.

Bornmann, L. "Bias Cut." *Nature* 445 (Feb. 1, 2007), 566.

Bourdieau, P. "Cultural Reproduction and Social Reproduction." In *Power and Ideology in Education*, edited by J. Karabel and A. Halsey. New York: Oxford University Press, 1997, pp. 130–143.

Bowen, W., and D. Bok. *The Shape of the River: Long-term Consequences of Considering Race in College and University Admissions.* Princeton, NJ: Princeton University Press, 1998.

Boyle, P., and R. Boice. "Systematic Mentoring for New Faculty Teachers and Graduate Teaching Assistants." *Innovative Higher Education* 22 (1998), 157–179.

Bradley, J. *The Imperial Cruise: A Secret History of Empire and War.* Boston: Little Brown, 2009.

Brender, A. "In Japan, Education for Koreans Stays Separate and Unequal." *Chronicle of Higher Education* (Feb. 9, 2001), A40–41.

Brent, R., R. Felder, and S. Rajala. *Preparing New Faculty Members to be Successful: A No-Brainer and yet a Radical Concept.* Proceedings of the 2006 ASEE Conference. Washington, DC: ASEE.

Brodkin, K. *How Jews Became White Folks and What that Says About Race in America.* Piscataway, NJ: Rutgers University Press, 2000.

Bronstein, P., E. Rothblum, and S. Solomon. "Ivy Halls and Glass Walls: Barriers to Academic Careers for Women and Ethnic Minorities." In *Building a Diverse Faculty*, edited by J. Gainen and R. Boice. San Francisco: Jossey Bass, 1993.

Brown, K. "African-American Immersion Schools: Paradoxes of Race and Public Education." In *Critical Race Theory,* edited by R. Delgado and F. Stefancic. Philadelphia: Temple University Press, 1993, pp. 415–428.

Bruner, J. The *Culture of Education.* Cambridge: Harvard University Press, 1996.

Budden, A., L. Aarssen, J. Koricheva, R. Leimu, C. Lortie, and T. Tregenza. "Does Double-Blind Review Favor Female Authors?" *Frontiers in Ecology and the Environment* 6 (2008), 356–357.

Burgess, D. "The President's Comments on Diversity Issues: Barriers to Graduate School for Minority-Group Students." At the 1998 meeting of the Society for the Advancment of Chicanos and Native Americans in Science. See website www.sacnas.org. [Burgess laments the preference of campus researchers for graduate students and post-doctoral fellows who are immigrant and international in background. He explains why this "out-sourcing" pattern happens and why it must stop.]

Caplan, N., J. Whitmore, and M. Choy. *The Boat People and Achievement in America.* Ann Arbor: University of Michigan Press, 1989.

Carter, T. *Mexican Americans in School: A History of Educational Neglect.* Princeton, NJ: College Entrance Examination Board, 1970.

Carter, T., and R. Segura. *Mexican-Americans in School: A Decade of Change.* Princeton, NJ: College Entrance Examination Board, 1979.

Chang, R. "Toward an Asian American Legal Scholarship." In *Critical Race Theory*, edited by R. Delgado and J. Stefancic. Philadelphia: Temple University Press, 1993.

Charles, C., M. Fisher, and D. Massey. "Affirmative Action Programs for Minority Students: Right in Theory, Wrong in Practice." *Chronicle of Higher Education* (March 27, 2009), A29.

Charles, C., M. Fischer, M. Mooney, and D. Massey. *Taming the River: Negotiating the Academic, Financial, and Social Currents at Selective Colleges and Universities.* Princeton, NJ: Princeton University Press, 2009.

Chavez, J. *The Lost Land, The Chicano Image of the Southwest.* Albuquerque: University of New Mexico Press, 1984.

Chubin, D., and E. Hackett. *Peerless Science.* Albany: State University of New York Press, 1990.

Clance, P. *The Imposter Phenomenon: When Success Makes You Feel like a Fraud.* New York: Bantam Books, 1985.

Clark, S., and M. Corcoran, "Perspectives on the Professional Socialization of Women Faculty: A Case of Accumulative Disadvantage?" *Journal of Higher Education* 57.1 (1989), 20–43.

Clayman Institute for Gender Research. *Dual-Career Academic Couples: What Universities Need to Know.* Authors: L. Schiebinger, A. Henderson, and S. Gilmartin. Stanford, CA: Stanford University, 2008.

Cohen, J. "Time to Shatter the Glass Ceiling for Minority [Medical] Faculty." *JAMA* 280 (1998), 821–822.

Colbeck, C., and R. Drago. "*Accept, Avoid, Resist*: Faculty Members' Responses to Bias against Caregiving—And How Departments Can Help." *Change* 37.6 (2005), 10–17.

Cole, S. *Making Science*. Cambridge, MA: Harvard University Press, 1992.

Cole, J., and S. Cole. *Social Stratification in Science*. Chicago: University of Chicago Press, 1973.

Coleman, D., R. Goyatzis, and A. McKee. *Primal Leadership: Learning to Lead With Emotional Intelligence*. Cambridge, MA: Harvard Business Press, 2004.

Connor, K., and E. Vargyas. "The Legal Implications of Gender Bias in Standardized Testing." *Berkeley Women's Law Journal* 7 (1992), 13–89.

Cooper, J., and D. Stevens, eds. *Tenure in the Sacred Grove: Issues and Strategies for Women and Minority Faculty*. Albany: State University of New York Press, 2002.

Correspondents of the New York Times. *How Race is Lived in America*. New York: Holt, 2001.

Creighton, J. "The S.A.T. Solution: None of the Above." *Boston Globe* (Sept. 29, 1997), A15.

Croskerry, P. "The Cognitive Imperative: Thinking about How We Think." *Academy of Emergency Medicine* 7 (2000), 1223–1231.

Croskerry, P. "The Importance of Cognitive Errors in Diagnosis and Strategies to Minimize Them." *Academic Medicine* 78 (2003), 775–780.

Cruz, D. "Struggling with the Labels That Mark My Ethnic Identity." In *The Leaning Ivory Tower: Latino Professors in American Universities*, edited by R. Padilla and R. Chavez. Albany: State University of New York Press, 1995.

Cummins, B. *Dominion from Sea to Sea: Pacific Ascendancy and American Power*. New Haven, CT: Yale University Press, 2011.

Dahl, R. *How Democratic is the American Constitution?* New Haven, CT: Yale University Press, 2001.

Daley, S., D. Wingard, and V. Reznik. "Improving the Retention of Underrepresented Minority Faculty in Academic Medicine." *Journal of the National Medical Association* 98.9 (2006), 1435–1440.

Daniell, E. *Every Other Thursday: Stories and Strategies from Successful Women Scientists*. New Haven, CT: Yale University Press, 2006.

Davis, P. "Law as Microaggression." *Yale Law Review* 98.8 (2000), 1989–2020.

Dawson, V., and H. Arkes. "Systematic Errors in Medical Decision Making: Judgment Limitations." *Journal of General Internal Medicine* 2.3 (1987), 183–187.

Delgado, R. "Mexican Americans as a Legally Cognizable Class." In *The Latino/a Condition*, edited by R. Delgado and J. Stefancic. New York: New York University Press, 1998.

Deloria, V. "Identify and Culture." In *From Different Shores*, edited by R. Takaki. New York: Oxford University Press, 1987.

Dettmar, K. J. H. "What We Waste When Faculty Hiring Goes Wrong." *Chronicle of Higher Education* (Dec. 17, 2004), B6.

Detsky, A., and M. Baerlocher. "Academic Mentoring—How to Give It and Get It." *Journal of the American Medical Association* 297 (2007), 2134–2136.

DeVos, G. "Essential Elements of Caste: Psychological Determinants in Structural Theory." In *Japan's Invisible Race*, edited by G. DeVos and H. Wagatsuma. Berkeley: University of California Press, 1967.

DeVos, G., and C. Lee. *Koreans in Japan*. Berkeley: University of California Press, 1981.

DiTomaso, N., G. Farris, and R. Cordero. "Diversity in the Technical Work Force: Rethinking the Management of Scientists and Engineers." *Journal of Engineering and Technology Management* 10 (Jan./Feb.1993), 101–127.

Doane, A. "Dominant Group Ethnic Identify in the United States: The Role of 'Hidden' Ethnicity in Intergroup Relations." In *Majority and Minority: The Dynamics of Race and Ethnicity in American Life,* edited by N. Yetman. Needham Heights, MA: Allyn and Bacon, 1999.

Dunham, S. *Surviving Against the Odds: Village Industry in Indonesia*. Durham, NC: Duke University Press, 2009.

Duster, T. "The Structure of Privilege and its Universe of Discourse." *American Sociologist* 11 (1976), 73–78.

Dyer, T. *Theodore Roosevelt and the Idea of Race*. Baton Rouge: Louisiana State University Press, 1960.

Dyson, M. *Race Rules: Navigating the Color Line*. Reading, MA: Addison-Wesley, 1996.

Epps, E. "Academic Culture and the Minority Professor." *Academe* 36 (1989), 23–26.

Espinoza-Herold, M., and V. Gonzalez. "The Voices of Senior Scholars on Mentoring Graduate Students and Junior Scholars." *Hispanic Journal of Behavioral Sciences* 29 (2007), 313–335.

Essien, V. "Visible and Invisible Barriers to the Incorporation of Faculty of Color in Predominantly White Law Schools." *Journal of Black Studies* 34.1 (2003), 63–71.

Exum, W., R. Menges, B. Watkins, and P. Berglund. "Making It at the Top: Women and Minority Faculty in the Academic Labor Market." *American Behavioral Scientist* 27 (1984), 301–324.

Fain, P. "Diversity Is Still Largely Missing from Colleges' Governing Boards." *Chronicle of Higher Education* (Dec. 10, 2010), A19.

Fair, B. *Notes of a Racial Caste Baby: Color Blindness and the End of Affirmative Action*. New York: New York University Press, 1997.

Fang, D. "Racial and Ethnic Disparities is in Faculty Promotion in Academic Medicine." *JAMA* 284 (2000), 1085–1092.

Farquhar, R. "Faculty Renewal and Institutional Revitalization in Canadian Universities." *Change* (July/Aug. 2001), 13–20.

Feagin, J., and K. McKinney. *Systemic Racism*. New York: Routledge, 2006.

Feagin, J., and M. Sikes. *Living with Racism: The Black Middle-Class Experience*. Boston: Beacon Press, 1994.

Feagin, J., and H. Vera. *White Racism, the Basics*. New York: Routledge, 1995.

Fernández-Aráoz, C., B. Groysberg, and N. Nohria. "The Definitive Guide to Recruiting in Good and Bad Times." *Harvard Business Review* 87.5 (2009), 74–84.

Feugen, K., and M. Biernat. "Reexamining the Effects of Solo Status for Women and Men." *Personality and Psychological Bulletin* 28.7 (July 2002), 913–925.

Fine, M., ed. *Off White: Readings on Race, Power, and Society.* New York: Routledge, 1997.

Fink, D. *The First Year of College Teaching.* San Francisco: Jossey-Bass, 1984.

Fischer, C., M. Hunt, M. Jankowski, S. Lucas, A. Swidler, and K. Vos. *Inequality by Design: Cracking the Bell Curve Myth.* Princeton, NJ: Princeton University Press, 1996.

Fiske, S. "Intent and Ordinary Bias: Unintended Thought and Social Motivation Create Casual Prejudice." *Social Justice Research* 17.2 (2004), 117–127.

Fiske, S. *Social Beings: Core Motives in Social Psychology.* New York: Wiley, 2010. [Professor Susan Fiske has a number of publications—check her website at Princeton University's Psychology Department.]

Fitzgerald, T. "Held Back by the Glass Border." *Boston Globe* (Feb. 4, 2001), B4.

Foner, N. "West Indian Migration to New York." In *Islands in the City: West Indian Migration to New York,* edited by N. Foner. Berkeley: UCA Press, 2001, pp. 1–22.

Foote, T. *Black and White in Manhattan 1624–1781: The History of Racial Formation in Colonial New York City.* New York: Oxford, 2004.

Frampton, M, I. Lopez, and J. Simon. *After the War on Crime: Race, Democracy, and a New Reconstruction.* New York: New York University Press, 2008.

Frank, F. "Taking Up a Professorial Line at Florida A&M University" In *Affirmed Action: Essays on the Academic and Social Lives of White Faculty Members at HBCUs,* edited by L. Foster, J. Guydes, and A. Miller. Lanham, MD: Rowman and Littlefield, 1999.

Frankenberg, R. *White Women, Race Matters: The Social Construction of Whiteness.* Minneapolis: University of Minnesota Press, 1993.

Franklin, J. "The Worlds of Race: A Historical Perspective." Republished in *Daedalus* (Winter 2011), 28–43.

Franklin, R. *Shadows of Race and Class.* Minneapolis: University of Minnesota Press, 1991.

French, L. *Native American Justice.* Chicago: Burnham Press, 2003.

Fried, L., C. Francomano, S. MacDonald, E. Wager, E. Stokes, K. Carbone, W. Bias, M. Newman, and J. Stobo. "Career Development for Women in Academic Medicine: Multiple Interventions in a Department of Medicine." *Journal of the American Medical Association* 276 (Sept. 18, 1996), 898–905.

Gaertner, S., and Dovidio, S. "The Aversive Form of Racism." In *Prejudice, Discrimination, and Racism,* edited by S. Gaertner and J. Dovidio. Orlando, FL: Academic Press, 1986. [Dovidio's later studies are listed at the website for Yale University where he is a psychology professor.]

Gallagher, J. "Thinking about Thinking." *Annals of Emergency Medicine* 41 (2003), 121–122.

Gallagher, A., and C. Trower. "The Demand for Diversity." *The Chronicle of Higher Education* (Feb. 4, 2009).

Gallos, J., and J. Ramsey. *Teaching Diversity.* San Francisco: Jossey-Bass, 1997,

Gappa, J., and D. Leslie. *The Invisible Faculty: Improving the Status of Part-Timers in Higher Education.* San Francisco: Jossey-Bass, 1993.

Garcia, E. "Where's the Merit in the S.A.T.?" *New York Times*, Dec. 26, 1991, 28.

Garcia, H. "Toward a Postview of the Chicano Community in Higher Education." In *The Leaning Ivory Tower: Latino Professors in American Universities*, edited by R. Padilla and R. Chavez. Albany: State University of New York Press, 1995.

Garcia, M. "Introduction." In *Succeeding in an Academic Career: A Guide for Faculty of Color*, edited by M. Garcia. Westport, CT: Greenwood Press, 2000.

Garvey, J., and N. Ignatiev. "Toward a New Abolitionism—A Race Traitor Manifesto." In *Whiteness, A Critical Reader*, edited by M. Hill. New York: New York University Press, 1997.

Garza, H. "Second-Class Academics: Chicano/Latino Faculty in U.S. Universities." In *Building a Diverse Faculty*, edited by J. Gainen and R. Boice. San Francisco: Jossey Bass, 1993.

Gates, H. "Forty Acres and a Gap in Wealth." *New York Times* (Nov. 18, 2007), 43.

Gawande, A. *The Checklist Manifesto: How to Get Things Right.* New York: Henry Holt, 2009.

Gibson, M. "The School Performance of Immigrant Minorities: A Comparative View." *Anthropology and Education Quarterly* 13 (1987), 3–27.

Gibson, M. *Accommodation Without Assimilation: Sikh Immigrants in an American High School.* New York: Cornell University Press, 1988.

Gibson, M. "Minorities and Schooling: Some Implications." In *Minority Status and Schooling: A Comparative Study of Immigrant and Involuntary Minorities*, edited by J. Ogbu and M. Gibson. New York: Garland, 1991.

Ginorio, A. *Warming the Climate for Women in Academic Science.* Washington, DC: Association of American Colleges and Universities, 1995.

Giroux, H. *Border Crossings: Cultural Workers and the Politics of Education.* New York: Routledge, 1992.

Giroux, H. "Racial Politics and the Pedagogy of Whiteness." In *Whiteness, A Critical Reader*, edited by M. Hill. New York: New York University Press, 1997.

Gladwell, M. "The Art of Failure." *The New Yorker* (Aug. 21–28, 2000), 92.

Glazer-Raymo, J. *Shattering the Myths: Women in Academe.* Baltimore: Johns Hopkins University Press, 1999.

Glenn, D. "At Selective Colleges, Many Black Students Are Immigrants, Study Finds." *Chronicle of Higher Education* (Feb. 9, 2007), A29.

Gonzales, P., H. Blanton, and K. Williams. "The Effects of Stereotype Threat and Double-Minority Status on the Test Performance of Latina Women." *Personality and Social Psychology* 28.5 (2002), 658–670.

Goodman, D. *Promoting Diversity and Social Justice: Educating People from Privileged Groups.* San Francisco: Sage, 2001.

Goodwin, D. *Team of Rivals.* New York: Simon and Schuster, 2005.

Graham, H. Collision Course: *The Strange Convergence of Affirmative Action and Immigrant Policy in America*. New York: Oxford University Press, 2002.

Graham, L. *Member of the Club: Reflection on Life in a Racially Polarized World*. New York: Harper, 1995.

Gray, H. *We Can't Teach What We Don't Know*. New York: Teachers College, Columbia University, 1999.

Gray, P., and D. Drew. *What They Didn't Teach You in Graduate School*. Sterling, VA: Stylus, 2008.

Greenwald, A., and L. Krieger. "Implicit Bias: Scientific Foundations." *California Law Review* 94 (2006), 945–965.

Gregory, S. *Black Women in the Academy*. Lanham, MD: University Press of America, 1995.

Grillo, T., and S. Wildman. "Obscuring the Importance of Race." In *Critical Race Theory*, edited by R. Delgado and F. Stefancic. Philadelphia: Temple University Press, 2000.

Groopman, J. *How Doctors Think*. New York: Houghton-Mifflin, 2007a.

Groopman, J. "What's the Trouble? How Doctors Think." *The New Yorker* (Jan. 29, 2007b), 36–41.

Grosfoguel, R. *Colonial Subjects: Puerto Ricans in a Global Perspective*. Berkeley: University of California Press, 2003.

Grosfoguel, R., and C. Georas. "*Coloniality of Power* and Racial Dynamics: Notes toward a Reinterpretation of Latino Caribbeans in New York City." *Identities* (2000), 85–125

Guinier, L., and S. Sturm, eds. *Who's Qualified?* Boston: Beacon Press, 2001.

Guinier, L., and G. Torres. *The Miner's Canary: Enlisting Race, Resisting Power, Transforming Democracy*. Cambridge, MA: Harvard University Press, 2000.

Guterman, L. Peer Review Conference. *Chronicle of Higher Education* (Sept. 19, 2005), A19.

Hardwick, S. "Mentoring Early Career Faculty in Geography: Issues and Strategies." *Professional Geographer* 1 (2005), 21–27.

Harleston, B., and M. Knowles. *Achieving Diversity in the Professoriate: Challenges and Opportunities*. Washington, DC: American Council on Education, 1997.

Harlow, R. "Race Doesn't Matter, but … : The Effect of Race on Professors' Experiences and Emotion Management in the Undergraduate College Classroom." *Social Psychology Quarterly* 66 (2003), 348–363.

Haro, R. "The Dearth of Latinos in Campus Administration." *Chronicle of Higher Education* (Dec. 16, 2001), 48.

Harris, C. "Whiteness as Property." In *Black on White: Black Writers on What It Means To Be White*, edited by D. Roediger. New York: Schocken Books, 1993. [Harris's original article appeared in the 1993 *Harvard Law Review*.]

Harvey, W. "African American Faculty in Community Colleges." In *Creating and Maintaining a Diverse Faculty*, edited by W. Harvey and J. Valadez. San Francisco: Jossey Bass, 1994.

Harvey, W. ed. *Grass Roots and Glass Ceilings: African-American Administrators on Predominantly White Colleges and Universities.* Albany: State University of New York Press, 1999.

Haynes, B. *Red Lines, Black Spaces.* New Haven, CT: Yale University Press, 2001.

Haynes, R. "An Exploration and Assessment of Mentoring within the American Law Professoriate." *Academy of Human Resource Development* International Conference 35 (2006), 724

Heath, C., R. Larrick, and J. Klayman. "Cognitive Repairs: How Organizational Practices Can Compensate for Individual Shortcomings." *Research in Organizational Behavior* 20 (1998), 1–37.

Hemami, S., and M. van der Meulen. "But You Don't Look Like an Engineer...." *Chronicle of Higher Education* (Jan. 29, 2010), A31.

Hewlett, S., K. Peraino, L. Sherebin, and K. Sumberg. "The Sponsor Effect: Breaking Through the Last Glass Ceiling." In *Harvard Business Review Research Materials.* Cambridge, MA: Harvard Business School, 2011.

Hill, H. "Black Labor and Affirmative Action." In *The Question of Discrimination: Racial Inequality in the U.S. Labor Market,* edited by S. Shulman and W. Darity, Jr. Middletown, CT: Wesleyan University Press, 1989.

Hitchcock, J. *Lifting the White Veil.* Roselle, NJ: Crandall, Dostie, and Douglass Books, 2002.

Hochschild, J. *Facing Up to the American Dream: Race, Class, and the Soul of the Nation.* Princeton, NJ: Princeton University Press, 1995.

Hollinger, D. *Science, Jews, and Secular Culture.* Princeton, NJ: Princeton University Press, 1996.

Hollinger, D. "The One Drop Rule and the One Hate Rule." *Daedalus* (Winter 2005), 18–28.

Hollinger, D. *Cosmopolitanism and Solidarity: Studies in Ethnoracial, Religious, and Professional Affiliation in the United States.* Madison: University of Wisconsin Press, 2006a.

Hollinger, D. "From Identity to Solidarity." *Daedalus* (Fall 2006b), 23–31.

Hollinger, D. "Rich, Powerful, and Smart: Jewish Overrepresentation Should Be Explained Rather than Mystified or Avoided." *Jewish Quarterly Review* (Fall 2004), 595–592. [This article also included in Hollinger's *Cosmopolitanism* book, 2006a.]

Hollinger, D. "The Concept of Post-Racial: How Its Easy Dismissal Obscures Important Questions." *Daedalus* 140.1 (Winter 2011), 174–184.

hooks, b. *Yearning: Race, Gender, and Cultural Politics.* Boston: South End Press, 1990.

Horning, L. ed. *Unequal Rites: Unequal Outcomes for Women in American Research Universities.* New York: Plenum, 2008.

Howard, G. *You Can't Teach What You Don't Know.* New York: Teachers College, 1999.

Hu-DeHart, E. "Introduction: Asian American Formations in the Age of Globalization." In *Across the Pacific: Asian Americans and Globalization,* edited by E. Hu-DeHart. Philadelphia: Temple University Press, 1999.

Hu-DeHart, E. "Office Politics and Departmental Culture." In *Succeeding in An Academic Career: A Guide for Faculty of Color,* edited by M. Garcia. Westport, CT: Greenwood Press, 2000.

Humphrey, J. "The Best of Intentions." In *Harvard Business School Case Studies.* Cambridge, MA: Harvard Business School, 2002, pp. 31–42.

Ibarra, R. *Latino Experiences in Graduate Education: Implications for Change.* Washington, DC: Council of Graduate Schools, 1996.

Ignatiev, N. *How the Irish Became White.* New York: Routledge, 1995.

"Impact of Census' Race Data." *USA Today* (March 13, 2001), 1A–2A.

Isenbert, A. *Mining California.* New York: Hill and Wang, 2005.

Jackson, J. "Teaching Controversial Issues." Highlights from the Blog of *The Chronicle Review. The Chronicle Review* (March 5, 2010), p. B2.

Jackson, K. *Crabgrass Frontier,* New York: Oxford University Press, 1985.

Jackson, B., and R. Hardiman. "Stages in the Development of a Multicultural Organization" distributed at B. Jackson's and L. Marchesani's Institute on Multicultural Organizational Development. Institute held at the National Conference on Race and Ethnicity. San Francisco, 2003.

Jacobs, J. *Revolving Doors: Sex Segregation and Women's Careers.* Palo Alto, CA: Stanford University Press, 1989.

Jacobson, M. *Whiteness of a Different Color: European Immigrants and the Alchemy of Race.* Cambridge, MA: Harvard University Press, 1998.

Jarvis, D. *Junior Faculty Development: A Handbook.* New York: Modern Language Association, 1991.

Jayakumar, U., M. Howard, W. Allen, and J. Han. "Racial Privilege in the Professoriate: An Exploration of Campus Climate, Retention, and Satisfaction." *Journal of Higher Education* 80 (2009), 538–563.

Johnson, A. *The Gender Knot: Unravelling our Patriarchal Legacy.* Philadelphia: Temple University Press, 1997.

Johnson, W. *On Becoming a Mentor: A Guide for Higher Education Faculty.* Mahwah, NJ: Erlbaum, 2007.

Johnson, B., and W. Harvey. "The Socialization of Black College Faculty: Implications for Policy and Practice." *Review of Higher Education* 25 (2002), 297–314.

Jordan, D. *Sisters in Science: Conversations with Black Women Scientists on Race, Gender, and their Passion.* West Lafayette, IN: Purdue University Press, 2006.

Kahlenberg, R. *Affirmative Action for the Rich: Legacy Preferences in College Admissions.* Washington, D.C.: Brookings Institution, 2010.

Kahneman, D. "Bounded Rationality: A Perspective on Judgment and Choice." *American Psychologist* 58.9 (2003), 697–720.

Kahneman, D., P. Slovic, and A. Tversky. *Judgment under Uncertainty: Heuristics and Biases.* Cambridge, UK: Cambridge University Press, 1982. [Kahneman won the Nobel Prize in Economics. He is a psychologist who has never taken an economics course.]

Kain, J. *Race and Poverty: The Economics of Discrimination.* Englewood Cliffs, NJ: Prentice-Hall, 1969.

Kanter, R. *Men and Women of the Corporation.* New York: Basic Books, 1997.

Karabel, J. "Community Colleges and Social Stratification in the 1980s." In *The Community College and Its Critics*, edited by S. Zwerling. San Francisco: Jossey-Bass, 1986.

Katznelson, I. *When Affirmative Action Was White: An Untold History of Racial Inequality in Twentieth-Century America*. New York: W.W. Norton, 2005.

Kendall, F. *Understanding White Privilege*. New York: Routledge, 2006.

Kiang, P. "Issues of Curriculum and Community for First-Generation Asian Americans in College." In *First-Generation Students: Confronting the Cultural Issues*, edited by S. Zwerling and H. London. San Francisco: Jossey-Bass, 1992.

Kobrynowicz, D., and M. Biernat. "Decoding Subjective Evaluations: How Stereotypes Provide Shifting Standards." *Journal of Experimental Social Psychology* 33 (1997), 579–601.

Kozol, J. *Savage Inequalities: Children in America's Schools*. New York: Harper, 1991.

Kram, K. *Mentoring at Work: Developmental Relationships in Organizational Life*. Glennview, IL: Scott, Foresman, 1985.

Kramer, B. "Education and American Indians: The Experiences of the Ute Indian Tribe." In *Minority Status and Schooling: A Comparative Study of Immigrant and Involuntary Minorities*, edited by J. Ogbu and M. Gibson. New York: Garland, 1991.

Kramer, V., A. Konrad, and S. Erkut. *Critical Mass on Corporate Boards: Why Three or More Women Enhance Governance*. Wellesley, MA: Wellesley Center, 2006.

Krieger, L. "The Content of Our Categories: A Cognitive Bias Approach to Discrimination and Equal Employment Opportunity." *Stanford Law Review* 47 (1995), 1161–1222.

Kushnick, L. "Racism and Class Consciousness in Modern Capitalism." In *Impacts of Racism on White Americans*, edited by B. Bowser and R. Hunt. Beverly Hills, CA: Sage, 1981.

Lamont, M. *How Professors Think: Inside the Curious World of Academic Judgment*. Cambridge, MA: Harvard University Press, 2009.

Law, J. "The Psychology of Tokenism: An Analysis." *Sex Roles* 1 (1975), 209–223.

Lee, A., C. Dennis, and P. Campbell. "*Nature*'s Guide for Mentors." *Nature* 447 (June 14, 2007), 781–787.

Lee, J., and F. Bean. "Reinventing the Color Line: Immigration and America's New Racial/Ethnic Divide." *Social Forces* 86.2 (2007), 561–586.

Lee, Y. "Koreans in Japan and the United States." In *Minority Status and Schooling: A Comparative Study of Immigrant and Involuntary Minorities*, edited by J. Ogbu and M. Gibson. New York: Garland, 1991.

Lemann, N. *The Big Test: The Secret History of the American Meritocracy*. New York: Farrar, Straus and Giroux, 1999.

Lewin, T. "Study Finds Family Connections Give Big Advantage in College Admissions." *New York Times* (Jan. 8, 2011), 36.

Leonhardt, D. "Larry Summer's Evolution." *New York Times Sunday Magazine* (July 19, 2007), 22–29.

Lieberson, S. *A Piece of the Pie: Blacks and White Immigrants Since 1880*. Berkeley: University of California Press, 1980.

Light, I. "Ethnic Enterprise in America: Japanese, Chinese, and Black." In *From Different Shores: Perspectives on Race and Ethnicity in America,* edited by R. Takaki. New York: Oxford University Press, 1987.

Lipsitz, G. *The Possessive Investment in Whiteness: How White People Profit from Identity Politics*. Philadelphia: Temple University Press, 1998.

Loewen, J. *The Mississippi Chinese: Between Black and White*. Prospect Heights, IL: Waveland Press, 1988.

Lopez, I. "Colorblind to the Reality of Race in America." *Chronicle of Higher Education Review* (Nov. 3, 2006a), pp. B6–B8.

Lopez, I. *White By Law: The Legal Construction of Race*. New York: New York University Press, 2006b.

Loury, G. *Race, Incarceration, and American Values*. Cambridge, MA: MIT Press, 2008.

Lutz, F. "The Deanship: Search and Screening Process." *Educational Record* 60 (Summer 1979), 261–271.

MacQuarrie, B. "Black Drivers Describe Harassment by Police." *The Boston Globe* (April 13, 1999), A1, A9.

Maddox, L. *Citizen Indians: Native American Intellectuals, Race, and Reform*. Ithaca, NY: Cornell University Press, 2005.

Madera, J., M. Hebl, and R. Martin. "Gender and Letters of Recommendation for Academia: Agentic and Communal Differences." *Journal of Applied Psychology* 94 (2009), 1591–1599.

Maher, F., and M. Tetreault. *Privilege and Diversity in the Academy*. New York: Routledge, 2007.

Marabel, M. *Beyond Black and White: Transforming African-American Politics*. New York: Version, 1995.

Marcus, H., C. Steele, and D. Steele. "Colorblindness as a Barrier to Inclusion: Assimilation and Nonimmigrant Minorities." *Daedalus* 129.4 (2000), 233–259.

Margolis, E., and M. Romero. "'The Department Is Very Male, Very White, Very Old, and Very Conservative': The Functioning of the Hidden Curriculum in Graduate Sociology Departments." *Harvard Educational Review* 68 (Spring 1998), 1–32.

Martell, R. "Sex Bias at Work: The Effects of Attentional and Memory Demands on Performance Ratings for Men and Women." *Journal of Applied Psychology* 21 (1991): 1939–1960.

Martell, R., D. Lane, and C. Emrich. "Male-Female Differences: A Computer Simulation." *American Psychologist* 51 (1991), 157–158.

Martinez-Alemán, A. "Actuando." In *The Leaning Ivory Tower: Latino Professors in American Universities,* edited by R. Padilla and R. Chavez. Albany: State University of New York Press, 1995.

Martinez, O. *Mexican-Origin People in the United States*. Tucson: University of Arizona Press, 2001.

Mason, M., and E. Ekman. *Mothers on the Fast Track*. New York: Oxford University Press, 2007.

Massachusetts Institute of Technology (MIT). "A Study on the Status of Women Faculty in Science at MIT," 1999, at campus website. Also at website: "Report of the Initiative for Faculty Race and Diversity," 2010. Updates are periodically posted.

Massey, D. "The Past and Future of American Civil Rights." *Daedalus* 140.2 (Spring 2011), 37–54.

Massey, D, C. Charles, G. Lundy, and M. Fischer. *The Source of the River: The Social Origins of Freshmen at America's Selective Colleges and Universities.* Princeton, NJ: Princeton University Press, 2003.

Massey, D., and N. Denton. *American Apartheid: Segregation and the Making of the Underclass.* Cambridge, MA: Harvard University Press, 1993.

Massey, D., M. Mooney, K. Torres, C. Charles. "Black Immigrants and Black Natives Attending Selective Colleges and Universities in the U.S." *American Journal of Education* 111 (2007), 243–271. [This article indicates the reasons why admission officers often prefer to admit immigrant Blacks rather than non-immigrant African Americans.]

Matasar, R. "The Ten Commandments of Faculty Development." *University of Toledo Review* 31.4 (2000), 65–67.

Matute-Bianci, E. "Ethnic Identities and Patterns of School Success and Failure among Mexican-Descent and Japanese-American Students in a California School." *American Journal of Education* 95 (1989), 233–255.

Matute-Bianchi, M. "School Performance among Mexican-Descent Students." In *Minority Status and Schooling: A Comparative Study of Immigrant and Involuntary Minorities,* edited by J. Ogbu and M. Gibson. New York: Garland, 1991.

McCarthy, R. "Negative Stereotypes, A Personal View." *Monitor on Psychology* (April 2001), 31.

McIntosh, P. *White Privilege and Male Privilege.* Working Paper No. 189. Wellesley, MA: Wellesley College Center for Research on Women, 1988.

McIntosh, P. "White Privilege: Unpacking the Invisible Knapsack." *Peace and Freedom* (July/August 1989), 10–14.

McKay, N. "Minority Faculty in [Mainstream White] Academia." In *The Academic's Handbook,* edited by A. DeNeef and C. Goodwin. Durham, NC: Duke University Press, 1995.

McWhorten, J. *Losing the Race: Self-Sabotage in Black America.* New York: Free Press, 2000.

Meier, D. *The Power of Their Ideas: Lessons for America from a Small School in Harlem.* Boston: Beacon Press, 1995.

Menchaca, M. "Chicano Indianism." In *The Latino/a Condition,* edited by R. Delgado and J. Stefancic. New York: New York University Press, 1998.

Menges, R., and Associates. *Faculty in New Jobs: A Guide to Settling in, Becoming Established, and Building Institutional Support.* San Francisco: Jossey Bass, 1999.

Menges, R., and W. Exum. "Barriers to the Progress of Women and Minority Faculty." *Journal of Higher Education* 54 (1983), 123–143.

Merton, R. "The Matthew Effect in Science." *Isis* 79 (1988), 606–623.

Meyerson, D., and J. Fletcher. "A Modest Manifesto for Shattering the Glass Ceiling." *Harvard Business Review* 278 (Jan. 2000), 127–135

Miles, R. *Warren Buffett Wealth*. Hoboken, NJ: Wiley, 2004.

Misra, J., J. Lundquist, E. Holmes, and S. Agiomavritis. "The Ivory Ceiling of Service Work." *Academe Online* 97.1 (Jan.–Feb. 2011).

Mitchell, R. *The Korean Minority in Japan*. Berkeley: University of California Press, 1967.

Model, S. *West Indian Immigrants: A Black Success Story*. New York: Russell Sage Foundation, 2008.

Montero-Sieburth, M. "An Overview of the Educational Models Used to Explain the Academic Achievement for Latino Students." In *Effective Programs for Latino Students*, edited by R. Slavin and M. Calderon. Mahwah, NJ: Erlbaum, 2001, 331–368.

Moody, J. "Demystifying the Profession: Helping Early-Stage Faculty Succeed (Resources for Medical, Law, & Business Schools and Colleges & Universities)." San Diego: Author, revised 2010. Info at www. diversityoncampus.com

Moody, J. "Mentoring Early Stage Faculty at Medical, Law, and Business Schools and Colleges and Universities." San Diego: Author, revised 2010.

Moody, J. "Rising Above Cognitive Errors: Improving Searches, Evaluations, and Decision-Making (Resources for Medical, Law, & Business Schools and Colleges & Universities)." San Diego: Author, revised 2010.

Moody, J. "*Solo* Faculty at Colleges, Universities, and Professional Schools: Improving Retention and Reducing Stress (Resources for Mentors & Mentees; Provosts, Deans, & Department Chairs; Organizers & Evaluators of Formal Mentoring Programs, & Solos Themselves)." San Diego: Author, revised 2010.

Moody, J. "Vital Info for Graduate Students." San Diego: Author, edition 1996.

Moody, J. *Faculty Diversity: Problems and Solutions*. New York: RoutledgeFalmer, 2004.

Moore, J. *Mexican Americans*. Englewood Cliffs, NJ: Prentice-Hall, 1970.

Moore, W., and L. Wagstaff. *Black Educators in White Colleges*. San Francisco: Jossey Bass, 1974.

Morena, J., ed. *The Elusive Quest for Quality: 150 Years of Chicano/Chicana Education*. Cambridge, MA: Harvard Educational Review, 1999.

Morena, J., D. Smith, A. Clayton-Pedersen, S. Parker, and D. Teraguchi. "The Revolving Door for Underrepresented Minority Faculty in Higher Education." Washington, D.C.: American Association of Colleges and Universities, 2006.

Morrison, A., R. White, and E. Van Velsor. *Breaking the Glass Ceiling: Why Women Don't Reach the Top of Large Corporations*. Reading, MA: Addison-Wesley, 1992.

Morrison, T. *Playing in the Dark: Whiteness and the Literary Imagination*. New York: Random House, 1992.

Moskowitz, G., P. Gollwitzer, and W. Wasel. "Preconscious Control of Stereotype Activation through Chronic Egalitarian Goals." *Journal of Personality and Social Psychology* 77.1 (1999), 167–184.

Nahavandi, A., and A. Malekzadeh. *Organizational Behavior: The Person-Organization Fit*. Upper Saddle River, NJ: Prentice Hall, 1999.

National Research Council. *Gender Differences at Critical Transitions in the Careers of Science, Engineering, and Mathematics Faculty.* Washington, D.C.: National Academies Press, 2009.

Neimann. Y. "The Making of a Token: A Case Study of Stereotypical Threat, Racism, and Tokenism in Academe." *Frontiers* 20.1 (1999), 111–134.

Nelson, D. *Nelson Diversity Surveys.* Washington, D.C.: Diversity in Science Association. [New data collected, interpreted, and released on a regular basis; see Nelson's website.]

Nelson, D., and C. Brammer. *A National Analysis of Minorities in Science and Engineering Faculties at Research Universities.* Washington, D.C.: Diversity in Science Association, 2010.

Nieto, O. *Puerto Rican Students in U.S. Schools.* Mahwah, NJ: Erlbaum, 2000.

Nieves-Squires, S. *Hispanic Women: Making Their Presence on Campus Less Tenuous.* Washington, D.C.: Association of American Colleges, 1991.

Nugent, W. *Crossings: The Great Transatlantic Migrations, 1870–1914.* Bloomington: Indiana University Press, 1992 and 1995.

Nunez-Smith, M., L. Curry, J. Bigby, D. Berg, H. Krumholz, and E. Bradley. "Impact of Race on the Professional Lives of Physicians of African Descent." *Annals of Internal Medicine* 146 (Jan. 2, 2007), 45–51.

Oakes, J. *Keeping Track: How Schools Structure Inequality.* New Haven, CT: Yale University Press, 1985.

Obama, B. *Dreams of My Father: A Story of Race and Inheritance.* New York: Three Rivers Press (Random House), 1995.

O'Brien, E. *Whites Confront Racism: Antiracists and Their Paths to Action.* Landam, MD: Rowman and Littlefield, 2001.

Ogbu, J. *Minority Education and Caste: The American System in Cross-Cultural Perspective.* New York: Academic Press, 1978.

Ogbu, J. "Immigrant and Involuntary Minorities in Comparative Perspective." In *Minority Status and Schooling: A Comparative Study of Immigrant and Involuntary Minorities,* edited by J. Ogbu and M. Gibson. New York: Garland, 1991.

Ogbu, J. "Understanding Cultural Diversity and Learning." *Educational Researcher* 21 (Nov. 1992), 413–423.

Ogbu, J., and M. Matute-Bianchi. "Understanding Sociocultural Factors: Knowledge, Identity, and School Adjustment." In *Beyond Language: Social and Cultural Factors in Schooling Language Minority Students.* Sacramento, CA: Bilingual Education Office, California State Dept. of Education, 1986.

Ogbu, J., and H. Simons. "Voluntary and Involuntary Minorities: A Cultural-Ecological Theory of School Performance with Some Implications for Education." *Anthropology and Education Quarterly* 29 (1998), 155–188.

Olivas, M. "The Attack on Affirmative Action." *Change* (March/April 1993), 16–20.

Oliver, M., and T. Shapiro. *Black Wealth/White Wealth: A New Perspective on Racial Inequality.* New York: Routledge, 1995.

Olsen, D., S. Maple, and F. Stage. "Women and Minority Job Satisfaction: Professional Role Interests, Professional Satisfactions, and Institutional Fit." *Journal of Higher Education* 66 (1994), 267–293.

Operario, D., and S. Fiske. "Racism Equals Power Plus Prejudice." In *Confronting Racism: The Problem and the Response*, edited by J. Eberhardt and S. Fiske. Thousand Oaks, CA: Sage, 1998. [Also see Professor Susan Fiske's website at Princeton University]

Oquendo, A. "Re-Imagining the Latino/a Race." In *The Leaning Ivory Tower: Latino Professors in American Universities*, edited by R. Padilla and R. Chavez. Albany: State University of New York Press, 1995.

Orchowski, P. "*Diverse* Faculties, Increasingly Foreign." *Hispanic Outlook* (March 24, 2008), 38.

Padilla, R., and R. Chavez, eds. *The Leaning Ivory Tower: Latino Professors in American Universities*. Albany: State University of New York Press, 1995.

Parker, L. *Native American Estate: The Struggle over Indian and Hawaiian Lands*. Honolulu: University of Hawaii Press, 1989.

Patterson, O. "Affirmative Action: Opening Up Workplace Networks to Afro-Americans." *The Brookings Review* (Spring 1998a), 17–23.

Patterson, O. *Rituals of Blood: Consequences of Slavery in Two American Centuries*. New York: Perseus, 1998b.

Peterson-Hickey, M., and W. Stein. "Minority Faculty in Academe: Documenting the Unique American Indian Experience." In *Keeping Our Faculties* 1998 conference papers. Minneapolis: University of Minnesota, 1998.

Piore, M. "Diversity and Capitalism." In *Who's Qualified?*, edited by L. Guinier and S. Sturm. Boston: Beacon Press, 2001.

Pinker, S. *The Blank Slate*. New York: Viking Press, 2002.

Pololi, L., and Knight, S. "Mentoring Faculty in Academic Medicine." *Journal of General Internal Medicine* 20 (2005), 866–870.

Powell, C. *My American Journey*. New York: Random House, 1995.

Pronovost, P. "Champion of Checklists in Critical Care." *The Lancet* 374 (2009), 443.

Rains, F. "Is the Benign Really Harmless?" In *White Reign: Deploying Whiteness in America*, edited by J. Kincheloe et al. New York: St. Martin's Griffin Press, 1998a.

Rains, F. "Is the Price Worth the Cost of Survival in Academic Apartheid? Women of Color in a [White] Research University." In *Keeping Our Faculties* 1998 conference papers. Minneapolis: University of Minnesota, 1998b.

Rains, F. "Dancing on the Sharp Edge of the Sword: Women Faculty of Color in White Academe." In *Everyday Knowledge and Uncommon Truths*, edited by L. Smith and K. Kellor. Boulder, CO: Westview Press, 1999.

Ramos, I., and S. Benitez. "Advancing Women Science Faculty in a Small Hispanic Undergraduate Institution." In *Transforming Science and Engineering: Advancing Academic Women*, edited by A. Stewart, J. Malley, and D. LaVaque-Manty. Ann Arbor: University of Michigan Press, 2007, pp. 243–261.

Randall, V. *Dying While Black: An In-Depth Look at a Crisis in the American Healthcare System*. Dayton, Ohio: Seven Principles Press, 2006.

Redelmeier, D. "The Cognitive Psychology of Missed Diagnoses." *Annals of Internal Medicine* 142.2 (Jan. 18, 2005), 115–120.

Reder, M., and E. Gallagher. "Transforming a Teaching Culture through Peer Mentoring: Connecticut College's Johnson Teaching Seminar for Incoming Faculty." *To Improve the Faculty* 25 (2007), 327–345.

Reiman, J. *The Rich Get Richer and the Poor Get Prison.* Boston: Allyn and Bacon, 1998.

Reis, R. *Tomorrow's Professor* Listserv. Quote from Yale Professor Joan Steitz: Message 349, Aug. 30, 2001. To subscribe to this Listserv, send an email message to majordomo@lists.stanford.edu.

Reiss, S. "Nell Painter: Making It as a Woman of Color in the Academy." In *Diversity Digest* (Fall 1997), 6–7.

Remnick, D. "The Joshua Generation: Race and the Campaign of Barack Obama." *The New Yorker* (November 17, 2008).

Rendon, L., and R. Hope. *Educating a New Majority: Transforming America's Educational System for Diversity.* San Francisco: Jossey-Bass, 1996.

Reyes, M., and J. Halcon. "Practices of the Academy: Barriers to Access for Chicano Academics." In *The Racial Crisis in American Higher Education*, edited by P. Altback and K. Lomotey. Albany: State University of New York, 1991.

Rimer, S., and K. Arenson. "Top Colleges Take More Blacks, But Which Ones?" *New York Times*, June 24, 2004. [Included in this article are quotations from Harvard Professors Lani Guinier and Henry Louis Gates, Jr. who underscore the troubling pattern that two-thirds of Black students at Harvard are in fact West Indian and African immigrants or their children. Very few are *non-immigrant*, domestic African Americans.]

Robinson, E. *Disintegration: The Splintering of Black America.* New York: Knopf, 2010.

Rodriguez, C. "An Educated Move—Top School Systems Draw Asians to Wealthy Suburbs." *The Boston Globe* (May 7, 2001), B1, B3.

Rodriguez, G. *Mongrels, Bastards, Orphans, and Vagabonds: Mexican Immigration and the Future of Race in America.* New York: Vintage Press, 2007.

Rodriguez, R. *Brown: The Last Discovery of America.* New York: Viking, 2002.

Roediger, D. *Toward the Abolition of Whiteness: Essays on Race, Politics, and Working-Class History.* London: Verso, 1994.

Roediger, D. *Black Writers on What It Means To Be White.* New York: Schocken Books, 1998.

Roediger, D. *The Wages of Whiteness: Race and the Making of the American Working Class.* London: Verso, 1999.

Rohlen, T. "Education, Policies, and Prospects." In *Koreans in Japan*, edited by G. DeVos and C. Lee. Berkeley: University of California Press, 1981.

Rosenbaum, J. *Making Inequality: The Hidden Curriculum of High School Tracking.* New York: Wiley, 1976.

Rosser, S. *The Science Glass Ceiling.* New York: Routledge, 2004.

Roth. L. "The Social Psychology of Tokenism: Status and Homophily Processes on Wall Street." *Sociological Perspectives* 47 (2004), 189–214.

Rothblum, E. "Leaving the Ivory Tower: Factors Contributing to Women's Voluntary Resignation from Academia." *Frontiers* 10 (1988), 14–17.

Rothenberg, P. *Invisible Privilege: A Memoir About Race, Class, and Gender.* Lawrence: University of Kansas Press, 2000.

Ryn, S. "Freedom in His Blood, Frederick Douglass IV." *Boston Globe* (Feb. 26, 2001), B7, B11.

Sacks, K. "The G.I. Bill: Whites Only Need Apply." In *Critical White Studies,* edited by R. Delgado and J. Stefancic. Philadelphia: Temple University Press, 1997.

Sacks, P. *Standardized Minds: The High Price of America's Testing Culture and What We Can Do To Change It.* Cambridge, MA: Perseus, 1999.

Sagaria, M. "An Exploratory Model of Filtering in Administrative Searches: Toward Counter-Hegemonic Discourses." *Journal of Higher Education* 73 (2002), 677–704.

Sanchez, G. *Becoming Mexican American: Ethnicity, Culture, and Identity in Chicano Los Angeles, 1900–1945.* New York: Oxford University Press, 1993.

Sanchirico, C. "Evidence, Procedure, and the Upside of Cognitive Errors." *Stanford Law Review* 57 (2004), 291–330.

Sanders, K., K. Ward, and E. Bensimon. "The Department Chair's Role in Working with Junior Faculty." *The Department Chair* (Winter 1996), 7–8.

Sandler, B. *The Campus Climate Revisited: Chilly for Women Faculty, Administrators and Graduate Students.* Washington, DC: Association of American Colleges, 1992.

Scandura, T. "Dysfunctional Mentoring Relationships and Outcomes." *Journal of Management* 24.3 (1998), 449–467.

Schoenfeld, C., and R. Magnan. *Mentor in a Manual: Climbing the Academic Ladder to Tenure.* Madison, WI: Atwood Publishing, 2004, 3rd edition.

Schuster, J., and M. Finkelstein. *The American Faculty.* Baltimore: Johns Hopkins University Press, 2006.

Schuster, J., and D. Wheeler. *Enhancing Faculty Strategies for Development and Renewal.* San Francisco: Jossey Bass, 1990.

Seldin, P. *Coping with Faculty Stress.* San Francisco: Jossey-Bass, 1987.

Scott, J. *A Singular Woman: The Untold Story of Barack Obama's Mother.* New York: Riverhead Books (Penguin), 2008.

Sekaquaptewa, D., and M. Thompson. "The Differential Effect of Solo Status on Members of High- and Low-Status Groups." *Personality & Social Psychology Bulletin* 28.5 (2002), 694–707.

Seldin, P. *Coping with Faculty Stress.* San Francisco: Jossey-Bass, 1987.

Sevo, R., and D. Chubin. "Bias Literacy: A Review of Concepts in Research on Discrimination." Washington, D.C.: AAAS, 2008.

Seymour, E., and N. Hewitt. *Talking about Leaving: Why Undergraduates Leave the Sciences.* Boulder, CO: Westview Press, 1997.

Schwartz, J. "Thousands of Prison Terms in Crack Cases Could Be Eased." *New York Times* (June 30, 2011), 42.

"Shattering the Silences: The Case for Minority Faculty" [videotape]. San Francisco: California Newsreel, 1997.

Shibutani, T., and M. Kwan. *Ethnic Stratification.* New York: MacMillan, 1965.

Shiller, R., and G. Akerlof. *Animal Spirits: How Human Psychology Drives the Economy, and Why It Matters*. Princeton, NJ: Princeton University, Press, 2009.

Shimahara, N. *Politics of Classroom Life in International Perspective*. New York: Routledge, 1998.

Shin, A. "The Lily-White University Presses." *Journal of Blacks in Higher Education* (Summer 1996), 78–82.

Singh, H., L. Petersen, and E. Thomas. "Understanding Diagnostic Errors in Medicine: A Lesson from Aviation." *Quality Safety Health Care* 15.3 (2006), 159–164.

Shorris, E. *Latinos: A Biography of the People*. New York: Norton, 1992.

Skrentny, J. *The Ironies of Affirmative Action*. Chicago: University of Chicago Press, 1996.

Skrentny, J. *The Minority Rights Revolution*. Cambridge, MA: Harvard University Press, 2002.

Slezkine, Y. *The Jewish Century*. Princeton, NJ: Princeton University Press, 2004.

Smith, C. *The Cost of Privilege (Taking on the System of White Supremacy and Racism)*. New York: Camino Press, 2007.

Smith, D. *Achieving Faculty Diversity: Debunking the Myths*. Washington, D.C.: Association of American Colleges and Universities, 1996.

Smith, D. "How to Diversify the Faculty." *Academe* (Sept.–Oct. 2000), 48–52.

Smith, D. *Diversity's Promise for Higher Education*. Baltimore: Johns Hopkins University Press, 2009.

Solem, M., and K. Foote. "Concerns, Attitudes, and Abilities of Early-Career Geography Faculty: Research Content and Future Directions." *Journal of Geography in Higher Education* 30.2 (2007), 195–198.

Sorcinelli, M. "New and Junior Faculty Stress: Research and Responses." In *Developing New and Junior Faculty*, edited by M. Sorcinelli and A. Austin. San Francisco: Jossey Bass, 1992. [Also see additional Sorcinelli articles at the U. Mass-Amherst website.]

Sorcinelli, M., and J. Near. "Relations between Work and Life Away from Work Among University Faculty." *Journal of Higher Education* 60 (Jan.-Feb. 1989), 59–81.

Sorcinelli, M., and J. Yun. "From Mentor to Mentoring Networks: Mentoring in the New Academy." *Change* 39.6 (2006), 58–61.

Stanley, C. "Cross-Race Faculty Mentoring." *Change* 37.2 (2005), 44–50.

Stanley, C. ed. *Faculty of Color: Teaching in Predominantly White Colleges and Universities*. Boston, MA: Anker, 2006.

Stannard, D. *American Holocaust: The Conquest of the New World*. New York: Oxford University Press, 1993.

Stanton-Salazar, R. "A Social Capital Framework for Understanding the Socialization of Racial Minority Children and Youths." *Harvard Educational Review* 67 (Spring 1997): 1–40.

Stanton-Salazar, R. "The Development of Coping Strategies among Urban Latino Youth." In *Making Invisible Latino Adolescents Visible: A Critical Approach to Latino Diversity*, edited by M. Montero-Sieburth and R. Villarruel. New York: Falmer Press, 2000.

Stanton-Salazar, R. *Manufacturing Hope and Despair: The School and Kin Support Networks of U.S. Mexican Youth.* New York: Teachers College Press, 2001.

Stanton-Salazar, R., and S. Spina. "The Network Orientations of Highly Resilient Urban Minority Youth." *The Urban Review* 32 (2000), 227–261.

Stavans, I. "How Elite Universities Fail Latino Students." *Chronicle of Higher Education* (Jan. 20, 2006), p. B20. [Professor Stavans notes that immigrant "Latinos" are from well-to-do families and rarely perceive themselves as Latinos and in fact rarely identify with those who are domestic U.S. non-immigrants.]

Steele, B. "In a Seller's Market, Cornell Needs to Recruit Hundreds of New Faculty, Putting Years-Long Pressure on Budget." Article in Chronicle Online at the website of Cornell University, Ithaca, New York, Oct. 26, 2006.

Steele, C. "Race and the Schooling of Black Americans." *Atlantic Monthly* (April 1992), 68–75.

Steele, C. "High-Stakes Testing." Presentation at Harvard University's Graduate School of Education, Cambridge, MA, October 25, 2000.

Steele, C. "Understanding the Performance Gap." In *Who's Qualified?*, edited by L. Guinier and S. Sturm. Boston: Beacon Press, 2001.

Steele, C. "Secrets of the SAT." "Frontline" Interview in 2001 with Steele, at Steele's website

Steele, C., and J. Aronson. "Stereotype Threat and the Intellectual Test Performance of African Americans." *Journal of Personality and Social Psychology* 69 (1995), 797–811.

Stein, W. "The Survival of American Indian Faculty." *Thought and Action* 10 (1994), 101–115.

Strum, S. "Gender Equity as Institutional Transformation: The Pivotal Role of Organization Catalysts." In *Transforming Science and Engineering: Advancing Academic Women*, edited by A. Stewart, J. Malley, and D. LaVaque-Manty. Ann Arbor: University of Michigan Press, 2007, pp. 262–280.

Sturm, S., and L. Guinier. "The Future of Affirmative Action: Reclaiming the Innovative Ideal." *California Law Review* 84 (1996), 953–1036.

Suarez-Orozco, M. "Becoming Somebody: Central American Immigrants in U.S. Inner City Schools." *Anthropology and Education Quarterly* 18 (1987), 287–299.

Suarez-Orozco, C., and M. Suarez-Orozco. *The Children of Immigration.* Cambridge, MA: Harvard University Press, 2001.

Sue, D., C. Capodilupo, G. Torinio, J. Bucceri, A. Holder, K. Nadal, and M. Esquilin. "Racial Micro-Aggressions in Everyday Life." *American Psychologist* 62 (2007), 271–286.

Sunstein, C. *Infotopia: How Many Minds Create Knowledge.* New York: Oxford University Press, 2006.

Sunstein, C., and R. Thaler. *Nudge: Improving Decisions about Health, Wealth, and Happiness.* New Haven, CT: Yale University Press, 2008.

Suskind, R. *Hope in the Unseen.* New York: Broadway Books, 1998.

Swingle, A. "Poised for Power." *Hopkins Medical News* (Spring/Summer 2002), 8.

Takaki, R. "To Count or Not to Count By Race and Gender?" In *From Different Shores: Perspectives on Race and Ethnicity in America*, edited by R. Takaki. New York: Oxford University Press, 1987.

Takaki, R.. *Strangers from a Different Shore, A History of Asian Americans*. Boston: Little, Brown, 1989.

Takaki, R. *A Different Mirror: A History of Multicultural America*. Boston: Little, Brown, 1993.

Tapia, R "Minority Students and Research Universities: How to Overcome the *Mismatch*." *Chronicle of Higher Education* (March 27, 2009), A72.

Tapia, R "True Diversity Doesn't Come From Abroad." *Chronicle of Higher Education* (Sept. 28, 2007), B34–B35.

Tapia, R. "To Test or Not To Test." *The Magazine of Rice University*. Houston, TX: Rice University, 2008.

Tatum, B. "Talking About Race, Learning About Racism: The Application of Racial Identity Development Theory in the Classroom." *Harvard Educational Review* 62 (1992): 1–24.

Tatum, B. "Talking About Race, Learning About Racism." In *Whiteness, A Critical Reader*, edited by M. Hill. New York: New York University Press, 1997a.

Tatum, B. *Why Are All the Black Kids Sitting Together in the Cafeteria? and Other Conversations about Race*. New York: Basic Books, 1997b.

Taylor, A. *American Colonies: The Settling of North America*. New York: Penguin, 2001.

"Teaching Science Collaboratively" [videotape featuring science professor Art Muzer]. Cambridge, MA: Derek Bok Center for Teaching and Learning, Harvard University.

Tenure Denied: Cases of Sex Discrimination in Academia. Washington, D.C.: American Association of University Women, 2004.

Thaler, R., and S. Bernartzi. "Save More Tomorrow: Using Behavioral Economics to Increase Employee Savings." *Journal of Political Economy* 112 (2004), S164–S187. [Professor Thaler has provided a list of his articles at the University of Chicago website.]

Thelin, J. *A History of American Higher Education*. Baltimore: Johns Hopkins University Press, 2004.

Thomas, L. "Moral Deference." *Philosophical Forum* 24 (Fall-Spring 1992–93), 233–250.

Thomas, A., J. Thomas, and R. Thomas. "Lingering Racism Calls for Reflection and Action." *Annals of Internal Medicine* 147.4 (2007), 282.

Thompson, G., and A. Louque. *Exposing the Culture of Arrogance in the Academy: A Blueprint for Increasing Black Faculty Satisfaction in Higher Education*. Sterling, VA: Stylus, 2005.

Thurow, L. *Poverty and Discrimination*. Washington, D.C.: Brookings Institute, 1969.

Tierney, W. *Official Encouragement, Institutional Discouragement: Minorities in Academe—The Native American Experience*. Norwood, NJ: Ablex, 1992.

Tierney, W., and E. Bensimon. *Promotion and Tenure: Community and Socialization in Academe*. Albany: State University of New York Press, 1996.

Tomaskoviv-Devey, D., M. Thomas, and K. Johnson. "Race and the Accumulation of Human Capital Across the Career: A Theoretical Model for Fixed-Effects Application." *American Journal of Sociology* 111 (2005), 58–89.

Tonn, J. *Understanding the Other Person: Skillful Interpersonal Communication.* Wellesley Hills, MA: Educational Planning Services Corp., 1985.

Travis, E. ed. *Legends and Legacies: Personal Journeys of Women Physicians and Scientists at M.D. Anderson Cancer Center.* Houston, TX: Anderson Cancer Center, 2009.

Trix, F., and C. Psenka. "Exploring the Color of Glass: Letters of Recommendation for Female and Male Medical Faculty." *Discourse and Society* 14 (2003), 191-220.

Trower, C. "Alleviating the Torture of the Tenure Track: All It Takes Is a Little Show and Tell." *The Department Chair* 1 (Spring 1999), 16–17.

Trower, C. "Towards a Greater Understanding of the Tenure Track for Minorities." *Change* 41 (2009), 38–45.

Trower, C., and A. Gallagher. "A Call for Clarity." *Chronicle of Higher Education* (Sept. 19, 2008), A37–A40.

Trower, C., and R. Chait. "Faculty Diversity: Too Little for Too Long." *Harvard Magazine* (March-April 2002), 33–36. [At the website www.harvard-magazine.com are data tables that accompany Trower's and Chait's article.]

Turner, C. "Defining Success: Promotion and Tenure—Planning for Each Career Stage and Beyond." In *Succeeding in an Academic Career: A Guide for Faculty of Color,* edited by M. Garcia. Westport, CT: Greenwood Press, 2001.

Turner, C. *Diversifying the Faculty: A Guidebook for Search Committees.* Washington, D.C.: Association of American Colleges and Universities, 2002.

Turner, S., and J. Bound. "Closing the Gap or Widening the Divide: The Effects of the G.I. Bill and World War II on the Educational Outcomes of Black Americans." *Journal of Economic History* (March 2003), 145–177.

Turner, C., and J. Thompson. "Socializing Women Doctoral Students: Minority and Majority Experiences." *The Review of Higher Education* 16 (1993), 355–370.

Turner, C., M. Garcia, N. Amaury, and L. Rendon, eds. *Racial and Ethnic Diversity in Higher Education.* Needham Heights, MA: Simon & Shuster, 1996.

Turner, C., J. Gonzalez, and J. Wood. "Faculty of Color in Academe: What 20 Years of Literature Tells Us." *Journal of Diversity in Higher Education* 1 (2008), 139–168.

Turner, C., and S. Myers, Jr. *Faculty of Color in Academe: Bittersweet Success.* Needham Heights, MA: Allyn & Bacon, 2000.

Twombly, S. "The Process of Choosing a Dean." *Journal of Higher Education* 63 (1992), 653–693.

University of Michigan Faculty Work-Life Study Report. Ann Arbor: University of Michigan, 1999. [Every 1–2 years, the campus undertakes a Work-Life Survey].

Valenzuela, A. *Subtractive Schooling: U.S.-Mexican Youth and the Politics of Caring*. Albany: State University of New York Press, 1999.

Valian, V. "Sex, Schemas, and Success—What's Keeping Women Back?" *Academe* (Sept.-Oct. 1998a), 50-55.

Valian, V. *Why So Slow? The Advancement of Women*. Cambridge, MA: MIT Press, 1998b.

Vargas, L. "Why Are We Still So Few and Why Has Our Progress Been So Slow?" In *Women Faculty of Color in the White Classroom: Narratives on the Pedagogical Implications of Teacher Diversity*, edited by L. Vargas. New York, Peter Lang, 2002, pp. 35–47.

Vélez-Ibáñez, C. *Border Visions: Mexican Cultures of the Southwest United States*. Tucson: University of Arizona Press, 1996.

Vicker, L., and H. Royer. *The Complete Academic Search Manual: A Systematic Approach to Successful and Inclusive Hiring*. Sterling, VA: Stylus, 2006.

Wade, K., and A. Kinicki. "Examining Objective and Subjective Applicant Qualifications within a Process Model of Interview Selection Decisions." *Academy of Management Journal* 38 (1995), 151–155.

Waldinger, R. "Immigration: The New American Dilemma." *Daedalus* 140.5 (Spring 2011), 215–225.

Waldinger, R. "The Ethnic Division of Labor Transformed: Native Minorities and New Immigrants in Post-Industrial New York." *New Community* 14 (1998), 319–332.

Waltman, J., and C. Hollenshead. "Creating a Positive Departmental Climate: Principles for Best Practices." Ann Arbor: University of Michigan's Center for the Education of Women, 2005.

"Wanted: A Better Way to Boost Numbers of Minority PhDs." *Science* 281 (1998), 1268–1270.

Washington V., and W. Harvey. *Affirmative Rhetoric, Negative Action: African-American and Hispanic Faculty at Predominantly White Institutions*. ASHE-ERIC Higher Education Report. Washington, D.C.: George Washington University, 1989.

Waters, M. "Growing Up West Indian and African American: Gender and Class Differences in the Second Generation." In *Islands in the City: West Indian Migration to New York*, edited by Nancy Foner. Berkeley: University of California Press, 2000.

Waters, M. *Ethnic Options: Choosing Identities in America*. Berkeley: University of California Press, 1990.

Waters, M. *Black Identities: West Indian Immigrant Dreams and American Realities*. Cambridge, MA: Harvard University Press, 1999.

Weiner, M. The *Origins of the Korean Community in Japan, 1910–1923*. Manchester, UK: Manchester University Press, 1989.

Weis, L. *Between Two Worlds: Black Students in an Urban Community College*. New York: Routledge, 1985.

Wenneras, C., and A. Wold. "Nepotism and Sexism in Peer Review." *Nature* 387 (1997), 341–343.

Wenneras, C., and A. Wold. "A Chair of One's Own: The Upper Reaches of Academe Remain Stubbornly Inaccessible to Women." *Nature* 408 (2000), 647.

Wheeler, M., and S. Fiske. "Controlling Racial Prejudice: Social-Cognitive Goals Affect Amygdala and Stereotype Activation." *Psychological Science* 16.1 (2005), 56–63.

Whetten, D., and K. Cameron. *Developing Management Skills, 5th ed.* Upper Saddle River, NJ: Prentice Hall, 2002.

White, J., and J. Cones. *Black Man Emerging: Facing the Past and Seizing a Future in America.* New York: W.H. Freeman, 1999.

Wildman, S. *How Invisible Preference Undermines America.* New York: New York University Press, 1996.

Williams, C. *Technology and the Dream: Reflections on the Black Experience at MIT, 1941–1999.* Cambridge, MA: MIT Press, 2001.

Williams, C. L. "The Glass Escalator: Hidden Advantages for Men in the 'Female' Professions." *Social Problems* 39 (1992), 253–267.

Williams, P. *The Alchemy of Race and Rights.* Cambridge, MA: Harvard University Press, 1991.

Williams, P. *Seeing a Color-Blind Future: The Paradox of Race.* New York: Farrar, Straus and Giroux, 1997.

Williams, J. *Unbending Gender: Why Family and Work Conflict and What to Do About It.* New York: Oxford University Press, 2000.

Williams, J. *Reshaping the Work-Family Debate: Why Men and Class Matter.* Cambridge, MA: Harvard University Press, 2010.

Willie, C. *The Ivory and Ebony Towers.* Lexington, MA: Heath, 1981.

Willie, C. *The Caste and Class Controversy on Race and Poverty.* Dix Hills, NY: General Hall, 1990.

Wilson, T., and N. Brekke. "Mental Contamination and Mental Correction: Unwanted Influences on Judgments and Evaluations." *Psychological Bulletin* 116 (1994), 117–142.

Wingard, D, K. Garman, and V. Reznik. "Facilitating Faculty Success: Outcomes and Cost Benefit of the UCSD National Center of Leadership in Academic Medicine." *Academic Medicine* 79.10 (2004), S9–S11. [More articles by these authors can be found at the NCLAM website.]

Wise, T. *White Like Me: Reflections of a Privileged Son.* Brooklyn: Soft Shell Press, 2008.

"Women Make Gains in Getting Canadian Research Chairs." *Chronicle of Higher Education* (Nov. 26, 2004), A38.

Women of Color in the Academy Project at the University of Michigan. "Through My Lens" [videotape]. Ann Arbor: Center for the Education of Women, University of Michigan, 1999.

Woodward, C. *The Strange Career of Jim Crow.* New York: Oxford University Press, 1966.

Wu, F. *Yellow: Race in America Beyond Black and White.* New York: Basic Books, 2002.

Wunsch, M., ed. *Mentoring Revisited: Making an Impact on Individuals and Institutions.* San Francisco: Jossey Bass, 1990. [In this collection, Professor Wunsch provides an invaluable checklist for developing mentoring programs; she also contributes two articles.]

Yetman, N. ed.. *Majority and Minority: The Dynamics of Race and Ethnicity in American Life.* Needham Heights, MA: Allyn and Bacon, 1999.

251

Yoder, J. "Looking Beyond Numbers: The Effects of Gender Status, Job Prestige, and Occupational Gender-Typing of Tokenism Processes." *Social Psychology Quarterly* 57 (1994), 150–165.

Yoder, J. "Looking Beyond Gender: Effects of Racial Differences on Tokenism Perceptions." *Sex Roles* 35 (1996), 15–22.

Yoder, J. "Understanding Tokenism Processes and their Impact on Women's Work." Presidential Address. *Psychology of Women Quarterly* 26 (2002), 1–8.

Yoder, J., J. Adams, S. Grove, and R. Priest. "The Price of a Token." *Journal of Political and Military Sociology* 11 (1983), 325–333.

Yoder, J., J. Adams, S. Grove, and R. Priest. "To Teach is to Learn: Overcoming Tokenism with Mentors [at West Point]." *Psychology of Women Quarterly* 9 (1985), 119–131.

Yoshinga-Itano, C. "Institutional Barriers and Myths to Recruitment and Retention of Faculty of Color: An Administrator's Perspective." In *Faculty of Color: Teaching in Predominantly White Colleges and Universities*, edited by C. Stanley. Boston: Anker Publishing, 2006.

Zackary, L. *The Mentor's Guide.* San Francisco: Jossey Bass, 2000.

ABOUT THE AUTHOR

JoAnn Moody, PhD, JD, is a national specialist in faculty development and diversity who consults with a variety of colleges, universities, and professional schools (such as the Universities of Virginia, Texas, Wisconsin, Stanford Medical School, Purdue and New Mexico State Universities as well as Middlebury and Harvey Mudd Colleges). Dr. Moody is a former college professor and higher education administrator. Her problem-based retreats and workshops engage leaders across the country in collective analysis, problem-solving, and the construction of action steps. Leaders and groups include campus presidents and their executive committees, provosts and their academic staff, deans, department chairs, search and tenure/promotion committees, post-docs and medical residents, mentors and mentoring programs, emerging leaders, faculty affairs officers, teaching and learning center directors, faculty senates, diversity officers and equity councils, boards of trustees, and at times staff and student leaders. Dr. Moody conducts not only on-site sessions and executive coaching for her clients but also provides off-site advice and follow-up assistance with new policies, reports, and action implementations.

Details about Dr. Moody's consulting practice and publications are available at the website: www.diversityoncampus.com.

INDEX